Turmoil in the Peaceable Kingdom:
The Quebec Sovereignty Movement and Its Implications for Canada
and the United States

Since the Meech Lake episode in Canadian political life, several volumes focusing on the future of Canada and the role of Quebec have appeared. *Turmoil in the Peaceable Kingdom* differs from these in that it is written by a Montrealer who now works in Washington and observes the movement towards sovereignty in Quebec from both U.S. and Canadian points of view. Jonathan Lemco's study evaluates the various policy options and considers the possible economic consequences of sovereignty. He argues that the political sovereignty of Quebec would bring significant immediate economic dislocation in Canada and Quebec.

Lemco suggests that the short-term cost of sovereignty for Quebec – which has not been carefully examined by sovereigntists – could be substantial: an increased debt burden, higher deficits and interest rates, deepening unemployment, little or no say in Canadian monetary policy, the emigration of some of Quebec's best and brightest, foreign-investor suspicion of Quebec's planning priorities, and instability. In the medium- and long-term, however, a sovereign Quebec and Canada might well be able to work out an acceptable economic relationship.

The economic effects of Quebec sovereignty on the rest of Canada would be felt mostly in Ontario because of the proximity of the two provinces and their substantial economic integration. About 80 per cent of interprovincial trade in Canada is between Ontario and Quebec. Ontario, however, has manufacturing, resource, and service industries that would enable it to thrive as one of the world's most diversified and powerful economies, and in the medium and long term its economy would perform better than Quebec's.

As for the United States, its vital interests inevitably would be affected by changes in Canada, but American officials have no long-term plans connected with Canada's constitutional plight. Only if Quebec should attain sovereignty, would the U.S. government decide on what constitutes its best interests.

While the future of Quebec in uncertain, Lemco says it is clear that Canada's provinces will grow stronger and the Canadian federation will become further decentralized. The comfort he offers is that whatever the choices made by Quebecers and Canadians, they will likely be made in a democratic, non-violent manner.

JONATHAN LEMCO is Executive Director of the International Centre for Family Enterprises, Montreal. He was previously Senior Fellow, National Planning Association, Washington, DC.

JONATHAN LEMCO

Turmoil in the Peaceable Kingdom:
The Quebec Sovereignty Movement and Its Implications for Canada and the United States

UNIVERSITY OF TORONTO PRESS
Toronto Buffalo London

© University of Toronto Press Incorporated 1994
Toronto Buffalo London
Printed in Canada

ISBN 0-8020-0532-2 (cloth)
ISBN 0-8020-6970-3 (paper)

Printed on acid-free paper

Canadian Cataloguing in Publication Data

Lemco, Jonathan
   Turmoil in the peaceable kingdom: The Quebec
   sovereignty movement and its implications for
   Canada and the United States

   Includes bibliographical references and index.
   ISBN 0-8020-0532-2 (bound)
   ISBN 0-8020-6970-3 (pbk.)

   I. Quebec (Province) – History – Autonomy and
   independence movements.   I. Title.

   FC2925.9.S4L4 1994   971.4'04   C94-931594-X
   FI053.2.L4 1994

University of Toronto Press acknowledges the financial assistance to its publishing
program of the Canada Council and the Ontario Arts Council.

Contents

TABLES AND FIGURES vii

PREFACE ix

INTRODUCTION xi

1
Quebec's Place in Canada 3

2
From Meech Lake to Charlottetown:
The Evolution of Constitutional Proposals 18

3
Sovereignty-Association – A Viable Alternative? 62

4
Quebec's Economic and Political Development since 1976 80

5
Political Sovereignty for Quebec – The Economic Costs and Benefits 91

6
Investment in Quebec after the Failure of the Meech Lake
and Charlottetown Accords 113

7
Quebec Sovereignty and the Debt 128

8
Quebec Sovereignty and Currency Concerns 137

9
The U.S. View of Post-Sovereignty Quebec–U.S. Relations 146

10
Where Is the Peaceable Kingdom Headed? 164

APPENDICES

Appendix A Bill 101: Charter of the French Language 173
Appendix B Canadian Charter of Rights and Freedoms 183
Appendix C Future Institutional Structures as Discussed by Ronald L. Watts 186
Appendix D Roadmap Summary Statements 191
Appendix E A Roadmap for National Unity 206
Appendix F Text of the Charlottetown Agreement 210

NOTES 233

INDEX 251

Tables and Figures

TABLES

1 Highlights of the constitutional proposal of the Quebec Liberal party 34
2 How the Allaire proposals would shift power to Quebec 36
3 Recommendations of the commission on the political and constitutional future of Quebec 38
4 Highlights of the federal government's proposals 46
5 Arguments for and against the Charlottetown Agreement 50
6 Support in Quebec for the secessionist idea, 1960–90 75
7 Comparison of Quebec's and Ontario's relative importance in the Canadian manufacturing sector using three criteria 94
8 Ontario's manufacturing shipments, 1974 and 1989 95
9 Quebec's manufacturing shipments, 1974 and 1989 95
10 Estimates of Quebec's budget deficit in Year 1 of independence 135

FIGURES

1 Unemployment rates for the city of Montreal and the provinces of Quebec and Ontario, 1985–90 87
2 Personal income per capita, Quebec and Ontario, 1979–89 96

Preface

Canada is engaged in a wrenching and emotional constitutional struggle. As of April 1994, it is not clear whether Quebec will attain sovereignty or not, but what seems clear is that, no matter what the result, Canada's provinces will grow stronger and the Canadian federation will become further decentralized. This study is an effort to provide a balanced and comprehensive view of the issue. It is also the work of an ex-Montrealer who, until recently, was resident in the United States. To the extent that this reveals a bias of any sort, that is inevitable.

There are many government officials who agreed to be interviewed for this work, under conditions of anonymity. I am grateful for their help. I would also like to express my gratitude to Richard Belous, Stéphane Dion, Joseph Jockel, Frank Lemco, Kelly McClenahan, Gregory Marchildon, Edward Masters, Leo Paré, Rick Uslaner, and two anonymous referees for their insightful comments on a version that appeared in *Canada–U.S. Outlook*. I would like to thank Virgil Duff of the University of Toronto Press for his skilful editing and Jane Broderick for preparing the index. All errors of fact or interpretation are my own of course.

I would also like to thank my family for their love and support. My son David came into the world while this was being written. My father-in-law, Daniel, fell ill during its completion. This study is for David and Daniel.

Introduction

Canada is in serious trouble. It faces an economic slump, and debt levels are substantially higher than those of the United States and several of its major trading partners. The heretofore stable Canadian party system has been restructured. There is a crisis of national leadership, widespread cynicism in the land, and demands for greater political decentralization from most areas of the country.

There is one ongoing development, however, that threatens to dwarf the others in its financial implications, one which makes Canada's plight among the most fascinating in the world today. Quebec is threatening to leave the Canadian federation to become a new nation-state. If it does, the political and economic consequences for Canada, Quebec, and the United States will be substantial. That is the focus of this book.*

The failure of the Charlottetown Agreement in October 1992 and the national election results in October 1993 have revealed national malaise and constitutional exhaustion. Canada's economic problems are so substantial that, for most Canadians, constitutional concerns are on the back-burner. But the possibility of Quebec's sovereignty remains quite real and must be addressed. According to Parti Québécois leader Jacques Parizeau, sovereignty-association is dead. The choice for Quebecers is now only sovereignty/separatism or the status quo. Even if he is mistaken, as is very possible, and a restructured federation remains a viable option, the long-term prospects for a politically stable Canada are mixed at best.

Should Quebec attain sovereignty, it will become a new, highly industrialized, economically viable, well-educated, French-speaking nation directly bordering the United States. It will be a friendly, democratic, relatively prosperous ally, but it will still be worrisome to American policymakers. Quebec's sover-

---

* An earlier version of this book was published as a monograph in the *Canada–U.S. Outlook* series of the National Planning Association.

eignty might force changes in North American trading links, strategic ties, and political relations. In the long run, these problems are all manageable. But in the short run, a sovereign Quebec would force American politicians, public servants, and investors to deal with uncertainty, a most unpalatable situation. American public and private sector leaders favour stability and predictability. This is not surprising. The Canada–U.S. relationship is characterized by few crises. Most problems are solved amicably. Quebec's political sovereignty, should it occur, would present a new, unwelcome challenge to American leaders whose interests and profits depend on working with Quebec and Canada.

Should Quebec not become sovereign, the United States would likely still have to deal with a sharply decentralized Canada. The provinces will probably assume more constitutional powers than they currently have. Federal authority will diminish. Various symbols of Canadian national unity will vanish. This might or might not be a good thing for Canadians and Quebecers in the long run, but it would be disconcerting to many Americans who tend to regard Canada as safe, friendly, and stable. It would remain all of these things, of course, but the profound changes north of the border that may well emerge in the next decade will provoke a widespread sense of shock for many Americans who are genuinely fond of Canadians, if a little bored by Canadian affairs. From an American perspective, this rapidly changing, dizzying series of events is a bit perplexing and not a little unnerving.

This being said, Canadian and American policymakers and senior public servants are pragmatic and likely to adapt to whatever new political, constitutional, or economic structure emerges in Canada in the next few years. The United States is very concerned about the situation in Canada, but it will not overtly interfere beyond acknowledging its support for a strong and united Canada. U.S. officials worry about the strategic changes accompanying Quebec sovereignty. They fret about political instability so close to home. They are particularly interested in the implications of Quebec's possible sovereignty for the North American Free Trade Agreement. But the United States government will do nothing to aggravate existing tensions in Canada and will not commit itself to any future binational Quebec–U.S. policies. U.S. officials will adapt to changes as they occur and, thus far, they have handled their vital interests in Canadian affairs with tact and sensitivity.

This is fortunate for all parties involved, for Quebec's challenge to the stability of the Canadian federation has never been stronger nor more politically sensitive. In various 1991 and 1992 polls, a majority of Quebecers voiced support for some form of political sovereignty with or without economic association with Canada. By sovereignty, most Quebecers refer to an ability to manage their economy, administer their laws exclusively, and negotiate international treaties. The perceived benefits of sovereignty for Quebec include the certainty that its distinctive language, culture, and civil law will be protected and promoted in perpetuity. This would provide the people with an enormous degree of pride and security. Quebec sovereigntists also maintain that they can manage its economy best. The federal government's apparent failure in managing the nation's finances are an obsession with many Quebecers. Quebec's emergence as a confident nation has been the result of various factors, including a more politically sophisticated population, a militant trade union movement, a more enterprising business class, better educated state élites, examples of successful nationalist movements elsewhere, perceived slights or injustices committed by officials in the rest of Canada and best exemplified by the failure of the Meech Lake Accord, ambitious politicians with their own political motives, and a sense that francophone and non-francophone goals are incompatible.

In addition, it is certainly true that Quebec's language laws have served to protect and promote the French language and culture in the face of a low birth rate, declining immigration, increased consumption of English language products and culture, and economic opportunities elsewhere. However, whether a Quebec sovereign state is the next necessary step to ensure the maintenance of the distinct Quebec society is a highly debatable point. In fact, the costs of sovereignty could be prohibitive, but these costs have not been carefully examined by sovereigntists.

The economic costs might include an increased debt burden, higher deficits and interest rates, deepening unemployment problems, little or no say on Canadian monetary policy if the Canadian dollar is shared or great risks associated with creating Quebec's own currency, emigration of many of Quebec society's brightest and best, foreign investor suspicion of Quebec's political, economic, and industrial-planning priorities, and the instability that necessarily accompanies independence anywhere. Politically, a sovereign Quebec might have less clout in international affairs outside Canada. It might have particular difficulty negotiating advantageous political and economic agreements with the rest of Canada or with other nations. Strategically, it would be a weaker player than it now is. Its territorial integrity might be threatened by challenges from Quebec's native peoples and other non-francophones. The rest of Canada might well be angry and spiteful in the short run, although it would probably be accommodating in the long run. Nevertheless, negotiating treaties between a sovereign Quebec and Canada will be difficult and bitter. Ironically, as the disparate nations of the European Community grow closer, Canada joins unattractive models like the former Soviet Union and Yugoslavia in a trend leading to dissolution, although this comparison should not be pursued too far, since unlike the others

Canada is a liberal democracy and a wealthy modern welfare state. Overall, the greatest short-term cost to Quebec is uncertainty. This is a cross that all of its allies will have to bear as well.

The failure of the Canadian public to support the Charlottetown Agreement constitutional proposals, which were designed to keep Quebec in Canada among other goals, guarantees that the decentralization will continue. Most confederations fall apart eventually as constituent units realize that the costs in terms of giving up sovereignty outweigh the benefits of common defence, coordinated economic policies, and political coordination.[1]

A main purpose of this study is to help observers understand the context in which Quebec's constitutional challenge to Canada has occurred. It presents an overview of Quebec's development and the sources of its dissatisfaction with Canada. Various models for Quebec's and Canada's future are then examined, with particular attention devoted to the political implications of sovereignty or sovereignty-association. The study goes on to describe the process whereby sovereignty might occur and the likely response of the rest of Canada. Particular attention is extended to the economic environment in Canada and the possible ramifications of sovereignty for the economies of Quebec and Canada. Finally, attention is paid to U.S. interests in Quebec and to what Quebec's sovereignty might mean for the U.S.–Quebec relationship.

This is by no means a definitive evaluation of the future of North America's political relations. There are too many intangible factors for that. Existing data about the implications of sovereignty are incomplete or of poor quality. Personal biases characterize many of the available studies because the Canadian constitutional crisis has produced strong emotions. This study, however, is an honest effort to evaluate the current situation and to suggest likely choices. It is easy to be sympathetic to the Quebec sovereigntists' motives. It is not so easy to be encouraged about their chances of success. Their political goals may be necessary to ensure the protection and promotion of Quebec's distinct character. The economic costs of sovereignty, however, may make the whole exercise unproductive.

Nevertheless, no matter what choices Quebecers and Canadians make, they will likely adopt them in a democratic, non-violent manner. Furthermore, whether Quebec remains within the Canadian federal structure or departs from it, Canada will be changed fundamentally. It will become more decentralized, more reminiscent of a highly peripheralized federation or even a confederation with powers concentrated in the provinces. And history teaches us that most confederations eventually dissolve.

TURMOIL IN THE PEACEABLE KINGDOM:

THE QUEBEC SOVEREIGNTY MOVEMENT AND ITS
IMPLICATIONS FOR CANADA AND THE UNITED STATES

1

Quebec's Place in Canada

Many Quebecers have long felt ambivalent about their place in Canada. Montreal comedian Yvon Deschamps's joke is on the mark: 'I don't know why the English think we're inconsistent. All we want is an independent Quebec within a strong and united Canada.' As far back as 1839, Lord Durham could note that Canada was 'two nations warring in the bosom of a single state.' What has created this ambivalence in Quebec?

To some Quebecers, the fear of cultural disintegration emerges from the province's declining fertility rate and from fears that it will become increasingly difficult to attract French-speaking immigrants to Quebec. The province has one of the lowest birth rates in North America, currently 1.7 children per woman of child-bearing age. A 2.1 rate is needed to replace the population. So, population growth is near zero – a complete reversal from the prolific growth in Quebec earlier this century. Furthermore, Quebec's share of the Canadian population is decreasing and this means that its political weight will not increase within federal institutions. In addition, English-language television, radio, and magazines are very popular. Furthermore, the language of business outside Quebec is English. At the same time, French culture in Quebec has never been stronger. Its music, films, television, and literature have never been more vibrant. Many Quebec scientists and industrialists compete effectively in the international marketplace. The imposition of French-only official language legislation in 1977 sharply reduced the fears of cultural assimilation for many Quebecers. Indeed, at least at first glance, it is hard to understand the bitterness that some French Quebecers harbour towards English Canada.[1]

If one probes deeper, however, it becomes easier to comprehend the anger and the reasons for the emergence of Quebec nationalism. Several factors are at work, although they will be addressed only briefly here, since they have been discussed in detail elsewhere.[2]

Stéphane Dion of the Université de Montréal highlights three explanations for the ongoing sovereignty movement in Quebec. First is the common fear among francophone Quebecers that their language and culture are vulnerable to loss through assimilation in English-speaking North America. Second is the new confidence fuelled by the perception that Quebecers' standard of living will improve with sovereignty. Third is the sense of rejection following the failed Meech Lake Accord.[3]

Quebec nationalism is not new. In part, the anger was a response to the widespread discrimination practised by non-francophones and directed at francophones since the last century. With the 1976 election of the separatist Parti Québécois (PQ) to power in Quebec, many supporters of the independence movement proceeded to settle a few scores. But the PQ's election did not just happen; it owed much to a remarkable evolution in Quebec's economy and society begun in the early 1960s and referred to as the Quiet Revolution.

Ushered in by Liberal Premier Jean Lesage, the Quiet Revolution of the 1960s galvanized a Quebec mired in outdated agrarian and theological traditions – a Quebec in which francophones comprised 80 per cent of the province's population but owned a mere 22 per cent of its manufacturing businesses and only 26 per cent of its financial institutions.[4] The Quiet Revolution was a cultural revolution in business-averse Catholic Quebec and among its hallmarks was the establishment of the Société générale de financement du Québec, a state-owned investment agency targeted to francophone businesses, and the Caisse de dépôt et placement du Québec, the provincial investment corporation that invests savings (mainly public sector pension funds) in Quebec enterprises. These moves were augmented by the nationalization of about 82 per cent of the province's hydroelectric resources under the aegis of the crown corporation Hydro-Québec. Other crown corporations, among them the Société de développement industriel (set up under the 1970–6 Robert Bourassa Liberal government) and the Société québécoise d'initiatives petrolières (1969), were established. By providing capitalization for provincial businesses, giving francophones more opportunities to work in the business sector, and bringing most resource sectors (mining and forestry excepted) under firm government control, these initiatives served as the first steps to provincial economic self-reliance. A further push by the provincial government consisted of encouraging young Québécois to attend business school – a policy that eventually gained Quebec the distinction of graduating more MBAs than any other province in Canada and enrolling twice as many business students as the national average.

The Quiet Revolution signalled Quebec's emergence from a relatively poor, largely agrarian population to a modern industrialized society. Various conditions brought it about. First, a Quebec bureaucratic élite developed that had confidence in its ability to guide the future of the province, whether within or outside Canada. Second, an independent and politicized trade union movement emerged. Third, an intellectual class of writers, teachers, professors, and students began to think seriously about nationalism. Fourth, the provincial Liberal party provided new leadership and confidence in the human and natural resources of the province. In this regard, the nationalization of the province's hydroelectric resource promoted an awareness that Quebec could develop the economic infrastructure to sell its products and services to the world and thereby control its own destiny. In a similar vein, big industry and small business, all controlled by francophones, created jobs, prosperity, and confidence in the province's economic future. These French-speaking, university-trained business leaders introduced modern managerial techniques to the Quebec economy. Fifth, the 1967 declaration by President Charles de Gaulle of France – 'Vive le Québec Libre' – offered Quebec nationalists a measure of legitimacy in that the French mother country, from which Quebec had been largely divorced for almost two hundred years, was now recognizing and applauding developments. Sixth, there was a recognition that if Quebec's population growth stayed near zero, and if French-speaking immigration remained limited, then the future of Quebec's distinctive language and culture would be uncertain.

The Quiet Revolution fostered a stronger Quebec identity and greater economic and political power for French-speaking Quebecers. In turn, Quebec nationalists grew more confident that they could take concrete steps to protect and promote the French language and culture. This massive social change had the effect, however, of undermining two of the three most prominent institutions in French Quebec life.

First, as Quebec society changed, more women entered the workforce, put off having children, or decided to have fewer children. The influence of the extended family declined, and birth rates diminished from one of the highest levels in North America to one of the lowest. In addition, the Roman Catholic Church, which had been vital to Quebec society, declined in importance. Church attendance fell dramatically, and the recruitment of priests became difficult. Only the state bureaucratic élites remained as active protectors and promoters of the French presence in Quebec.

In the 1960s, the federal government sought to redress Quebec's fears of cultural assimilation by promoting a national policy of bilingualism in federal government institutions. The notion that Canada could be a truly bilingual nation, in fact as well as in theory, had long been a goal of national political leaders. Bilingualism was made official government policy in federal institutions following the recommendations of the Royal Commission on Bilingualism and Biculturalism in the mid-1960s and, most explicitly, within the policy

agenda of Prime Minister Pierre Elliott Trudeau. In 1969, Trudeau's government passed legislation, the Official Languages Act, that, for the first time,
gave French equal standing with English in the federal government. All federal
government services were made available in both official languages and bilingual government employees were favoured for promotion. Labels of all consumer goods were to be written in both languages. French immersion classes
became widely available.

There were at least four components to Mr Trudeau's strategy. The first was
official bilingualism, which entrenched language rights throughout the country.
The second was multiculturalism, which reflected Trudeau's uneasiness about
the previous emphasis on only two founding cultures. The third was the constitutional equality of the provinces, rather than just two founding nations. The
fourth was to be the eventual incorporation of a charter of rights into the
Canadian constitution.

The federal government's rationale was that national bilingualism would
circumvent the emerging nationalist movement in Quebec and would calm the
fears of francophone Quebecers who worried that their culture and language
would be absorbed into English-speaking North America. In his 1969 book,
Federalism and the French Canadians, Trudeau stressed that federalism would
only work if two things happened. 'First, French Canadians must really want it.
That is to say, they must abandon their role of oppressed nation and decide to
participate boldly and intelligently in the Canadian experience.' Second, Trudeau
wrote, 'if French Canadians abandon their concept of a national state, English
Canadians must do the same.' That is, English-speaking Canadians should not
be pursuing the goal of an English-speaking Canada. The prime minister believed that the Canadian federation should be based on pluralism and the
protection of rights and freedoms rather than a state based on language or race.

Nevertheless, one would be hard-pressed to make the case that Trudeau's
vision has been realized, although the latter three points of Mr Trudeau's
strategy have become vital to Canadians outside of Quebec.[5] Most Canadians
remain unilingual. The national capital area (comprising Ottawa-Hull) along
with Montreal and parts of New Brunswick are the only truly bilingual parts of
Canada, although most federal government services are available in both official languages. There is a general recognition that you cannot impose a language on a people who do not want to speak it.

In fact, Quebecers have not been entirely sympathetic to Ottawa's bilingualism policy. In 1977, the sovereigntist Parti Québécois government made French
the province's only official language with the passage of Bill 101 (see appendix A). It passed legislation mandating that all road and commercial signs
would be in French only. Almost all new immigrants to the province were

compelled to send their children to French schools. All large companies were required to handle internal correspondence in French. These policies were distasteful to many English-speaking Canadians who resented legislation that substantially restricted their institutions. Some rejected the idea that French should receive a special status. Others feared the loss of federal jobs to francophones. Some anglophones were annoyed that French was imposed upon them, even if few local residents spoke the language. Official bilingualism was attractive to many Canadians in theory, but its practical problems have become quite evident. Subsequent developments, such as the passage of the 1982 Constitution Act including the Charter of Rights (now central to English Canada's sense of identity) without Quebec's signature, the inclusion of a notwithstanding clause to the constitution that permitted the Quebec government to sustain its language legislation after court challenge, and the failure of the Meech Lake Accord (to be discussed later) all reinforced Quebec's sense of isolation and English Canada's bitterness.

So language is a key. It is always just below the surface as an issue. It can be a unifying device bringing about a collective interest. In general, in a modern industrialized and diverse polity like Quebec's, the French language is by far the most tangible confirmation of Quebec's distinctive character. Language can be divisive as well, of course. Official language policy can alienate minorities. It can inhibit a sense of national identity. Canada's official languages policy and Quebec's official language policy have not been instruments of multi-ethnic harmony.

Camille Laurin, the PQ education minister and the architect of Bill 101, espoused a variety of goals for the legislation: to end the economic inferiority of francophone Quebecers, to redistribute economic opportunities, to promote the assimilation of immigrants into the francophone community, and to make it clear to all concerned that Quebec was French-speaking.[6] These concerns were and are understandable. Outnumbered by anglophones in North America, 260 million to 6.5 million, the francophones also have the lowest birth rate on the continent and virtually no population growth, since it has been difficult to attract French-speaking immigrants to Quebec. French Canadian children are exposed to English-language media, culture, and business, and they find it attractive. Many francophones fear, quite legitimately, that unless steps are taken to protect and promote their language and culture, it will disappear in the not-too-distant future. Also, it should be noted that some francophone Quebecers have a desire to retaliate against the English in their province, viewing them, rightly or wrongly, as intruders and oppressors. Finally, francophone Quebecers have but to look at the plight of francophones in other provinces to conclude that only in Quebec can their distinctive character be protected.

Bill 101 affected almost every aspect of Quebec society, including the courts, the legislature, the civil service, education, health and social services, and private business. Government services in the language of the anglophone minority (numbering over one million) were curtailed, although English-language materials would be provided on request. The instruction of English-speaking students was to be increasingly in the French language, with anglophone public schools available only to those whose parents had been educated in English in Quebec. Street and commercial signs were to be in French only, and reported violations would be investigated by government bureaucrats, commonly referred to as 'language police.' Most professionals would now have to pass a French language–proficiency test. Clearly, there was complete inconsistency between the bilingual policies of Ottawa and the unilingual policies emanating from Quebec City.

Nevertheless, Bill 101 was enormously popular in the province. Many francophones began to feel that their distinctive language and culture was secure. Although Canada is a country where the protection of individual rights is considered mandatory, collective rights are regarded as almost as important in both English-Canadian and French-Canadian political culture. By world standards the francophone minority is remarkably homogeneous, and its history in Canada dates back as far as the anglophones'. Both factors contribute to a sense of cohesion and legitimacy.

Furthermore, the Canadian federal system grants so many discretionary powers to the provinces that Quebec can legally declare French its official language, play a determining role in immigration policy, and maintain separate public school systems based on religion and language. The Canadian Supreme Court and the Quebec Superior Court had ruled that much of the language legislation was unconstitutional. But the provincial government led by Premier Robert Bourassa had been able to disregard those rulings by using the 'notwithstanding' clause of Canada's constitution,[7] arguing that Bill 101 was in the best interests of Quebec's distinctive character.

Following the passage of Bill 101, Minister of Education Laurin announced that a 50 per cent reduction in the number of children attending English-language schools would be appropriate.[8] In fact, the reduction has been even greater. The Protestant School Board of Greater Montreal had lost 60 per cent of its anglophone students by 1984, substantially more than the natural decline suffered by all schools at the end of the baby boom. In 1993, the entire education system in Quebec was changed as religious school boards were abolished (Catholic as well as Protestant) and restructured along linguistic lines.[9] Many anglophones strongly resisted losing the constitutional guarantee for Protestant schools without gaining in return an equally strong protection for English schools. This protection appears to have been granted.

A major rationale for the educational provisions of Bill 101 was the fear that most immigrants to Quebec would choose English-Protestant schools for their children. This was perceived as a threat to French-language dominance in the province, and for good reason. Immigrants tended to concentrate in Montreal, where English was a powerful attraction. In 1972, according to the Gendron Commission, 89.3 per cent of the allophone children (of neither French nor English heritage) under the jurisdiction of the Montreal Catholic School Commission were enrolled in English schools.[10] A variety of factors have been cited to explain this preference among immigrants: the relatively poor quality of French-language education, including the teaching of English as a second language; perceived prejudice against allophone children in French schools; the ethnic and religious heterogeneity of English schools;[11] the importance of English in North America; and the economic supremacy of English in Quebec. However, by 1993 it had become clear that immigrants to Quebec who spoke neither of Canada's official languages had turned increasingly to French. Between 1976 and 1991 almost two-thirds of allophone immigrants to Quebec had learned French. These immigrants are two and a half times more likely to speak French at home than English.[12] Bill 101, changes in immigration patterns, and constant media attention to language issues have combined to bring about this change.

Neither the place of English in the province nor any special educational provisions for English-speaking migrants from other parts of Canada was mentioned in Bill 101. The latter omission conflicted with the right to minority education set forth in Canada's 1982 constitution. One consequence of Quebec's language legislation is that Quebec anglophones can no longer rely, as they once did, on their economic power to ensure the protection of their rights within the province. As a result, they have become articulate proponents of administrative, legislative, and constitutional action to extend appropriate educational and other public services to linguistic minorities.

Bill 101 had important implications for business and employment in Quebec, as well. Despite promises by the PQ government in 1977, some jobs were lost as a result of the legislation. Section 20 of the bill, for example, created obstacles to the hiring, promotion, and transfer of English-speaking Quebecers in the public sector. Section 35 (among others) impeded access by English-speaking Quebecers to an increasingly French workplace. For a time the Office de la langue française proposed that some firms restrict the number of positions in which business contacts outside Quebec were required, a policy that would have been particularly punitive to the tourist industry.

Most importantly, businesses were required to undertake 'francization' programs aimed at making French the predominant language of industry and commerce. Bill 101 established the fundamental right of every Quebecer to work in French, in both the public and private sectors.[13] Every firm with over fifty employees had to prepare a francization plan covering such concerns as French communications with employees and French-language proficiency at managerial levels. Penalties would be imposed where French was not sufficiently promoted and where merchants advertised their products in languages other than French. Public administration, health and social services, professional corporations, and employees' associations were now obliged to inform and serve in French.

Francophones, now guaranteed that workplaces and schools would operate in French, could more effectively control their cultural and linguistic destiny. The two-thirds of Quebecers who speak only French could feel more secure that their jobs in Quebec would be protected.[14] By the same token, however, Quebec was the only province in Canada to restrict the legal rights of a minority to work, study, and function freely in its own language. Bill 101 was possible in a society that had accepted the principle of state intervention in relation to language and had mobilized to withstand a perceived threat to its survival as a majority within Quebec. The resulting climate of fear and mistrust between the English and the French, especially in Montreal, gave rise to a worsening environment for economic investment. Most observers would agree, however, that Bill 101 has served to reduce, if not totally eliminate, the economic disparity between French-speaking and English-speaking Quebecers. The francization of private enterprise has also contributed to the emergence of a French-speaking entrepreneurial class.

Amid the enormous level of popular support for Quebec's language legislation, many non-francophones felt bitter and charged that, even when they spoke French, they were being discriminated against by the provincial bureaucracy. The *Montreal Gazette*, the leading English-language newspaper in the province, has systematically listed episodes of discrimination against Quebecers of English heritage. Alliance Quebec was organized to protect English-language minority rights in the province. In 1989, for the first time, an anti–Bill 101, anti-Meech Lake, English rights party, the Equality party, won four seats in the provincial legislature. Two of the four elected members did not speak French, a frequent pattern among Quebec's anglophones – which proved interesting, since all debates in the National Assembly are conducted in French. One could argue that denying the rights of anglophones hurts francophones as well, by limiting their exposure to English and thus their social mobility. Quebec's economy depends heavily on exports to the United States and almost all bilateral contracts are written in English. Also, English predominates in advanced technologies, where French terms often do not exist. And yet, Quebec's education department has expressed concern that children not learn a second language at too early an age for fear it would hinder their learning of French. One apparent result is that anglophone children in Quebec are more likely to speak French than are francophone children to speak English. This is a complete reversal from the pre–Bill 101 era.

Since 1976, more than 200,000 Quebecers have emigrated, principally anglophones and often the best educated, most skilled members of Quebec society. For reasons most often cited for this are the consequences of Bill 101 and the high level of income tax. Similarly, many individuals and businesses refuse to relocate to the province because of perceived language problems. Many corporations regard Quebec as a distribution area rather than a manufacturing centre or home-office location. These circumstances do not bode well for Quebec's economic future.

However, from a Quebec sovereigntist's perspective, Quebec will always hold the minority position in what is seen as its non-compromising position with Canada. Quebec will never be treated as an equal, as indicated by its uncertain constitutional status and disdain for the 1982 Constitution Act. Quebec will never be able to bargain as an equal, and its low birth rate would make it weaker still within Canada as its population declines.

This notion of equality should be stressed. In general, francophone Quebecers see the federation as a pact between two equals, English and French. By contrast, most anglophone Canadians see Canada as a federation of ten provinces. French-speaking Quebec, although extremely important, is still only one of ten. Canadians outside Quebec see Canada as a multicultural society where special status for any one group is a 'constitutional affront.'[15]

The Charter of Rights reflects an emphasis on protecting and promoting individual rights in Canada. In fact, the Charter is now immensely popular and is the most tangible evidence of a Canadian ethic for many Canadians today outside Quebec. By contrast, francophone Quebecers place less emphasis on the Charter. If the French fact is to survive, then collective rights must be protected and promoted. This is a fundamentally different perspective than that evident in the rest of Canada.

Alain Dubuc, a columnist with Montreal's *La Presse*, would add another explanation. He stresses that many Quebecers see the Canadian federal structure as hindering the growth and fulfilment of Quebec's political and economic evolution. Dubuc notes that new generations of francophone Quebecers are not angry at Canada. They have not known oppression first-hand. But Canadian institutions are inflexible and are largely inaccessible to francophones.[16] Daniel Latouche, a columnist for *Le Devoir* and a professor at the Université du Québec à Montréal, sees this new interpretation of Quebec nationalism as a case of 'deregulation.' Sovereignty would eliminate a stifling and expensive level of government. Of course, this begs the question of whether there exists evidence to demonstrate that money can be saved and efficiency promoted by removing a layer of government. Nor can most Quebecers identify the areas where the removal of the federal government would serve their interests. In fact, Quebecers are more dissatisfied with basic public services like health, education and policing – all of which are delivered by the provincial or local governments – than Canadians in any other province.[17]

Furthermore, even as PQ leader Jacques Parizeau denounces the multiple overlapping jurisdictions between Quebec and Ottawa, the policy platform of the Parti Québécois creates many new structures between the local, regional, and provincial levels of government. In addition, Mr Parizeau has guaranteed employment for all federal bureaucrats who live in Quebec. This will not make sovereignty cheaper or more efficient for Quebecers. Also, Quebec is the only province that duplicates such services as personal income tax and the administration of the Canadian and Quebec pension plans. This Quebec-inspired duplication does not promote efficiency either. In truth, we do not know how to measure the effect of overlap on governmental efficiency. The debate may be more about competition for power than bureaucratic duplication.[18]

Nevertheless, many Quebec sovereigntists insist that the Canadian federal structure 'shackles' Quebec. If Canada is in poor financial shape, then this inhibits Quebec's ability to prosper. Canada does not invest enough in training and research programs, technology or agricultural development, or health and post-secondary education. There is truth to this critique. Manufacturing investments in Quebec have declined steadily from 1990 to 1993. From 1990–1 to 1992–3, only 7.8 per cent of the $275 million in tax credits earmarked by the Quebec government for manpower training have been granted to companies. Money spent for research and development had remained at less than 1.5 per cent of the province's gross domestic product, below the 2 per cent the government had targeted.

Also, sovereigntists insist that 45 per cent of the operations of 119 federal departments, crown corporations, and other bodies, involving 453 different federal programs, directly overlap similar provincial programs. Bloc Québécois leader Lucien Bouchard has asserted that as much as $40 billion is wasted annually. It should be noted that Bouchard's assertions have been challenged by prominent federalists.

Quebec is quite generous in offering business tax credits. But these are taxed by Ottawa and this is frustrating to many in Quebec. Quebec initiates various programs that, once reviewed by Ottawa, are essentially emasculated. Among sovereigntist intellectuals, the duplication/inefficiency motive for independence is as compelling, if not more so, than the language and culture concern. The

federal Liberal government of Jean Chrétien has pledged to address the duplication issue in concert with the provincial premiers. But reinventing government is an extremely difficult exercise.

The 'shackling' argument is really a complaint about federal inefficiency.
Presumably, a sovereign Quebec with a unitary constitutional structure would
promote less duplication and clearer direction and action. However, this may
be wishful thinking. There is no empirical evidence to demonstrate that unitary
states in large countries are any more or less efficient than federal ones.[19]

The most compelling motive for sovereignty remains the fear of linguistic assimilation. Nearly two of three French-speaking Quebecers believe that
the French language is threatened in Quebec, while only two of ten non-
francophones share that view.[20] André Blais and Élisabeth Gidengil find in a
survey that linguistic fear of assimilation is a significant determinant of support
for sovereignty. For example, the mayor of Quebec City, Jean-Paul L'Allier,
while testifying before the Quebec National Assembly committee holding hearings on relaxing the Bill 178 commercial sign law, stated that the ban on all
minority languages should be maintained. But if it were repealed, then Quebec
City should be exempted and remain French only. He said that the capital
region must express itself in French, or social peace and linguistic harmony
and tolerance would be threatened. Mr L'Allier warned that vandalism could
result. So, public policy would be dictated by mythical vandals. This view is
not easily dismissed. Many Quebecers are increasingly concerned about any
perceived threats to their distinctive language and culture.

The various strains of nationalism in Quebec have produced a situation in
which French-speaking Quebecers are twice as likely to identify themselves as
Québécois than as French Canadians and more than six times as likely to
identify themselves as Quebecers than as Canadians. This said, a significant
majority of Quebec francophones – 62 per cent in 1991 – feel profoundly
attached to Canada.[21] It is interesting to note that Canadians outside Quebec are
increasingly likely to call themselves Canadian in census reports, rather than
listing their ethnic background.[22] It may be that for many Canadians ethnicity
is no longer relevant.

Sovereignty advocates insist that sovereignty-association would allow Quebec to adapt to new global imperatives.[23] Entire societies are in competition
with each other worldwide, and their success depends on their capacity for
social compromises and rapid adaptation to changing economic conditions. Yet
federal-provincial competition inhibits Quebec's ability to compete. Sovereignty-association would allow Quebec greater policy-making authority, and
thereby offer it a chance to compete freely without obstructive federal obstacles, supporters stress.

Quebec has emerged as a powerful French-speaking polity. It has a stock exchange where French is the predominant language of work, its own universities, and a substantial cultural industry. Most French-speaking Quebecers can trace their roots back to a few thousand settlers in the 1600s. They have their own customs, system of civil law, tastes, and national holidays. In the terms of the failed Meech Lake Accord, Quebec is a 'distinct society.' Furthermore, there is now in Quebec a viable, energetic, and moderately successful business class.

In addition, the sovereigntist Parti Québécois has emerged as an important component of the Canadian political élite. This is unusual. One would be hard-pressed to find a sovereigntist party in any western industrialized country that is so fully integrated into the nation's political life. Quebec's unique cultural history, coupled with its apparent economic strength, gave the sovereigntists reason to believe that an independent Quebec could thrive.

Several observers argue that, in some ways, francophones and anglophones in Canada are not so different. Both French-speaking and English-speaking Canadians are said to have more of a collective orientation than do Americans, who are said to favour more individualistic values. This is a popular belief in Canada. It may or may not be true.[24] Notwithstanding the difficulty of testing this proposition empirically, it is certainly possible that Canada's collective orientation might be manifested in the widespread support for comprehensive national health insurance, generous unemployment and social security benefits, gun control, and the willingness to pay higher taxes to meet these expenses. Nowhere in Canada (with Newfoundland the possible exception) is this collective orientation more pervasive than in Quebec, where politicians and the mass public commonly refer to Quebecers (in French) as constituting a 'nation.' If there is a perception that this 'nation' is threatened by Canada's English-speaking majority or by demographic factors, the first instinct for many Québécois is to call for the creation of a sovereign state that could best protect what makes Quebec a distinctive society.

Quebec is not entirely unique of course. Other parts of the world – the Basque region of Spain, Belgium, and much of Africa and Asia – have national minorities that are concentrated in particular areas where they are majorities. In many of these areas, the people think that their interests would be best served if they had more independence. Quebec is special for a number of reasons, however.

First, it is by world standards an ethnically homogeneous place outside the Montreal region. Second, it enjoys one of the highest standards of living in the world. Third, it is one of just ten provinces in the Canadian federation. This relatively small number, and Quebec's position as the province with the second largest population base, gives it enormous political and economic clout within Canada. Fourth, Canada's decentralized federal structure, in combination with its centralized parliamentary system, provides incentives for the provinces to seek greater measures of economic and political autonomy.[25] The Canadian parliament represents only population, not regional communities. Unlike the U.S. Congress, which has an upper legislative body that includes two senators per state and thus balances the regions, Canada has no such balance. As a result, the provinces with the largest populations, Ontario and Quebec, have dominated the national agenda while western and Atlantic regional interests have been underrepresented in the institutions of power. Similarly, Ontario and Quebec manufacturers have historically been protected while western and Atlantic consumers have paid premium rates for imports.

In addition, critics of Canada's decentralized structure make the reasonable case that Ottawa has become incapable of instituting national policies in technology enhancement, export promotion, education, and retraining. Quebec sovereigntists have been in the forefront of those groups who criticize Ottawa's lack of leadership. Instead, the sovereigntists claim that only they could plan a coherent policy agenda for a modern Quebec. The combination of a weak parliament and senate, poor federal public policy direction, an electoral system that favours the centre and hurts third parties, and possibly the most powerful constituent units (provinces) in any federation in the world today all work to promote national fragmentation and strong regional identities.

This is not a new phenomenon in Canada. It has long been clear that there is nothing sacrosanct about Canada's constitutional structure. Quebec has been looking for an altered administrative role since it first became a colony of Great Britain in the mid-eighteenth century. Quebec has promoted substantial changes in Canada's constitutional structure many times in the past (in 1763, 1774, 1791, 1840, and 1867). The new arrangement that might emerge in the 1990s has had some precedent then, although the proposed changes have never been so sweeping.[26]

In the long run, regional disaffection with Ottawa may prove as destructive as the constant battles over language in Canada. In the Atlantic region, as well as in the West and the North, the longstanding complaints that the country's affairs are unfairly dominated by Quebec's constitutional demands and Ontario's economy are becoming more insistent. In addition to the increasing sense of ambivalence about national identity, there is also a growing confidence that Quebec, Ontario, and the West could survive economically as separate nations. In fact, it is worth noting that former Ontario attorney general Ian Scott has acknowledged that, if Quebec were to leave the federation, Ontario might contemplate entering into a new, two-province union with Quebec that could exclude the rest of present-day Canada.[27] This is a minority view, of course, but it is a recognition that Ontario does not look forward to being left with the primary responsibility for supporting the 'have-not' Maritime provinces.

As noted, Canada has long been a fairly decentralized nation-state. What is now different is the extent to which Canada has become not just politically but economically decentralized. For example, the federal government controls only 40 per cent of public sector expenditures, the other 60 per cent being held by other levels of government. Furthermore, the larger provinces are better able to regulate their own economies. Market forces are increasingly being controlled by global multinationals. Centralizing institutions in transportation sectors have been drastically cut back, as in the case of the Via Rail train service, or are being privatized, as in the case of Air Canada. The unifying symbols of the nation are increasingly rare. In addition, until recently, when provinces flouted federal regulations, Ottawa penalized them by withholding transfer payments. But with a crippling federal debt, the federal government has systematically reduced the cash flow to the point where it has little clout left to enforce compliance. The federal deficit and debt burden are promoting decentralized policy making.

Indeed, a decentralized view of Canada has become the accepted vision of the nation. Ironically, this has occurred after the death of the Meech Lake constitutional accord, which was defeated by those who said that they were standing up for a strong central vision of the country. Their victory over the forces of decentralization appears to have been fleeting. Today, a Canada with more powers at the provincial level, organized according to economic realities, seems to be assumed in any political discussion about the nation's future. Both former prime minister Brian Mulroney and Prime Minister Jean Chrétien have declared that decentralization would be part of their respective constitutional programs. This is particularly ironic in Chrétien's case, given that he once proclaimed himself the champion of strong centralized federalism. Senior civil servants, academics, and the general public now regard federal decentralized public policy making as the only acceptable course to follow. The September 1991 federal government constitutional proposals and the July 1992 first ministers' agreement both address this issue directly, a point that will be discussed subsequently.

Furthermore, pollsters find that Canadians attach declining importance to such symbols of nationhood as the national anthem, the prime minister, the governor general, the queen, and bilingualism (although the 1982 Charter of Rights remains an important national symbol outside Quebec). Many Canadians establish their identity first in terms of their province or region and only second in terms of being Canadian. The obvious contrast is to the United States whose citizens, no matter their state or region, regard themselves as Americans first. In addition, when the Environics Research Group polled Canadians about the division of powers in nineteen areas of constitutional jurisdiction, they found that respondents favoured more provincial power in fifteen.[28] It is clear, then, that Canada has emerged as a decentralized federation with the provinces exercising many of Ottawa's traditional powers.

2

From Meech Lake to Charlottetown: The Evolution of Constitutional Proposals

In contrast to the vitality of the French-speaking majority in Quebec, the English-speaking minority in Quebec and the French-speaking minority outside Quebec are diminishing in number. According to census figures, between 1981 and 1986 the proportion of Quebec's population that spoke English at home fell from 12.7 per cent to 12.3 per cent. The proportion of the rest of Canada's population that spoke French at home fell from 3.8 per cent to 3.6 per cent. To ensure the protection and promotion of the French language in Quebec, politicians there have demanded greater control by the Quebec government of education, language policy, immigration, cultural policy, and many other sectors.

It should be noted, however, that Quebec has never been more French-speaking than it is today. Quebecers whose mother tongue is French make up 82 per cent of the province, and more than half of the remaining 18 per cent are functional in French. Only 8 per cent of Quebec residents speak no French. French is now the language of business in the province. More than 80 per cent of immigrant children voluntarily enter French language junior colleges after they finish high school. Eighty-eight per cent of persons born in Quebec stay in Quebec. By contrast only 60 per cent of Canadians born outside Quebec remain in their home province.

Repeated efforts to reconcile the English and the French factions within the Canadian federation have been made in the last forty years. Every major party, various royal commissions, Canadian senate investigations, and prominent interest groups have suggested a variety of federal, non-federal, unitary, special status, or sovereignty-association alternatives. Some have called for national bilingualism; others seek unilingualism in Quebec and in the rest of Canada. Efforts to promote national multiculturalism were once prominent as well. These blue-ribbon constitutional panels attracted national attention during their tenure, but concrete resolutions to Canada's constitutional ills have provided mixed results at best.

One important effort was the inclusion of the Charter of Rights and Freedoms in the 1982 Constitution Act, and the meeting at Meech Lake in 1987 which attempted to accommodate the only non-signatory to that constitution, Quebec. Quebec was legally bound to the terms of the Act, but it refused to offer its assent. Prime Minister Brian Mulroney decided that Canadian unity could be ensured only if Quebec's demands for an official recognition of its unique character were acknowledged by the federal government and enshrined in the constitution. As a result, in 1987, the prime minister and every provincial premier negotiated the Meech Lake constitutional accord which met all of Quebec's demands and simultaneously strengthened the policy-making authority of the other provinces vis-à-vis the federal government.

The Meech Lake Accord has been discussed in great detail elsewhere[1] and will not be discussed comprehensively here. It should be noted that the Meech Lake Accord was a proposed set of amendments to the 1982 Constitution Act designed to convince Quebec that it should sign the Constitution. According to the provisions of the accord, Quebec was to be recognized as a 'distinct society,' which referred to Quebec's interest in protecting its distinctive language, culture, and system of civil law. The distinct society clause implied to many analysts outside the province that Quebec was special and entitled to a greater share of responsibility for its own political and cultural future. Others saw the distinct society clause as recognition of an obvious reality, that Quebec was distinctive and that Meech Lake simply reaffirmed this. They pointed out that Quebec's uniqueness was recognized as long ago as 1774 with the acceptance of its distinct French civil law system rather than English common law. Canada's fathers of confederation further entrenched this view of Quebec's distinctiveness by officially recognizing the Civil Code and allowing the use of French in the province's courts and legislature.

Still other political analysts noted that if Quebec were constitutionally distinctive, if its provincial leaders were required to preserve and promote that distinctiveness, then other regions of the country would also have to be granted similar status. They worried that Quebec's special status would grant it constitutional powers unavailable to other regions or groups with an equally valid claim. Some worried that Quebec would invoke the distinct society clause as a lever to harm individual and minority rights. Also, many suggested that the exclusive focus on Quebec's distinctiveness within Canada demeaned the contribution of aboriginals and other ethnic communities to defining Canada's identity. The Meech Lake Accord failed, in part, because of opposition by the Newfoundland government and native Canadians in Manitoba who expressed these exact fears.

Quebec sees itself as one of two partners to the federal constitutional bargain. The rest of Canada sees Quebec as just one of ten provinces. Meech Lake failed to reconcile these two positions. The distinct society clause of the Meech Lake Accord, which would have balanced the Charter of Rights' individual rights focus with the collective rights interest of Canada's francophone minority, was of core importance. This clause was rejected by the majority of non-francophone Canadians who were wary of offering Quebec special powers unavailable in the rest of the nation.

This point is important. In English Canada, there is general agreement that all provinces deserve equal constitutional status, although this has not always been true in actual constitutional law. Also, all Canadians deserve equal rights and equal protection under the law. By contrast, francophone Quebecers regard the federal bargain as between two equal nations. One is French speaking and one is English speaking. Quebec is equal before the law to all of the others. Both interpretations relate to competing interpretations of the 'compact' theory, the notion that there were two 'founding nations' of Canada. One view sees the compact as between two peoples, English and French. The other sees it as consisting equally of the four original provinces in 1867 – Ontario, Quebec, New Brunswick, and Nova Scotia – and subsequently the remaining six.[2] From this perspective, the 1982 Charter of Rights is perfectly compatible with provincial equality; Quebec's use of the notwithstanding clause is not.

When the Meech Lake Accord was introduced in 1987, all ten premiers and the prime minister supported it. The provincial leaders pledged that the accord would be ratified in their respective legislatures, however, and it collapsed when Manitoba and Newfoundland had failed to ratify it by the three-year deadline of 23 June 1990. One can point to a number of frequently suggested flaws in the accord including: first, the élitist, non-consultative nature of the bargaining; second, the failure to recognize adequately the interests of native Canadians, English-speaking women, immigrants, and others; and third, the vague discussion of fundamental issues. Other reasons for its failure were the poor job of promotion that the federal government pursued, as well as the blatant manipulation of the media and the public by politicians on both sides of the debate. The public's attention and its passions were targeted by politicians for their own short-term political interests. What might have been a reasoned debate about the relative advantages and disadvantages of the Meech Lake Accord was instead a blatant manipulation of symbols and emotions resulting in widespread public cynicism concerning the accord, its architects, and its opponents.

The Meech Lake Accord was sold badly to the Canadian public by the Mulroney government. Indeed, the prime minister bragged of manipulating his political adversaries over the issue. In addition, because the two major federal opposition parties – the Liberals and the New Democrats – immediately supported the accord, there was virtually no parliamentary debate about its rationale and substance. It should also be noted that the media was obsessed with the personalities involved, not the content and possible consequences of the proposals.[3]

Ultimately Meech failed because Canadians could not agree on how Quebec should be regarded within Canada. It failed because many of its leaders were unwilling to negotiate the deal to a successful conclusion. It may have failed because the public was virtually excluded from the deliberations, as many critics maintain. Although one could make the equally plausible argument that, had the process been more open, it would have suffered from an excess of democratic voices, and amid the cacophony nothing would have been accomplished. Finally, it failed because most Canadians and their political leaders could not agree on what Canada represents as a nation, what rights its people should have, and how they should be governed. All these signs of a lack of national consensus had always been present, but the Meech Lake Accord brought the underlying tensions to the surface.

The accord's collapse was an indication, however legitimate, to French Quebecers that English Canada did not care about their most basic interests. For the first time ever, the rest of Canada had rejected a Quebec constitutional proposal. Prior to this, Quebec had been the one to say no to Canadian constitutional proposals.[4] As a result, an alternative constitutional arrangement within or outside Canada would become mandatory as far as Quebecers were concerned. For many English Canadians, the failure of the accord was a rejection of Prime Minister Brian Mulroney, or of Quebec's special status, or of the French language, or of élitism, or of any of Canada's other ills, both real and imagined.

For example, outside Quebec, the anti–Meech Lake Accord movement was fuelled by the realization that Premier Bourassa of Quebec had imposed the 'notwithstanding' clause of the Canadian Charter of Rights to set aside a Canadian Supreme Court ruling declaring unconstitutional some of Quebec's strict language laws. In the rest of Canada, Quebec was seen not as promoting national bilingualism but Quebec unilingualism. It did not respect the rule of law and would make use of every constitutional trick it could to reaffirm its distinctiveness from the rest of Canada. Quebec was not respecting the Charter of Rights which was so vital to the rest of Canada. It was not recognizing the constitutional protections afforded to all Canadians. The 'distinct society' clause of the Meech Lake Accord reinforced this Quebec intolerance, Meech opponents urged, for Quebec was alone in demanding recognition of its distinctiveness. In addition, Quebec would never be satisfied until it achieved political sovereignty. Distinctiveness was just the first step, then, towards sovereignty-association.

A successful Meech Lake Accord would not have been a tonic for Canada's problems, however. It was just a first step as far as many Quebecers were concerned. Demands for greater levels of political autonomy would have continued, but at a slower pace.

It should be stressed that the provisions of the Meech Lake Accord were the absolute minimum that Quebec would accept. Any new concessions by Ottawa would have to include far more widespread provincial powers. In addition, Quebecers interpreted Meech's failure as a loss of national pride or 'face.' Ottawa and the provinces would have to make substantial concessions to Quebec to make amends for Meech's failure. This loss of face is a driving force behind Quebec's sovereigntist push. Furthermore, it would be difficult for federal authorities to make the necessary concessions to Quebec without squandering what little political capital that they might still have in the rest of the country.

Ultimately, Meech's failure demonstrated that Canada's leaders and political institutions could not design and implement a new set of accommodations within the federation. It showed that the 'unanimity' rule whereby all of the provinces, and not just a substantial majority, had to ratify constitutional amendments, was unworkable. Most importantly, Meech's failure made clear the constitutional disputes between Canadians, and thereby prompted Quebec to pursue a more sovereigntist path.[5]

It is interesting to speculate about what might have happened had the Meech Lake Accord passed. Undoubtedly, the Quebec sovereigntist movement would still be strong, but it probably would have been unable to rally a majority of voters – at least in the short run. Secession was regarded by most observers as a radical alternative that was in sharp contrast to Quebec's conciliatory traditions. In addition, the independence movement had a limited constituency, as 20 per cent of the electorate – English-speaking Quebecers and first-generation immigrants – would never vote for sovereignty. The failure of Meech Lake was such a blow to the pride of French-speaking Québécois, however, that a majority began to demand dramatic restructuring. Those francophones who still considered themselves federalists – and they remained a significant number – became fairly quiet, for they could not say when asked how they could obtain a decent and honourable deal with the rest of Canada when even Meech's minimal conditions were not accepted. French-speaking federalists felt deprived of arguments against the sovereignty supporters, and this was almost entirely because of the Meech fiasco.

Because all of Canada's provinces failed to reach agreement at Meech Lake, Premier Bourassa of Quebec decided that his government would negotiate amendments only in Ottawa directly, and not with the other provinces. He also launched a parliamentary commission, the Bélanger-Campeau Commission, to explore Quebec's future relationship to Canada. The mandate of this panel was to consider all options for Quebec's future, except for retaining the status quo and applying to join the United States. The Bélanger-Campeau Commission will be discussed later in more detail, but it is important to note here that Bourassa expected it to come up with suggestions as to the scope of the powers to be taken from Ottawa, the ways to achieve this, and the means whereby the economic relationship between Quebec and Canada could be protected.

After the failure of Meech, the federal Conservatives continued to decline in popularity. The federal Liberals found themselves first in national polls, but their leader, Jean Chrétien, was unpopular in his native province, Quebec, and represented a New Brunswick constituency. An avowedly sovereigntist party, the Bloc Québécois, emerged as a popular federal alternative to the more established parties in Quebec. The governing provincial Liberal party had become almost as decentralist as the opposition sovereigntist Parti Québécois. Bourassa promised to hold a provincial referendum on sovereignty on federal government concessions to Quebec in October 1992. Clearly the fallout in Quebec from Meech Lake's failure had been extensive.

In addition, from the time of Meech's failure until 1993, the constitutional position of both the provincial Liberal party and the separatist Parti Québécois had become similar. Both advocated constitutional restructuring. Both were angry about Meech Lake's failure and were increasingly strident in their rhetoric. The PQ discussed independence or sovereignty-association. Their strategy would be to begin the sovereignty process after an election victory, negotiate a new economic agreement with the rest of Canada, and then submit a new constitutional proposal advocating sovereignty to a referendum.

The Liberals emphasized a substantially autonomous Quebec within a larger nation called Canada. It was reminiscent of a true confederation of powerful provinces and a weak central government. It was as if the Liberals wanted to achieve political sovereignty only after negotiating an economic association first. To some observers, the difference between the two parties was a matter of tactics and not ultimate goals. Although he was a federalist, Quebec Premier Robert Bourassa called for 'a new arrangement within the Canadian federation' that would give Quebec more economic clout.

Bourassa argued for renewed federalism because he believed that the Bank of Canada's high interest rate policy was unfair to Quebec, that the federal government made unacceptable demands on Quebec to reduce its expenses and raise taxes, and that the federal system forced too much costly duplication of public services.[6] Of course, a number of the other provinces had the same complaints. Problems of this kind are evident in almost any democratic federation. It is not clear that renewed federalism would ameliorate this situation.

After the failure of the Meech Lake Accord, many members of the provincial Liberal party voiced support for sovereignty-association. In November 1990, the then-president of the Liberal party's youth wing asserted that this group was willing to consider full political autonomy for Quebec. Liberal members in the provincial legislature openly questioned the existing federal structure. Premier Bourassa lauded as 'realistic and innovative' the youth wing's position. The only staunchly federalist provincial party, the Equality party, was an English-rights fringe group with only three elected members in 1993 who by virtue of their number had to sit as independents. In fact, there is no completely pro-federalist party in Quebec today.

Nevertheless, Premier Bourassa made it clear that he favoured keeping Quebec in Canada, but with a loosening of ties with Ottawa. Quebec would continue to use the Canadian dollar and to trade freely with the rest of Canada. It would continue to share the defence and foreign policy apparatus of the federal government, while retaining complete sovereignty over areas such as immigration, culture, education, and manpower training. Bourassa also suggested that a new 'supranational' parliament be formed as part of a transformed Canadian federation.

Bourassa's suggestions for a renewal of the federation brought him into conflict with the opposition Parti Québécois. PQ leaders said they also wanted Quebec to have close economic links with Canada, including a common currency, but rejected any form of political association. In their view, Quebec should be a fully independent state with its own laws, tax system, foreign policy, and military establishment.

Premier Bourassa had considerable ability to shape the outcome of the ongoing debate in Quebec. He was strengthened by his strong majority in the Quebec parliament and his popular support in the polls. On the other hand, the separatist Parti Québécois has set a clear agenda for sovereignty. A PQ government would enter negotiations with Ottawa on independence. A subsequent referendum would endorse the final independence agreement as well as a constitution for the new state. Indeed, PQ leader Jacques Parizeau vigorously opposed Premier Bourassa and the Liberal party's attempt to renegotiate the existing constitutional structure. By 1994, Bourassa's successor as premier, Daniel Johnson, had asserted that he and his party were federalists. The choice between his party and the sovereigntist PQ would now be clear.

Part of the PQ strategy is to argue that constitutional uncertainty is not good for the economy. They stress that English Canada is no longer a threat to Quebec's culture. Instead, they fear that Canada is no longer workable as a country. As noted earlier, however, this is by no means a unanimous position within the sovereigntist party, many of whose members still express concern about linguistic and cultural threats.

The Parti Québécois insists that an independent Quebec would adopt its own constitution, collect all taxes, sign international treaties, and apply for a seat at the United Nations. In addition, a Quebec citizen would be defined as a Canadian citizen living in Quebec at the moment of independence and all those born after. Persons born outside Quebec but whose parents were once Quebec residents would be eligible to become citizens. A Quebec passport would give them official citizenship status. Quebec would have its own army and remain a part of the North Atlantic Treaty Organization (NATO) and the North American Air Defence Agreement (NORAD). People and goods would circulate freely between Quebec and Canada, but customs offices would be set up along the border to collect duties on Canadian goods entering Quebec. Also, Quebec would share a common currency with Canada and become a minority shareholder in the Bank of Canada. If Canada refused such an arrangement, Quebec would establish its own currency or use the Canadian currency anyway. In addition, a special commission would study the possibility of setting up an American-type republican form of government, with a president and an upper house formed of regional representatives. As noted, all Quebec civil servants working for the federal government would automatically be hired by the Quebec government to run its embassies and manage its postal service, training, and other programs now under federal jurisdiction.

Until 1993, the Parti Québécois's policy for cultural and linguistic minorities was explicit and restrictive. To promote the French language and culture, the PQ would permit no bilingual signs, even inside stores. All firms with ten or more employees would be forced to demonstrate their primary usage of French. English-language health institutions would provide full services in French immediately. The federal government would be hindered from promoting bilingual projects in Quebec. All these policies would reinforce or carry further existing legislation. The collapse of the Meech Lake Accord further galvanized PQ support for these policies. It was noted that a Parti Québécois government might relax these laws somewhat after sovereignty, if a majority of Quebecers favoured such a move. But they might not have.[7] Bill 101, and the subsequent Bill 178 governing signs, are extremely popular measures in francophone Quebec.

However, at an August 1993 PQ policy convention, the sovereigntist party endorsed various policies on the role of anglophones in a sovereign Quebec, These include:

- The right to an education system run by anglophones.
- The right to speak English in the courts and the National Assembly.
- Bilingual status for health institutions historically linked to the English community.
- English programming on the state radio and television networks of an independent Quebec and licences for private English radio and television stations.
- Affirmative action to increase the number of anglophones in the Quebec civil service.

No policy on commercial signs was agreed upon.

MEECH LAKE'S FAILURE AND THE FEDERAL-PROVINCIAL
DIVISION OF POWERS

Meech Lake's failure aggravated the existing problem of how powers should be divided between Ottawa and the provinces. Prime Minister Mulroney insisted that any new powers that Quebec sought should be available to all of the provinces. He was not prepared to pursue an asymmetrical approach that would grant powers to Quebec that were not also available to the other provinces. Contrary to the expectations of Quebecers, the Constitution Act, 1982, reduced rather than increased some of the powers of the Quebec National Assembly and transferred power – including the authority to determine who can attend English-language schools in Quebec – to the Supreme Court of Canada through its decisions made under the Charter of Rights and Freedoms.

The Bélanger-Campeau Commission heard briefs that addressed the question of what new powers Quebec should have. Some argued that Quebec should assume virtually all of the powers of a sovereign state, sharing a common currency and armed forces with Canada. Others believed that Quebec should assert control of specific areas over which it has traditionally sought jurisdiction, including telecommunications, job training, unemployment insurance, language policy, and all aspects of health care.

Those who argue for an asymmetrical federation face two problems. First, there is little incentive for the other provinces to agree to a constitutional structure in which Quebec has powers unavailable to the other provinces. Also, if Quebec is given powers that the other provinces do not get, it will be difficult to justify Quebec MPs and ministers voting on laws and programs that only apply outside their province.

Nevertheless, because of the Meech Lake Accord's collapse, as well as escalating indebtedness and market-oriented economics, Quebec and the other provinces have demanded and received more powers from the federal government. Ottawa has, in turn, loosened restrictions on provincial income tax systems and rearranged federal-provincial finances. The federal government's program of deregulation, aggravated by Meech Lake's failure, has led to a steady withdrawal of federal agencies and institutions from directing the national economy.

Also, the government is attempting to contain the deficit by restricting the growth of transfer payments – the money Ottawa sends to the provinces to help pay for such services as health, welfare, and higher education. In return, Ottawa will give the provinces the responsibility – and the authority – to restructure and increase their own income taxes if they want to maintain or improve current levels of service. The result is an increasingly pronounced fragmentation of the centre of political gravity away from Ottawa and to the provinces.

Critics assert that this decentralization will lead to a patchwork federation of 'have' and 'have-not' provinces. In the absence of strong federal leadership, they maintain, richer provinces may have better medicare systems, for example, while poorer provinces will be able to afford only skeleton health programs. Analysts point to other recent examples of this federal government abdication of authority in fields like rail transportation, freedom of funding for hospitals and higher education, Ottawa's withdrawal from unemployment insurance programs, and federal government restrictions on payments to Ontario, British Columbia, and Alberta under the Canada Assistance Program, which helps fund welfare programs.

Although these reductions have clearly helped to slow the increase in Canada's national debt, the provinces have been unwilling to make up the shortfalls in order to maintain social spending. They do not have the money to take over these programs. Instead, several provinces have slashed their own transfers to municipalities, hospitals, and universities. In fact, some aspects of the medicare system are under severe financial strain in 1994.

In any case, it is clear that for political and economic reasons more public policy-making functions are being shifted to the provinces. In Quebec at least, this is a popular strategy, according to polls.[8] The Quebec government has been responsive. It now has jurisdiction over immigration (one of the provisions of the Meech Lake Accord) and might assume responsibility for communications and manpower training following subsequent constitutional proposals. This would accompany substantial autonomy in managing Quebec's education, legal code, and pension funds. Clearly, Quebec will be better able to make decisions in areas that directly affect its interests.

As was noted earlier, Quebec has received much greater authority to exercise immigration powers. Net emigration of the Quebec population reached

12,000 persons per year from 1976 to 1981, whereas from 1986 to 1989 Quebec recorded a gain of 13,000 persons per year. The new federal government agreement with Quebec on immigration gives Quebec greater control over the selection and integration of independent immigrants, along with the money needed for job training and French-language instruction. Quebec is 'guaranteed' a certain per centage of Canadian immigration, although the agreement is vague in its potential effort on immigration levels. As compensation for taking over these responsibilities, Quebec will receive $332 million from Ottawa over the period 1991–5. This is an exception to the federal government's policy of cutting transfer payments to the provinces.

This arrangement gives Quebec vital new instruments to help maintain, through immigration, its French character and its demographic weight in Canada.[9] Nevertheless, the Canadian Charter of Rights, including its mobility provisions, prevails. Ottawa maintains the ultimate power to admit or reject every applicant, although it is reluctant to exercise this power. Refugees and sponsored immigrants also remain under federal authority, as does exclusive responsibility for setting national standards and objectives for immigration. This being said, the immigration agreement with Quebec was a basic provision of the failed Meech Lake Accord. In the aftermath of its failure, the Mulroney government made every effort to accommodate its most dissatisfied province.

It should be noted that Meech's failure forced a dramatic shift in public attitudes towards French-English accommodation and provincial equality. It is now clear that certain accepted 'truths' are no longer valid. As one Quebec political scientist notes, there is no longer a reason to believe that Quebec francophones share the constitutional principles held by other Canadians, including 'the strict equality of all provinces, supremacy of judicial interpretation over political accommodation, a strong central government, and primacy of individual over collective rights.'[10] This statement may be a bit strong, as one could make the equally persuasive argument that French Quebecers are no less supportive of individual rights than are English-speaking Canadians with language the one clear exception.[11] Nevertheless, it should not be assumed that the survival of Canada depends on Quebec's participation; nor is it clear that Quebec independence will necessarily scare off potential investors or cause it to suffer in North American financial markets. It should not be assumed that political leaders in Canada can reach acceptable compromises, nor can the federal government be relied upon to enforce majority decisions. Most important, it has become clear that a spirit of mutual accommodation and a willingness to resolve disputes within the existing federal structure is more difficult to find than ever before.

The obstacles to national reconciliation are formidable. These include

Quebec's demand for a special status, for it does not see itself as a province like the others. Quebecers demand for a special status is also demonstrated in its insistence that it has a veto over constitutional amendments, and that it requires special constitutional powers in areas including language and culture. The larger provinces have made clear so far that they will frown on granting special status to Quebec unless they can have this special status as well. Equality of the provinces is an entrenched principle for many Canadians.

Another obstacle to national reconciliation is the opposition by the poorer 'have-not' provinces to a weaker federal government. They fear the economic and political costs to their interests that special status for Quebec, and greater demands for autonomy from the wealthier and more populous provinces, might bring. In particular, they worry that they might lose the equalization payments that are so important to their economic development and which are central to the practice of Canadian federalism.

Another obstacle relates to Canada's Charter of Rights and Freedoms entrenched in the Constitution Act, 1982. As noted earlier, outside francophone Quebec, the Charter is extremely popular, and because of it individual rights have been promoted more vigorously than previously. By contrast, francophone Quebecers continue to emphasize collective rights as a vehicle to protect the French language and culture. The Meech Lake Accord brought this tension to the surface.

Similarly, if it becomes clear that Quebec would be granted a special status, what would stop the other provinces from demanding the same privileges? Michael Walker, director of the conservative Fraser Institute, maintained that 'whatever Quebec gets, the other provinces will want in equal measure.'[12] The premiers of British Columbia and Alberta had also expressed this view. The western provinces developed their own set of demands to be made to Ottawa, the majority of which made the case for a reformed Senate to provide more regional representation in parliament, or a revamped fiscal relationship with Ottawa to promote western economic development. There was also a perception held by many westerners that, if Quebec were to go it alone, the West might consider autonomy as well.[13] However, a Canada without Quebec would force an imbalance between a dominant Ontario and every other province. Quebec's presence in the federation provides something of a balance. Its absence, so the argument goes, would make Ontario that much more politically and economically powerful. This would be an intolerable situation for many western Canadians.

The rift in interprovincial relations may render obsolete the concept of federal-provincial conferences because other provinces have indicated they are interested in following Quebec's lead in dealing on a one-to-one basis with the federal government. Whereas provinces used to band together to make demands from the federal government, the general belief now seems to be that provincial governments can gain more from Ottawa without the involvement of the other provinces. The rest of Canada has made it clear that it wants its fair share of any deal struck between Quebec City and Ottawa. On 24 June 1990, British Columbia's then-premier Bill Vander Zalm stated:

If Quebec can seek sovereignty association with Canada, other provinces should also have that option. I think (we) should commence the moment Quebec commences so we don't have them getting one particular package and everyone else looking at something different … B.C. will certainly seek a different type of confederation, perhaps similar to a Quebec-type association with Canada.[14]

Vander Zalm went on to explain that British Columbia would also deal with Ottawa on a one-to-one basis regarding matters left unresolved by the Meech Lake debate.[15]

From time to time there have emerged movements and parties seeking the West's political separation from the rest of Canada. Western anger with the federal government has been rooted in the perception that the federal government imposes unfair energy or economic policies. The Reform party is the most recent example of this. These parties do not benefit from the galvanizing effect that dissatisfaction over language, culture, and identity provides to French-speaking Quebecers. Quebecers' bitterness is more personal and emotional. Their rift with Ottawa could remain long after economic differences with Ottawa have been reconciled. By contrast, western grievances can probably be addressed successfully with political reform and increased levels of industrial investment. All of these difficult reforms to accommodate western Canada could possibly be instituted within the context of the existing federation, providing Quebec stays in.[16]

Western Canada is not the only dissatisfied region of the country since the Meech Lake Accord's failure. In Atlantic Canada, New Brunswick premier Frank McKenna has unveiled a proposal to create a European-style common market between the three Maritime provinces of New Brunswick, Nova Scotia, and Prince Edward Island. McKenna's argument centres on the idea that unifying the economy of the three provinces with their population of 1.5 million would give the Maritimes greater economic security in the event that the Canadian federation should crumble. 'Peering at the rest of Canada from behind Quebec, the region is worried the four Eastern provinces could be left high and dry if Meech Lake fails and Quebec separates.'[17]

The reasoning behind this idea is that the provinces must act if they are not to sink separately into economic irrelevance. Maritime economic union would entail the abolition of interprovincial trade barriers, the establishment of coordinated government relations and a common development fund. This is not as radical as separation of course, but it is a clear sign that the federal government's economic policies have not been adequate to the task of promoting economic development and prosperity in the Atlantic region.

There is no strong movement for both economic and political union, however. Polls conducted by both Baseline Research in Fredericton and Corporate Research Associates in Halifax demonstrate that people in all four of the Atlantic provinces are split over the idea of such a union.[18] Many groups oppose political union for a variety of cultural, economic, and political reasons. Nevertheless, most Atlantic Canadians agree that the region must prepare to face reduced federal spending and the possibility of Quebec leaving a vast geographic gap between the Maritimes and the rest of Canada. Economic union is one of several remedies being considered by Atlantic leaders.

The prospect of Quebec's sovereignty poses serious concerns to Ontario as well. Ontario is the province with the most to lose as a result of Meech's failure and the increased levels of decentralization in the country. It is the wealthiest, most populous province and the economic and political centre of the country. Quebec sovereigntist leader Jacques Parizeau has asserted that Toronto and Montreal are, to a significant degree, 'twinned' or co-dependent. Political and economic sovereignty for Quebec would have enormous repercussions for its neighbour. In response, Ontario's leaders have suggested that the province institute certain general principles to guide its thinking about the future shape of Canada. These include a strong national government, the abolition of the constitution's notwithstanding clause, stronger economic ties among provinces, and future changes worked out only between Ottawa and all of the provinces. Ontario Premier Bob Rae has also discussed his support for a federal constituent assembly consisting of non–professional politicians who would be expected to offer a more representative forum for the articulation of Canada's problems.

These are entirely predictable recommendations from Ontario; they are unacceptable to a Quebec focused on a less, not more, controlled federal government. Meech Lake's failure has severely damaged Quebec-Ontario relations. The new confident Quebec is focused almost wholly on itself. Its leaders are indifferent to Ontario's concerns. In the near term, Quebec will receive increased powers from the federal government in sectors including immigration, communications, and energy. It is discussing these issues directly with Ottawa and will not participate in any forum with the other provinces. As noted, the federal government is facing similar pressures from other provinces to relinquish some of its jurisdiction in these matters. Debates over the distribution of powers will likely grow more frequent and more acrimonious in the short term.

Canada's prospects after Meech Lake were complicated by the erosion of the national parties' ability to reconcile the major two language groups or the diverse regions of the country. The Mulroney Conservatives had the support of only a small minority of Canadians according to polls. Liberal party leader Jean Chrétien was not particularly popular among Quebecers. The New Democratic party held only one seat in Quebec but is the government party in Ontario, British Columbia, and Saskatchewan. The sovereigntist Bloc Québécois in Quebec and the conservative, decentralist Reform party in Alberta and British Columbia were gaining strength. In a country where the institutions of national integration are weak, the decline of the national parties was a further indication of the extent of the alienation felt in the country.

THE ALLAIRE REPORT

On 28 January 1991 the Quebec Liberal party released a report (Allaire report) recommending that the rest of Canada be given until the end of 1992 to negotiate a new deal with the province. If these talks were to fail, there would be a referendum on sovereignty.[19] The Allaire report also suggested that Quebec be given exclusive jurisdiction over many fields in which the federal government has been involved including regional development, energy, environment, agriculture, education, science, culture, justice, communications, health, social affairs, and manpower. The report called on Quebec to share jurisdiction with Ottawa in foreign affairs, native affairs, taxation, justice, fisheries, and transport. The federal government would control defence, customs, and currency. In total, twenty-two jurisdictions now shared or controlled by the federal government would come under Quebec's exclusive control. The federal structure would thus be made more decentralized, and efficient, and have its spending powers and ability to increase the national debt inhibited. The Allaire report noted that Quebec would negotiate agreements only with Ottawa and not directly with the other provinces. Quebec appeared to be giving the rest of Canada one more chance, until fall 1992, to negotiate a radically new constitutional arrangement.

There were problems with the Allaire report, however. One was that the Quebec Liberal party report called for the abolition of the constitutional Charter of Rights, planning instead to create its own constitution. The Senate would be abolished, thereby alienating those who wanted an elected Senate. Quebec would no longer play a substantial role in federal institutions. The report's demands for Quebec's exclusive jurisdiction in some areas might contribute to the abolition of medicare and the weakening of the federal government's redistribution function. To demand total control of agriculture suggested that Quebec farmers would not mind losing their access to the federal quota system by which they had prospered. To take control of energy might have cut Quebecers off from guaranteed access to Alberta's oil and natural gas. To demand that provinces have jurisdiction over language could be especially difficult for francophones outside Quebec. Quebec anglophones would have their rights protected, but francophones' linguistic rights in the rest of Canada would be vulnerable to unsympathetic provincial governments. It is hard to see how the Allaire report's demands would have been acceptable in the rest of Canada. In practice, according to the Allaire report, Quebec was demanding either complete sovereignty, or sovereignty with an economic association with the rest of Canada. Ottawa would be left with responsibility for just the debt, customs, currency, equalization policy, and defence. Quebec would claim equal authority over foreign affairs, including 'the right to establish direct relations with other states.' In short, the federal system would be gutted of most of its powers.

Quebec Premier Bourassa, in response to the Allaire report, said that there would be no final decisions on government policy before the Bélanger-Campeau report was released. His party was somewhat divided on the report's recommendations, in fact, although internal opposition to them was outnumbered and outmanoeuvred.

The Constitutional Committee of the Quebec Liberal party had concluded that one way to bring about effective changes in Canada's federal system was to proclaim Quebec an independent country – and only then should Quebec begin to negotiate with Ottawa. Premier Bourassa did not subscribe to this view, and the report was interpreted in various ways by the press. Furthermore, there was no agreement on how negotiations should proceed. (The main points of the Allaire report are summarized in tables 1 and 2.)

What purpose did the Allaire report have? First, Premier Bourassa wanted to avoid a split within the party, a substantial portion of which wished to pursue the sovereignty option in response to the rejection of the Meech Lake Accord. Second, he wanted to shock the rest of Canada into realizing that the Canadian federation had to be restructured. The report accomplished these goals. The report's recommendations were also unacceptable to most Canadians outside of Quebec, however. The *Globe and Mail* columnist Jeffrey Simpson pronounced them

dead on arrival outside Quebec. They would so emasculate the federal government, so radically dismember Canada and give so much particular latitude to one province –

TABLE 1
Highlights of the constitutional proposal of the Quebec Liberal party (Allaire report)

The Constitutional Committee of the QLP proposes a thorough reform of Quebec's political and constitutional structure.

To achieve this, the Committee proposes that the government undertake to:

- present this reform proposal to the Government of Canada as soon as possible;
- hold a referendum in Quebec before the winter of 1992 for the purpose of:
- ratifying the agreement, if one is reached with the rest of Canada on the proposed reform;
- ratifying Quebec's assumption of sovereign statehood, if the negotiations fail, along with an offer to form an economic union with the rest of Canada.

The reform proposed by the Constitutional Committee is based on the following three objectives:

1. The political autonomy of Quebec

This autonomy will be achieved through a thorough overhaul of the distribution of jurisdiction, according to the following principles:

Quebec will exercise full sovereignty in areas of authority:

(a) it already holds exclusively (social affairs, municipal affairs, culture, education, housing, recreation and sports, family policy, manpower policy, natural resources, health, tourism);

(b) that are currently under shared jurisdiction or under exclusive federal authority (agriculture, unemployment insurance, communications, regional development, energy, the environment, industry and commerce, research and development, public security, and income security);

(c) that are not specifically mentioned in the constitution (residual powers);

- the central government will continue to exercise exclusive authority in the following areas: defence and territorial security, customs and tariffs, management of the common debt, currency, equalization;
- Quebec and Canada will share, according to each one's respective areas of authority, the following powers: native affairs, taxation and revenue, immigration, financial institutions, justice, fisheries, foreign policy, the post office, telecommunications, transport;
- the federal government's spending power in Quebec's exclusive areas of authority will be eliminated;
- the National Assembly will pass a Constitution of Quebec; this constitution will safeguard the recognized historic rights of anglophone Quebeckers and specifically the right to their own social and cultural institutions along with the right to manage their development;
- the Quebec Charter of Human Rights and Freedoms will be entrenched in the new Constitution of Quebec.

2. Strengthening the Canadian economic union with:

- free mobility of persons, goods and capital; a customs union; a monetary union;
- restoring balance to Canadian public finances by reducing the size of the central state and introducing certain institutional limitations on its budgetary practices, including the establishment of specific targets to severely limit deficits and to restrict the taxation powers of the central state.

TABLE 1 (continued)

---

3. The establishment of a new Quebec-Canada structure, including:
- replacing the current constitution with a new constitution including the right of the parties to withdraw following advance notice and incorporating a charter of rights and freedoms, retaining the notwithstanding clause and ensuring that the application of this charter is consistent with the repatriation of powers stipulated in this reform;
- maintaining a common parliament, elected by universal suffrage;
- abolition of the Senate in its current form;
- implementation of a new amending formula providing that any constitutional amendment be subject to the approval of a substantial majority of the provinces together representing at least 50% of the population of Canada, Quebec necessarily being one of the provinces;
- creation of a community tribunal to ensure compliance with the Constitution and enforce legislation within the jurisdiction of the new central state.
- reform of the Bank of Canada to ensure regional representation, while maintaining its independence from political authorities.

SOURCE: English version of the report as presented in *Maclean's*, 18 February 1991

Quebec – that Canadians would be suckers or idiots to even contemplate a deal. Better separation, with all the anguish and bitterness it would bring, than the laughingstock of a country contemplated in this report. [20]

THE BÉLANGER-CAMPEAU COMMISSION REPORT

On 7 September 1990 a Quebec commission on the political and constitutional future of the province, the Bélanger-Campeau Commission, was created with a mandate to receive statements and briefs concerning Quebec's constitutional and political future from a wide variety of groups and individuals. With this information, the commission was to make recommendations to the provincial legislature.[21]

The Bélanger-Campeau Commission on the future of Quebec had to deal with the delicate problem of building a consensus on issues including Quebec's political options and the risks involved, the costs of sovereignty, the need for a referendum, the allocation of regional powers, and minority rights. The commission's representatives were balanced between members of the Quebec Liberal party, the Parti Québécois, the anglophone rights Equality party, representatives of the federal political parties, and various interest group representatives. The commission members' preferences also varied substantially. Prior to the final report, some advocated a 'renewed federalism' that would slightly modify the province's relationship with Ottawa. Others called for a

TABLE 2
How the Allaire proposals would shift power to Quebec

Current distribution	Allaire proposals
Quebec alone	**Quebec alone**
Social affairs	Social affairs
Municipal affairs	Municipal affairs
Culture	Culture
Education	Education
Housing	Housing
Recreation and sports	Recreation and sports
Family policy	Family policy
Natural resources	Manpower
Tourism	Natural resources
	Health
Shared	Tourism
Manpower	Agriculture
Health	Unemployment insurance
Agriculture	Communications
Communications	Regional development
Regional development	Energy
Energy	Environment
Environment	Industry and commerce
Industry and commerce	Language
Language	Research and development
Research and development	Public security
Public security	Income security
Taxation and revenue	
Immigration	**Shared**
Financial institutions	Native affairs
Justice	Taxation and revenue
Transport	Immigration
	Financial institutions
Ottawa alone	Justice
Defence, territorial security	Fisheries
Customs and tariffs	Foreign policy
Currency and common debt	Post office
Equalization	Telecommunications
Unemployment insurance	Transport
Native affairs	
Fisheries	**Ottawa alone**
Foreign policy	Defence, territorial security
Post office	Customs and tariffs
Telecommunications	Currency and common debt
	Equalization

SOURCE: Adapted from *Maclean's* 18 February 1991, 21

unilateral declaration of secession. Others sought a new Canada based on the emerging European model of economic union and loose political affiliation. All commission members agreed, however, that Meech's failure and the resulting lack of recognition of Quebec's distinctive character meant that maintaining the same federal-provincial relationship was out of the question.

The Bélanger-Campeau Commission travelled throughout the province, and its hearings became a forum for grievances of all sorts having, at times, nothing to do with the relative merits of sovereignty-association. The possibility of a fall 1992 referendum on independence was the focus of ongoing discussion, however.

One of the more influential briefs to the commission was from the Quebec Chamber of Commerce. This proposal asserted that many powers held by Ottawa should be taken over by the government of Quebec to end the wasteful overlapping of responsibilities between the two governments. The proposal maintained that such a move would save taxpayers billions of dollars annually and that cheaper, more efficient government was more important than political independence. The chamber recommended that Quebec be given sole control of manpower, unemployment insurance, research and development, education, justice, culture, communications, health, labour, and social affairs. It also recommended that Quebec's jurisdiction over immigration be enhanced and its power to regulate financial institutions be strengthened.

The final Bélanger-Campeau report, received on 27 March 1991, strove to promote province-wide consensus and was largely successful in this effort. Thirty of thirty-three commissioners voted to recommend passage of a law setting up a referendum on sovereignty by 26 October 1992. But more than twenty committee members added personal clarifications or dissents to various of the report's recommendations. Co-chairmen Michel Bélanger and Jean Campeau expressed satisfaction that on the basis of their report Quebecers could now make a democratic choice about the province's future. The text of the Bélanger-Campeau's recommendations is set out in table 3.

The Bélanger-Campeau report recommended that Quebecers vote on whether to break up Canada unless Canadians outside Quebec committed themselves, by October 1992, to a comprehensive proposal designed to address Quebec's demands. Such a proposal might still not be acceptable to Quebec, in which case the referendum would go ahead anyway. Gil Rémillard, Quebec's minister of intergovernmental affairs, stated that 'it's up to Canada to act' and that Quebec would make no more offers to the rest of the country. In fact, as will be discussed, Canada's proposal addressed the Quebec agenda, but it also addressed such regional and national concerns as parliamentary and Senate reform, and a better deal for Canada's aboriginal peoples.

TABLE 3
Recommendations of the commission on the political and constitutional future of Quebec (Bélanger-Campeau Commission Report)

The Commission recommends that the National Assembly adopt, in the spring of 1991, legislation to establish the process by which Quebec determines its political and constitutional future.

The legislation would contain three sections, that is, a preamble; a first part dealing with the organization of a referendum on Quebec sovereignty; and a second part dealing with the offer of a new constitutional partnership.

Preamble of the Act
1. Considering the report, the conclusions and the recommendations of the Commission on the Political and Constitutional Future of Quebec have been made public;
2. Whereas Quebecers are free to assume their own destiny, to determine their political status and to assure their economic, social and cultural development;
3. Whereas Quebecers wish to play an active part in defining the political and constitutional future of Quebec.
4. Whereas the *Constitution Act, 1982* was proclaimed despite the opposition of the National Assembly;
5. Whereas the 1987 Agreement on the Constitution, the aim of which was to allow Quebec to adhere to the *Constitution Act, 1982* failed;
6. Whereas it is necessary to redefine the political and constitutional status of Quebec.

Part 1 of the Act: The organization of a referendum on Quebec sovereignty
The Act will stipulate that:
- a referendum on Quebec sovereignty is to held, either between June 8 and 22, 1992, or between Oct. 12 and 26, 1992;
- should the outcome of the referendum be positive, Quebec will acquire the status of sovereign State one year, day for day, after the date of the referendum;
- special parliamentary committee of the National Assembly will be established, and its composition laid down, to examine questions related to Quebec's accession to sovereignty;
- the special parliamentary committee will study and analyze all questions related to Quebec's accession to full sovereignty, that is, Quebec's exclusive capacity, through its democratic institutions, to adopt laws, levy taxes within its territory and act on the international scene in order to conclude all manner of agreements or treaties with other independent States, and participate in various international organizations; the committee will make recommendations in this respect to the National Assembly;
- the committee will be granted a budget and authorized to have studies prepared and to conduct whatever consultations it deems necessary, and to hear all interested persons and organizations.

Part 2 of the Act: Offer of a new constitutional partnership
The Act will stipulate that:
- a special parliamentary committee of the National Assembly will be established, and its composition laid down, to assess any offer of a new constitutional partnership made by the Government of Canada and to make recommendations in this respect to the National Assembly;
- only an offer formally binding the Government of Canada and the provinces will be examined by the committee;
- the committee will be granted a budget and authorized to have studies prepared and conduct whatever consultations it deems necessary, and to hear all interested persons and organizations.

SOURCE: Michel Bélanger and Jean Campeau, *The Political and Constitutional Future of Quebec* (Quebec: National Library of Quebec 1991), 72–82

Coupled with the Liberal party's Allaire report, the Bélanger-Campeau report made clear that Quebecers could be persuaded to remain in Canada only if the federal government were to give up far more of its powers to Quebec, and probably to the other provinces as well. The Allaire report listed twenty-two powers it wanted turned over to Quebec. The Bélanger-Campeau Commission required Ottawa to give up all areas now shared with the provinces, including language, culture, social and economic policy. It also mandated a constitutional veto for Quebec, a recognition of Quebec's distinctiveness and the right to secede from the federation. If Quebec did not assume these powers, it would hold a referendum on sovereignty in October 1992.

It is worth stressing that Premier Bourassa of Quebec retained the freedom to seek a mutually satisfactory reform of the current federal system of government. His government retained its powers of initiative and evaluation of what might be in the best interests of Quebec. The National Assembly retained its sovereignty to decide on any referendum questions or appropriate legislative measures.

At this point, it was unclear whether Quebec's demands were compatible with new demands emerging from western Canada and from the aboriginal peoples of Canada. It remained for the rest of Canada to try to cobble together a proposal that would satisfy Quebec's demands without creating an unworkable federal union. Alternatively, the players might decide that it just was not worth the effort.

THE SPICER COMMISSION REPORT

Since Quebec appeared to be looking for some form of sovereignty-association, it was imperative that the rest of Canada consider its own position. There were a number of reasons why Canada had to formulate a series of specific policy proposals. First, Canadian officials had to be ready to respond to whatever measures that Quebec promoted. In addition, while Quebec was engaged in studying its future, the Canadian government needed to have some idea of what the rest of the country saw as priorities, possibilities for changes, and points of resistance.

The government of Canada faced challenges from the rest of Canada as well as Quebec, of course. The widespread public dissatisfaction in Canada with both the process and the content of the Meech Lake Accord demonstrated the profound changes in the distribution of political power in the country since the early 1980s and the 1982 Constitution and Charter of Rights. These changes have had repercussions throughout Canada.

The Spicer Commission was an effort to address these issues. Chaired by Keith Spicer, this blue-ribbon panel had a mandate to evaluate proposals for constitutional change and to consider strategies for negotiating with Quebec or other recalcitrant provinces. Also, the government thought such a highly viable and respected federal task force could be a powerful voice for federalism and national unity. Finally, such a commission could best respond to regional alienation outside Quebec. In the West, dissatisfaction with Ottawa was at a high point. The Maritime provinces were discussing greater forms of political and economic union. Native people were demanding settlement of their grievances. These pressures and others were to be addressed by the Spicer Commission.

This is not to say that the Spicer Commission had policy-making authority. It was there to listen to grievances and demonstrate the federal government's concern. It was there to listen to practical concerns such as how to accommodate multiculturalism in Canada without losing a distinct national identity, or how to reconcile both individual and collective rights given the Charter of Rights and Freedoms. It was interested in promoting dialogue among Canadians and in identifying the interests and concerns of Canadians of various regions and language groups.

Most Quebecers decided not to participate in the work of the Spicer Commission. They saw the Bélanger-Campeau Commission as the instrument to investigate Quebec's future. The Spicer Commission, for them, was a vehicle whereby the rest of Canada could articulate its views.

The commission had its share of problems, including cost overruns, weak leadership, poor organization, and internal bickering. All of these threatened to derail its purpose prior to the presentation of its 1 July 1991 report. Despite its myriad problems, however, the Spicer Commission was still the most important national forum for the articulation of grievances and the presentation of practical remedies.

At its hearings, the Spicer Commission learned about Canadians' resentment of the Meech Lake bargaining that had included only traditional élites. Commissioners discovered widespread support for a national referendum on sovereignty, a constituent assembly, or other forms of popular representation. In turn, the commission recommended that federal officials become more responsive to the wishes and aspirations of Canadians.

The report revealed that Canadians were confused and angry about the government's economic policies, were less then enthusiastic about official bilingualism or multiculturalism, and were not yet ready to grant Quebec special protections and powers. For most respondents outside Quebec, Quebec's continued presence in Canada could not be assured if it would mean the sacrifice of individual or provincial equality. Spicer did find, however, that Quebec's linguistic and cultural distinctiveness could be recognized so long as its government did not create two different definitions of the rights and obligations of

Canadian citizenship. The *Globe and Mail* presented the recommendations of the Spicer Commission as:

- Urging the government to review and co-ordinate its thinking on national institutions and symbols – in particular those with historic and communications value – to 'give them more evident importance and to avoid the impression among Canadians that they are losing their sense of country';
- Suggesting that people outside Quebec could accept that the province 'should have the freedom and means' to be its own unique self with a distinctive place in a 'renewed Canadian family,' if Canadians can be persuaded 'to place the emphasis on equity in the face of specific needs';
- Calling on federal and provincial governments, and the private sector, to tell Canadians of the economic, political, social, and international consequences of an independent Quebec;
- Urging an independent review of the application of the official languages policy 'to clear the air' and ensure it is not only fair, but sensible;
- Demanding 'prompt, fair settlement of the territorial and treaty claims of First Nations people' and suggesting that the Department of Indian and Northern Affairs and the Indian Act should be phased out as self-government is realized;
- Promoting travel and exchange programs and better teaching of Canadian history to address Canadians' ignorance about each other, their country and their history;
- Encouraging a new realism about the role – and limits – of government action;
- Recommending the elimination by the federal government of overlapping jurisdictions;
- 'Suggesting a careful review of Question Period' in the House of Commons so that it can be more productive. The forum report agrees with those who suggest that party discipline is too rigid. The commissioners also agree with what they call 'the vast majority of Canadians' who 'believe the Senate should either be fundamentally reformed or abolished.'[22]

There were a number of other commissions as well, some provincial, some representing the national interest, but all emerged as a response to the Meech Lake failure. Constitution Minister Joe Clark led a committee of cabinet ministers in trying to develop the federal government's constitutional proposals, while the Beaudoin-Edwards Committee of senators and members of parliament examined how the constitution might be changed. Finally, the federal New Democratic party created an 'Action Group' to study parliamentary reform first, and then constitutional reform. Clearly, political élites were taking seriously the threat posed by Quebec's constitutional challenge to Canada.

WHAT SORT OF CONSTITUTIONAL STRUCTURE MIGHT CANADA HAVE?

The tensions in the Quebec-Canada relationship are obvious. Quebecers want special powers for their province. A large majority of Canadians outside Quebec want equality for all the provinces. Most Quebecers would prefer more powers for the province. Outside Quebec, most Canadians find Quebec's demands for greater jurisdiction unpalatable.

The various proposals for Quebec's constitutional future range from the extreme of outright independence to a limited Quebec autonomy. Many Quebecers favour a drastic alteration of the political composition of Canada, with Quebec acquiring the status of a semi-independent nation-state.

Professor Ronald Watts of Queen's University has outlined various constitutional possibilities.[23] These include the retention of the existing federal system – an option that would be unacceptable to most Quebecers. Another possibility would be a more decentralized federation that would devolve more powers, including some taxing authority, to Quebec and give all the provinces control over many programs now run by the federal government. Alternatively, there might be created a confederation of regions, in which five regions would function autonomously under a central superstructure responsible for coordinating monetary, defence, and other major policy concerns. Watts also suggests the possibility of a 'bipolar' federation, consisting of Quebec and the rest of Canada. This is an unlikely scenario since the three-to-one population ratio between the two nations would probably lead to intractable disputes over representation on a central authority.

Another possibility is a loose 'sovereignty-association' confederation, which is advocated by many in Quebec and was the ultimate ambition of the 'yes' forces during the 1980 failed referendum. Quebec would be one constituent unit, the other provinces the other, and a central government would oversee a common market and the armed forces. However, Watts argues that the rest of Canada would not accept the provision of a Quebec veto on major issues, and the arrangement would almost certainly lead to repeated deadlocks. Finally, Watts considers complete Quebec independence, but notes that this would raise difficult questions about the allocation of Canada's assets and liabilities, boundary adjustments, and other issues. Subsequently, Ronald Watts revised his discussion and presented nine possibilities. These are offered verbatim from the original in appendix C.[24]

Following the failure of the Charlottetown Agreement (to be discussed below), no one can predict with any real confidence what sort of changes will ensue, although it is clear that eventually there will be a restructuring of the federal-provincial relationship. Further decentralization is likely.

Within Quebec, and in the rest of Canada, there is no one constitutional option preferred. In one (1991) poll of six available options, a plurality of Quebecers (27 per cent) favoured political independence for all of the provinces in a European Community–style common market. The choice of 22 per cent of Quebecers was a federal system giving Quebec special powers. The third most popular option of Quebecers (18 per cent) was a federal system giving all provinces much more power. By contrast, in the rest of Canada a plurality of respondents (41 per cent) declared that their first choice was a federal system giving all provinces much more power. Twenty-seven per cent called for no change to the existing system, and 14 per cent sought political independence for all provinces in an EC-like common market.[25]

Notwithstanding these differences, there is pessimism in Quebec and in the rest of the country about Canada's future prospects. Most of the pessimism is rooted in Canada's difficult economic plight. But there is simultaneous constitutional fatigue and dissatisfaction with the existing federal division of powers as well.

The various constitutional options have been presented briefly, but the most widely discussed deserve further attention. One possibility, however remote, is that Canada will muddle through with few, if any, constitutional changes. According to this scenario, the federal government will work out special arrangements with Quebec in the fields of culture and social policy, as they already have on immigration policy. This line of argument suggests that most Quebecers will decide that despite the failure of the Meech Lake Accord and the Charlottetown Agreement, the existing state of affairs is preferable to sovereignty.[26]

In fact, these Canadian federalists note that Canadian history is replete with episodes of sharp constitutional divisions, linguistic problems, regional strife. All of these are recurring parts of Canadian history, tradition, and culture. Amid terrible problems, Canadians have always muddled through.

Some observers maintain that English and French Canadians are not so much interested in constitutional change as they are focused on the possibilities of a new 'functional federalism.' Presumably, this would not address such red herrings as language rights, but instead would explore economic issues like the unpopular Goods and Services Tax, reducing interprovincial trade barriers, and other economic concerns. In the absence of constitutional concessions, they stress, it is best to address practical concerns.

Furthermore, status quo advocates argue that Canada's constitution is flexible enough to allow many or all of the changes that Quebec sought from the Meech Lake Accord and the Charlottetown Agreement. They claim that virtually everything that Quebec would have gained from these agreements could still be implemented by Ottawa unilaterally, whether by administrative practice, federal legislation, constitutional convention, or all three.

Since Ottawa has a veto on all constitutional amendments, it could stipulate that it will not agree to any constitutional changes unless Quebec consents – in effect, a veto for Quebec through Ottawa's veto. Similarly, the federal government could stipulate that Quebec senators and Supreme Court judges be appointed only from lists of names supplied by Quebec. In addition, Ottawa could stipulate that Quebec might opt out of national shared-cost programs and receive financial compensation if it establishes similar programs compatible with national objectives. Also, Ottawa could recognize Quebec as a distinct society and provide federal money and delegate federal power to help Quebec promote its distinctive character. Federal government representatives might hold annual conferences with their Quebec counterparts to discuss further constitutional reforms and economic development. Taken together, the provisions of the failed agreements might still be implemented by Ottawa.

In short, one could make the case that, since it has been so difficult to achieve national agreement on major constitutional change, the status quo or minor incremental changes may be the only viable alternative. There would be no sense to a 'constitutional fix.' Supporters argue that it is better to preserve a system that is known, however flawed, then get bogged down in endless constitutional squabbles. In fact, federalists charge that Meech was rejected by only two provinces, Newfoundland and Manitoba, despite the fact that most Canadians outside of Quebec opposed it, according to polls at the time. Nine of Canada's eleven legislatures, including the federal parliament, remained at least nominally for it. It remains to be seen, however, if this incremental approach can attract widespread support. In fact, this is a most unlikely prospect. Quebec francophones tend to blame the rest of Canada as a whole for Meech's collapse. Certain Quebec politicians perpetuate the belief that English Canada rejected Quebec to justify their own quest for power and their own rejection of the rest of Canada. The media promotes this 'abandonment' thesis.

However reasonable or practical the status quo option might seem, repeated polls reveal that the Quebec public rejects the status quo. Instead their political and many economic leaders are demanding fundamental changes. For example in an Institut de recherche sur l'opinion publique poll in March 1990, Quebecers were asked the same question that they rejected in the 1980 referendum: whether they would approve a mandate to negotiate sovereignty-association? In 1980, 60 per cent said no. This time 68 per cent said that they would vote yes. Most opinion polls up to fall 1992 revealed that a majority of Quebecers favoured some form of political sovereignty or at least a greater degree of federal decentralization. It should be noted, however, that most respondents were confused about what sovereignty or sovereignty-association means. Many of those who said they favoured sovereignty-association turned out, on further examination, to think that it was synonymous with renewed federalism. At the same time, a policy of slow, incremental transfer of power to the provinces is also problematic. This is because the Canadian constitution limits the powers and authority the federal government can give any province. Any change would require a revision of the constitution, although this is not an insurmountable obstacle. In fact, the amending formula in the Constitution Act, 1982, requires parliament and all provincial legislatures to amend the constitution together regarding the allocation of powers between Ottawa and the provinces.

THE FEDERAL GOVERNMENT'S PROPOSALS

The federal government's response to Quebec's constitutional challenge was the subject of great anticipation across Canada. In terms of their comprehensiveness and their effort to appeal to everyone, the proposals did not disappoint. Entitled *Shaping Canada's Future Together*, the proposals, to the surprise of some, addressed a number of the issues brought out in the Spicer report. They included a 'Canada clause' which identified in specific terms what constituted a Canadian identity and Canadian values. They addressed the issue of an elected Senate and parliamentary reform, including reduced political partisanship and more free votes and bipartisan cooperation. The proposals also noted the importance of increased economic efficiency and reduced barriers to interprovincial trade. Unlike the Spicer report, however, they called for a substantial devolution of constitutional, but not economic, powers to the provinces.

For those who favoured a stronger federal union, there was to be enhanced federal power to override provincial laws or practices of provincial governments that restrict the movement of capital or labour within Canada, but only with substantial provincial support and with an opt-out option for up to three provinces.[27] For supporters of an increased role for the provinces, Ottawa offered to cede residual power over areas not specifically delimited in the constitution to the provinces. It also proposed creation of a new body, a council of the federation, which would be comprised of representatives of the provincial, federal, and territorial governments, and would essentially institutionalize and provide a firm voting rule (two-thirds of the provinces having 50 per cent of the population) for formerly ad hoc arrangements of executive federalism. The proposals' highlights, as printed in the *Globe and Mail*, are listed in table 4.

The proposals did not please everyone. Immediately after their release, Quebec sovereignty leaders condemned them as too little and too late. The council

TABLE 4
Highlights of the federal government's proposals

• Charter amendments to guarantee property rights;

• Recognition of Quebec's distinctiveness and Canada's linguistic duality;

• Aboriginal participation in current constitutional deliberations;

• An amendment to the Constitution to entrench a right to aboriginal self-government within the Canadian federation;

• Guaranteeing aboriginal representation in a reformed Senate;

• A Canada clause in the Constitution acknowledging the following characteristics; the equality of women and men; a commitment to fairness and full participation in Canada's citizenship without regard to race, colour, creed, physical or mental disability or cultural background; recognition that the aboriginal peoples were historically self-governing; recognition of the responsibility of governments to preserve Canada's two linguistic majorities; the special responsibility borne by Quebec to preserve and promote its distinct society; preserving the environment for future generations; the free flow of people, goods, services and capital throughout Canada and the principle of equality of opportunity throughout Canada;

• A directly elected Senate providing more equitable provincial and territorial representation;

• On matters of language and culture, the Senate would have a double majority special voting rule;

• Constitutional amendments to call Canada an economic union within which persons, goods, services and capital may move freely without barriers or restrictions based on provincial or territorial boundaries;

• More control for provinces in immigration, culture and job-training;

• Creation of a Council of the Federation composed of federal, provincial and territorial appointees to determine shared-cost programs and national standards.

Following are proposals in Ottawa's new constitutional package that would have an impact on business and the economy:

• Amending the Bank of Canada Act so that its mandate is clearly 'to achieve and preserve prove stability.' Provinces would have input on new directors.

• Section 121 of the Constitution would be changed to remove barriers to trade within Canada and barriers to the mobility of people, capital and goods. Legislation promoting regional development would be exempt however.

• A constitutional amendment that would guarantee property rights.

TABLE 4 (continued)

• Closer co-operation between Ottawa and the provinces on securities regulation.

• Ottawa would consult the provinces on the issuing of new broadcast licences, allow operations of provincial governments and their agents to evolve into full public broadcasting undertakings with varied programming, further regionalize the operations of the Canadian Radio-television and Telecommunications Commission and allow provincial participation in the nomination of regional CRTC commissioners.

• The federal government would set up an annual timetable for setting provincial and federal budgets, and schedule annual finance ministers' meetings. Ottawa and the provinces would publish pre-budget outlooks and set up common accounting conventions.

• Ottawa would discuss with the provinces the creation of an independent agency to monitor and evaluate the macroeconomic policies of the federal and provincial governments.

• Provincial governments would be given sole responsibility for tourism, forestry, mining, and housing, and Ottawa will discuss responsibility for ferry services, small craft harbours, and some aspects of financial sector regulation, bankruptcy law and unfair trade practices.

• Labour market training would become a provincial responsibility only.

• A constitutional amendment that would allow Parliament to make laws for the efficient functioning of the economy.

SOURCE: Reprinted from the *Globe and Mail*, 25 September 1991

of the federation proposal was criticized as unwieldy and problematic by observers across the country. Quebec Premier Bourassa and many other Quebecers stressed that elements of the economic union proposal, and particularly Ottawa's spending power, were unacceptable as presented. Bourassa worried that Ottawa did not yet understand that Quebec's 'distinctiveness' extended beyond matters of language, culture, and civil law and into economic issues. He was concerned that the distinct society clause would be applicable only to the Charter of Rights and Freedoms. Nor was there a mention in the proposals of a Quebec veto on constitutional amendments or Supreme Court appointments. Federal officials countered that the proposals were not an assault on provincial authority, but merely a mechanism for facilitating federal-provincial cooperation. Of course, provinces disagreeing with particular federal government policies could opt out.

Unlike the failed Meech Lake Accord, which focused on Quebec's concerns, this document attempted to suggest remedies to grievances in the rest of Canada as well. It had to be a flexible paper with answers for everyone, acceptable to

Quebec and the rest of Canada. Quebec's distinct society status was entrenched, but so was recognition of an elected Senate.

There is much about the proposals that was vague, unclear, or controversial.[28] The economic union suggestions and the council of the federation proposition would have been particularly hard to implement. Initial polls in Quebec revealed that two-thirds of Quebecers with an opinion opposed the proposals,[29] although Canadians outside of Quebec appeared to be more optimistic. Subsequent polls revealed more support in Quebec, as much as 46 per cent.[30] Nationwide hearings were held to solicit the input of Canadians. These led to Charlottetown, the setting for the next stage of the winding road to constitutional reform. (A fairly comprehensive list and discussion of the constitutional reform suggestions offered since 1979 are found in appendices C, D, and E.)

THE CHARLOTTETOWN AGREEMENT

Since 1970 there have been five major attempts to reach a national constitutional accord. All have been less than wholly successful. During the 1984 election, Brian Mulroney promised to return Quebec to the constitutional fold with 'honour and enthusiasm.' He tried to accomplish this with the Meech Lake Accord and the Charlottetown Agreement. Both of these brought various squabbling, competing forces into the open. Both displayed the barely hidden wounds and animosities underlying Canadian political life. The failure of both agreements to be ratified aggravated tensions while exhausting its protagonists.

The Charlottetown Agreement was a complicated thing, and each provision depended on another for its viability. It was a lowest-common-denominator document – a document tailored to give something to everyone. The fragile trade-offs were everywhere – on Senate reform, on aboriginal self-government, on an amending formula, and on a distinct society clause. It was detailed and reasonably comprehensive, but it was not flexible. Too much was included in its provisions. Too many future political or administrative decisions would become constitutionalized. It was a risky proposition. The complete text of the Charlottetown Agreement is presented in appendix F. The main provisions included provisions for parliamentary reform, aboriginal self-government, a new division of federal-provincial powers, and a distinct society status for Quebec.

The Charlottetown Agreement's provisions with regard to parliamentary reform included reforms of the Canadian Senate with six members elected from each province and one each representing the territories. The Senate would have had an absolute veto power over natural resource taxation legislation. Laws affecting language and culture would have to receive the support of a double majority in the Senate, including the support of a majority of all francophone members. Furthermore, a Senate defeat of legislation passed by the House of Commons would prompt a bicameral session in which legislation would be sustained by a simple majority vote of the whole parliament. In addition, the provincial governments would decide how senators would be selected. The House of Commons would gain 42 seats to total 337 and Quebec would be guaranteed 25 per cent of all seats, even if its population were to fall below proportion.

The Charlottetown Agreement also provided that aboriginal self-government was to be constitutionally recognized. All governments would negotiate the jurisdiction of aboriginal governments, and all aboriginal government laws would be consistent with the national interest.

The agreement also outlined federal and provincial powers. Provincial governments could opt out of future shared-cost programs, with full fiscal compensation, provided they instituted compatible programs meeting national standards. There would also be a transfer of jurisdiction over labour-market training and culture to the provinces, but federal authority over major cultural institutions and unemployment insurance would be retained. The federal government would relinquish authority, on provincial request, over portfolios including forestry, mining, recreation, tourism, housing, and municipal and urban affairs.

Finally, most of the elements of the Meech Lake Accord would remain intact. Quebec would be constitutionally recognized as distinct. All provinces would be given a veto power on future constitutional reforms to federal institutions. As with Meech, the federal government would select Supreme Court justices from lists provided by the provinces.

The release of the Charlottetown Agreement prompted strong responses almost immediately from supporters and detractors alike. The *Globe and Mail* listed the major arguments for and against it (see table 5).

The opposition to the Charlottetown Agreement included the Reform party which maintained that it would give 'special status' to Quebec and aboriginal people. They insisted on the equality of all citizens and provinces in constitutional law. Former Prime Minister Pierre Trudeau and lawyer Deborah Coyne asserted that the agreement would have weakened the Charter of Rights and would have established a hierarchy of classes of citizens in which language and racial origin would be more important than the principle of equality of citizens and the inviolability of individual rights. In addition, the National Action Committee on the Status of Women worried that the Charlottetown Agreement could threaten the sexual equality provisions of the Charter of

TABLE 5

Arguments for and against the Charlottetown Agreement

The Yes argument	The No response

I Distinct society

1. Recognition of Quebec as a distinct society in the Canada clause and the constitutional right of the province to 'protect and promote' the distinct society, including language and culture. Protects Bill 101. (Article 1)

The distinct society grants no special legal power and could prove meaningless in future court rulings. Bill 101 is threatened and, therefore, so is the French language and culture.

2. An immediate increase in members of Parliament from the province, to 93 from the current 75, giving Quebec 28 percent of Commons seats. (Article 21)

Federal MPs vote along party lines, so the increased number will not guarantee that Quebec's interests are protected.

3. A minimum 25 percent of Commons seats guaranteed to Quebec. (Article 21.a)

Quebec held 28 percent of Commons seats when the Constitution was unilaterally repatriated in 1982, proving federal MPs do not necessarily act in Quebec's best interests.

4. A Senate double majority (of all senators and all francophone senators) is required for laws pertaining to French language and culture. (Article 14)

There is no guarantee that Quebeckers will dominate all francophone senators.

5. Three of nine Supreme Court of Canada judges will be from Quebec. (Article 18)

The federal government has no obligation to choose judges proposed by Quebec, as was the case in the Meech Lake accord.

II Veto rights

6. A veto on the existence and composition of the Supreme Court. (Articles 18 and 19)

But Quebec has lost its veto on the nomination of judges. (The Yes side replied that this is simply wrong.)

7. A veto on all future changes to the Senate. (Article 57)

The damage is done: Quebec has been reduced to having the same number of senators as Prince Edward Island.

8. A veto on all future changes to the House of Commons, in addition to the guarantee of 25 percent of seats for Quebec. (Article 57)

The veto is meaningless because the number of MPs will change after each census.

9. A veto on the increased representation of new provinces in the Senate. (Article 58)

9 and 10. The Meech Lake accord gave Quebec a veto on the creation of new provinces, not on

TABLE 5 (continued)

10. A veto on the participation of new provinces in the process for modifying the constitution. (Article 58)

the resultant technical changes. Further, the political pressure to respect the principle of provincial equality will be enormous.

11. Compensation for any transfer of provincial jurisdiction to the federal government. (Article 59)

Surrendering powers to Ottawa can never be considered a gain.

12. A provincial veto on the use of the federal government's declaratory power, which was used in 1950 when the federal government took control of uranium mining. (Article 39)

There has never been such a transfer since Confederation in 1867, and any transfer proposed would be to the advantage of the federal government. (The Yes side says that the declaratory power has in fact been used more than 500 times, although not since the 1950s.)

III Exclusive provincial jurisdictions

13. Labour market development. (Article 28)
14. Manpower training. (Article 28)
15. Forestry. (Article 30)
16. Mining. (Article 31)
17. Housing. (Article 33)
18. Municipal and urban affairs. (Article 35)
19. Tourism. (Article 32)
20. Recreation. (Article 34)
21. Culture. (Article 29)

13 to 21. These are already exclusive provincial jurisdictions. The limited list of minor powers also strips Quebec of jurisdiction it had in other sectors such as regional economic development, family policy and energy.

IV Limits on federal spending powers

22. The right to withdraw from federal-provincial programs, with full compensation. (Article 25)

There is no federal compensation for programs established by Quebec, even if they have the same goals as the federal programs.

23. The right of the federal government to spend in spheres of exclusive provincial jurisdiction will be limited by a process established by the first ministers, which will minimize overlap and respect provincial goals. (Article 25)

This is a gain for Ottawa because it constitutionalizes the ability of Ottawa to spend in provincial spheres of power. Quebec will be outnumbered 16 to 1 in negotiations.

V Agreements

24. Creation of a mechanism for the constitutional protection of intergovernmental agreements to prevent unilateral change. (Article 27)

The provision against unilateral change lasts five years, and afterwards all agreements can be renegotiated.

TABLE 5 (continued)

25. Constitutional protection of immigration agreements. (Article 26)	The Meech Lake accord gave Quebec a veto over the whole process of constitutionalization of agreements, not an equal vote in the negotiation of process.
26. Regional development agreements. (Article 36)	Must be renegotiated every five years. It is also stated in the accord that regional development is not an exclusive provincial jurisdiction as Quebec always considered it.
27. Culture agreements. (Article 29)	Quebec already has exclusive jurisdiction over culture and the agreement gives the province no additional powers over Radio-Canada or the Canada Council.
28. Telecommunications agreements, including the ability of Quebec to nominate members of the Canadian Radio-television and Telecommunications Commission. (Article 37)	Quebec gets no additional powers as the agreements are strictly technical in nature.
29. The repeal of the federal powers of disallowance and reservation. (Article 38)	A gain by default because the use of such powers ceased long ago.
30. A reinforcement of the federal commitments to correct regional disparities through equalization payments and regional development. (Article 5)	A statement of good intentions in areas that have previously been cut unilaterally by the federal government.
31. An agreement on aboriginal self-government. (Chapter V)	A gain for native people, not Quebeckers.

SOURCE: Compiled by André Picard of the *Globe and Mail*'s Quebec bureau, the *Globe and Mail*, 12 October 1993, p. A4

Rights. Various Quebecers worried that the distinct society clause would be meaningless. These disparate groups were united in their opposition to the agreement, but divided in their motives. The Reform party advocated provincial equality and provincial rights. The other opponents emphasized national equality. Feminist groups favoured affirmative action for women and visible minorities. The Reform party viewed this as 'special status' and was opposed. Mr Trudeau opposed the collective rights provisions of the accord, but feminists supported them as long as they didn't conflict with sexual equality rights. Deborah Coyne was concerned that the accord would not allow the federal government to implement national programs and policies effectively, resulting in excessive decentralization and national disunity. The Reform party would support strengthened provincial rights.

During the campaign leading up to the national referendum on the Charlottetown Agreement, some supporters of the deal predicted that a 'no' vote would prompt a sharp decline in the nation's stock markets. They were wrong. After it was defeated, Canadian stock and bond markets and the dollar rallied. The big banks cut their prime lending rates to reassure foreign investors. The markets responded so positively, in large part, because they had discounted the possibility of a no vote long before the 26 October referendum. In addition, investors appeared to take the agreement's broad rejection as a sign that Canadians were unhappy with the particular deal. They were not convinced that its failure would signal the dissolution of the country, as federal officials had warned. For many Canadians, the no vote promised the status quo, not sovereignty.[31] The referendum was defeated in 6 of 10 provinces, including Quebec, and by a margin of 54 per cent to 45 per cent.

The no victory represented a vindication, at least in English Canada, of Pierre Trudeau's vision of Canada. It made clear that anglophone priorities like provincial equality, individual equality, no special status, and, most importantly, the inviolability of the Charter of Rights and Freedoms would remain first principles. For Quebec sovereigntists, the failure of so many attempts to reform the Canadian constitution have appeared to leave just two alternatives in Quebec – the constitutional status quo or Quebec sovereignty. Pierre Trudeau had long maintained that Quebecers would always choose federalism over sovereignty. English Canada rejected a special status, or distinct character, for Quebec.

Canadians demonstrated a kind of perverse unity regarding Charlottetown. Most Canadians in six of ten provinces opposed the agreement. Interestingly, the no side won by greater margins in Alberta, British Columbia, and Manitoba than in Quebec. There was no one reason to explain why a majority of Canadians opposed the Charlottetown Agreement. In English Canada, 27 per cent disliked it because they felt it would give Quebec too many powers. Smaller numbers saw the no vote as a rejection of Prime Minister Brian Mulroney or opposed the agreement because of their resentment of the tactics used to promote it. Twenty-two per cent of respondents outside Quebec thought the deal was a 'poor one' but were not more specific. In Quebec, 44 per cent of those voting no did so because they felt their province did not gain enough concessions while 56 per cent of those voting no saw the accord as a poor deal.[32] In both English and French Canada, the no vote also reflected dissatisfaction with Canada's political and economic élites. But it also demonstrated that a majority of Canadians in every region, including Quebec, wanted Canada to remain intact.[33] In fact, 53 per cent disagreed with the proposition that it would be better in the long run if Quebec were sovereign, while 38 per cent agreed.[34]

Nevertheless, to accommodate Quebec in the long run would require giving the province more or special powers. This presumes that the constitution can still be revised. At present, there does not appear to exist the political will for constitutional change.[35] Even if there is to be change, the problem remains of how to grant special powers to Quebec without infuriating the western provinces which would want a strengthened upper house representing the provinces equally. Charlottetown's failure also points to the weaknesses of the referendum as a vehicle for change, and it also sets a precedent. It will be hard to reform the constitution in future without public input in the form of a referendum. To the extent that a reform has a chance of passage, it would have to be focused and specific. Constitutional demands are almost always complex. Furthermore, it may be difficult to convince the rest of Canada that it should again become so emotionally involved in negotiating with Quebec and trying to prevent its independence.

The October 1993 federal election revealed a massive political party restructuring in Canada. The Liberal government won a clear majority, but demonstrated weakness in Quebec and the West. The sovereigntist Bloc Québécois (BQ) captured fifty-four of seventy-five Quebec seats and formed the official opposition – a bizarre turn of events for a party dedicated to an independent Quebec. The ideologically based Reform party finished a close third with massive support only in western Canada. The New Democrats finished with only nine seats (but they remained a force on the provincial level by holding three provincial governments). Kim Campbell's governing Progressive Conservative party suffered the greatest drop in seats in the modern history of industrialized democracies. Only two PC candidates were elected. The prime minister lost her own seat. The party has a $3 million debt and is in danger of disappearing. From a Quebec perspective, the victory of the BQ futher represented the depth of that province's dissatisfaction with Ottawa.

The victory of the Bloc in Quebec might not signal majority support for sovereignty, however. According to a SOM poll in October 1993, 44 per cent of Bloc supporters wanted the Bloc to concentrate on job creation, while only 3 per cent chose independence. Although 62 per cent of Bloc supporters viewed sovereignty 'favourably' or 'very favourably,' this would not be sufficient to carry a majority of Quebec votes in a referendum on sovereignty.

However, most 1994 polls revealed that the next government party in Quebec is likely to be the Parti Québécois. Should it win, it has pledged to hold a referendum on sovereignty in the following year. This referendum might lose, however, and many Quebec sovereigntists have decided that the PQ, which now speaks only of complete independence, might be too hard line. A group of former Liberal party Quebec nationalists, soft-line sovereigntists, and academics have called for a new political union, based on Quebec sovereignty, with the rest of Canada. It argues that an alternative to both pure sovereignty and status quo federalism is needed. Called the Parti Action Québec (PAQ), this group would seek a new partnership between a sovereign Quebec and the rest of Canada. The two entities would share such jurisdictions as defence and native issues in a supranational parliament based on the European model. Of course, such a party, if it were to run candidates in the next election, might take enough votes away from the PQ to allow the provincial Liberals to be re-elected. This would be a federalist's dream. The Parti Action Quebec reflects the ambivalence of Quebecers who want 'a sovereign Quebec within a strong federal Canada.' It might also appeal to voters who are disenchanted with both the PQ and the Liberals. But it faces major hurdles. The PAQ has neither a firm electoral base nor a political organization of any consequence. It has a tough road to hoe.

For the foreseeable future, no major constitutional changes will occur in Canada. Quebec will need time to sort out its political options. Although it is hard to predict what sort of new constitutional structure might emerge, it is possible that an even more decentralized federation or a confederation will emerge. Perhaps we will witness the emergence of a European-style super-structure in which two sovereign countries delegate certain defined powers to a common parliament. Former Quebec premier Robert Bourassa has suggested this possibility.

The process of restructuring will be difficult and will require great care. There is no certainty that the rest of Canada will accept a sovereign Quebec. Nor is it clear that the rest of Canada will pursue relations with Quebec. Indeed, the rest of Canada might itself be restructured, forcing endless haggling with the resulting uncertainty. The negotiations for dividing Canada's assets and liabilities could be especially complicated. Nevertheless, constitutional change will come, in part because the rationale for federalism has changed.

As Canada has grown, as its provinces have come to blows with the federal government over jurisdiction in areas that they claim for themselves, and as certain provincial economies have strengthened dramatically (through the discovery and exploitation of new natural resources, or through innovative provincial economic policies), the economic arguments for federation have dwindled markedly. For well-to-do provinces such as Ontario, British Columbia, and Alberta, which have regularly generated surpluses for the federal government[36] – and which, by extension, end up 'subsidizing' equalization payments to poorer provinces – federation has come to mean an irritating drain on their finances. It has also meant that, owing to past federal measures that have ensured large 'Canadian' ownership of natural resources (such as Pierre Trudeau's National

Energy Policy) and that have kept prices within Canada artificially low, natural resources concentrated in a particular province – like oil in Alberta – have not always brought the returns that they might have otherwise. Such federal policies have helped to distribute the wealth of Canada and are in keeping with Canadian political ideals. However, they also serve to illustrate that the economic reasons for federation, at least for certain regions, are less than persuasive. Unlike the struggling Maritimes, which depend heavily on federal subsidies, the wealthier western provinces have looked elsewhere, particularly to the United States, for opportunities to enhance their economic prosperity.

Furthermore, Canadians are divided in their assessment of the present constitutional crisis and their view of the future. Seventy-two per cent of Quebecers think that the rest of Canada should grant Quebec powers other provinces do not have (an asymmetric federation) if that is what will be necessary to keep Quebec in Canada. However, 76 per cent of Canadians in the rest of Canada disagree. Nevertheless, there are also survey results which reveal that most Canadians inside and outside Quebec believe their nation to be the best country in the world in which to live.

Canada has important linguistic and regional tensions, but Canadians across the country share values and interests. Federal institutions, argue writers such as Richard Simeon, reinforce and exaggerate the tensions, and are unable to promote the common symbols and shared ideals of Canadians.[37] Simeon calls for a reformed Senate,[38] distinct status for Quebec, and an affirmation of Quebec's right to self-determination. He suggests that bilingualism be retained in federal government administration alone. The provinces would administer language policy as they see fit. After these tasks are completed, Simeon argues that constitutional change will be easier to enforce and implement. Economist Pierre Fortin of the Université du Québec à Montréal thinks that federal reform must also include provisions to make sure that discipline is imposed on federal finances, that monetary stability is established, that the federal government supports economic growth, and that government is further decentralized to promote efficiency in the provision of public services.[39]

If the constitution is to be reformed substantially, what form might it take? As noted, two of the most prominent models are asymmetrical federalism and a more general decentralization approaching a confederal structure. Asymmetrical federalism refers to a Canadian constitution characterized by Quebec exercising many functions of government unavailable to the other provinces, while Quebec has a reduced role and voice in federal affairs.[40] Quebec could elect MPs to Ottawa in proportion to its population, but they could only vote on matters that remained in the federal jurisdiction pertaining to Quebec. Presumably, such a system would be more responsive to Quebec's concerns than the

existing constitutional structure. On most issues, Quebec would be self-governing in practice.

There are problems with this model, however, not the least of which is the
weakened or second-class status of Quebec's MPs. Other questions also arise.
Why should the other strong provinces not demand the same opportunities?
How will provincial jealousies and legitimate differences be decided? To whom
will Quebecers owe their allegiance in practice? How would the Canadian
Charter of Rights apply if it is not implemented across Canada? How would
Quebec be represented, if at all, in central institutions such as the Supreme
Court or the Senate. Also, would not an asymmetrical federation become just
the first step to the inevitable dissolution of the federation into its constituent
parts?

In addition, how much credibility could a Canadian prime minister or cabinet minister from Quebec have if they were to govern the rest of the country in
jurisdictions they do not control in Quebec? What would be the relationship
with institutions like the Canadian Radio-television and Telecommunications
Commission (CRTC), that deal with issues in the areas of Quebec's unique
jurisdiction? It is hard to be optimistic about the survival chances of an asymmetric Canadian federation. It is difficult to find one example of a functioning
asymmetrical federation in the world, although this does not mean that it could
not work. It is likely that other Canadian provinces, at least the larger ones,
would also demand greater powers until the already weak central government
became emasculated.[41]

IS THE EUROPEAN COMMUNITY A MODEL FOR CANADA?

One widely suggested reform of the Canadian federation is to offer all the
provinces, and not just Quebec, much greater autonomy. The European Community (EC) or European Union (EU) is cited as a model of a structure in
which central institutions maintain an open market of people, goods and services, redistribution of resources between provinces, central taxation, foreign
and defence policy, and international trade. All other powers rest with the
individual countries.

So a restructured Canadian federation might resemble the European Community. That is, sovereignty-association might be a common market embracing
several sovereign states with a common currency. Certainly former Quebec
premier Robert Bourassa speaks of the possibility of a Canadian 'superstructure' of semi-autonomous constituent units. Bourassa argues that the European
Community can serve as a model of distinct cultures that form a strong economic union without forsaking their political sovereignty. The European model

also lies at the heart of the Allaire report, which called on the province to assume sole jurisdiction in twenty-two separate policy areas. Bloc Québécois leader Lucien Bouchard has noted that he would be happy if 'Quebec enjoyed the status of France in the European Community.'[42]

Many influential Quebecers have made references to Europe as a model, for if massive change can be taking place there, should independence for Quebec – a wealthy, democratic, sophisticated society – be any more threatening? Claude Castonguay, a former politician and head of a major Quebec-based insurance company, has noted that 'the recent events in Europe teach us an interesting lesson on the vitality of nationalism,' and he speculated about its possible applications to Quebec.[43] Bourassa made much of the fact that the European rush to a single market in 1992 was predicated on the belief that economic union is not incompatible with political sovereignty. The dissolution of Canada into semi-independent states, from Bourassa's perspective, might be as possible as the previously scoffed at idea of European economic unity. Bourassa expects that Quebec and Canada would continue to share a customs union, a common market, a monetary union, a parliament with some taxing powers, and perhaps a common environmental policy. If it came to that point, Bourassa appears to support a sovereign nation-state, which delegates some functions to a common parliament and which can also withdraw from the economic union. The Canadian federation would become a 'superstructure.' Bourassa told Quebecers that they were free to choose their future, without reference to the constitution of Canada. Indeed, this is stated in the preamble of the law establishing the Bélanger-Campeau Commission: 'Quebecers are free to choose their own destiny, to determine their political status and to ensure their economic, social and cultural development.'

However, the constitution is quite clear that major amendments affecting the country must have the approval of at least seven provinces representing at least half the population. If Quebec wants a major change in its constitutional relationship with the rest of Canada, then the other provinces will play a critical role in the process, at least according to the constitution. In practice, of course, the other provinces would play an extremely limited role if Quebec were to secede unilaterally.

If an EU-type system were adopted in Canada, each level of government would run and pay for its own programs. The provinces would have exclusive jurisdiction over education, health care, income support, industrial planning, and regional development. The provinces would give the municipalities complete control over roads, sewers, policing, and public transit. All bureaucratic duplication and inefficiency would be minimized or eliminated. In short, Ottawa would manage the economy, and the provinces would deliver all social services. Ottawa would administer the currency, the post office, citizenship, defence, and foreign policy. It is a view of government reminiscent of the Allaire report recommendations. Justice, transportation, and environmental policies would be responsibilities jointly shared by the federal and provincial governments. All other powers would be provincially controlled. Canada would resemble a confederation, with most powers held by the provinces, and not a federation with a roughly equal division of powers between the central and provincial governments. Without dwelling on the point, one could make the case that the 'confederation' of 1867 was really a 'federation,' for the central government in Ottawa held most of the constitutional powers. Over time, this dominance has eroded so that the Canadian provinces have more power than any other sub-units of government in the world.

Federal Liberals from Quebec have endorsed sweeping reforms that are reminiscent of this model. Their proposals include assigning powers to the level of government best able to deliver them, eliminating overlapping programs and services, giving Quebec veto power over free movement of people, goods, services, and capital, and claiming greater Quebec representation on the Bank of Canada. Former Conservative prime minister Mulroney also raised the possibility of offering a 'profound distribution of powers to Quebec and the other provinces' without making entirely clear what he meant.

Bourassa tried to cover all the options by keeping his proposals vague and by insisting that economic and political ties of some sort must be maintained with Canada. However, Quebec should be wary of emulating the European Union model. The European Union of 1994 is a system whose members, for their own financial good and military security, willingly agree to share power to establish fair competition, environmental rules, certain elements of foreign policy, and possibly even a single currency and European-wide interest rates. It began over forty years ago when French foreign minister Robert Schuman put forward the idea of France and West Germany pooling their coal and steel production in an organization any other European country could join. Slowly, the twelve members of the European Union have broken down barriers to create the biggest trading bloc in the world, a market of 320 million people.

To achieve their aim – the free movement between countries of people, money, and goods and services – each national government has agreed to give up substantial sovereign powers that had created a protective environment for local business. Each EU nation, for example, gives up the right to set special health and safety standards, favour local business for big government projects, regulate the price of milk, and restrict fellow Europeans from entering the country to travel or work. Instead, these powers are handed to European institutions that set uniform rules. In the coming years, it is even possible, although by no means assured, that a central bank and a single European currency, the ECU, will be introduced. If this happens, a country that wants to run up a large deficit might have to seek the approval of its European partners. The European Union is also involved in implementing social policy and coordinating the distribution of economic aid to eastern Europe. As Europe becomes more united, Jacques Delors, president of the European Union's executive arm, has predicted that 80 per cent of economic, and perhaps social and tax, legislation will be of common origin by the end of the century.

The Parti Québécois brief before the Bélanger-Campeau Commission praised the EC example. However, the single European Act, the legislative underpinning for Europe 1992, gives the European Union much broader powers than a PQ government would allow in a 'superstructure.' The European Union has a court to sort out disputes based on its laws and regulations. It is unclear if the PQ would permit the creation of such an arbiter. The union's charter gives residual power to the EU rather than to the national governments and notes that EU law supersedes national laws in the event of conflict. Independence advocates in Quebec would not tolerate such provisions.[44]

In addition, the European Union oversees a common agricultural policy for its member states. It has implemented a variety of environmental measures and sets regional policy on a community-wide basis. It plays a substantial role in education, culture, communications, and social policy. In all of these areas, Quebec demands exclusive control. The EU continues to centralize its policy implementation strategies, while Quebec seeks greater degrees of decentralization.[45]

Furthermore, in the EU most power rests in a twelve-member council that is not directly elected, is secretive, and can override the directly elected parliament. It is reminiscent of all of the negative aspects of 'executive federalism' as practised in Canada.[46] The European Union nations see the EU model as promoting greater centralization. Quebec sovereigntists would see the EU as a tool to promote decentralization.

A major decentralization of the Canadian federation could make central governance very complicated, however. Would there be ten sets of environmental regulations and health standards? What kind of national policies would be possible to encourage science and technology and regional development? Would the provinces compete more aggressively than at present for investment, and, if so, would they lower workplace or environmental standards? Who would set original national standards? Could the high quality of Canada's social programs be retained after decentralization of delivery systems is implemented? Would not the national commitment to equalization of services diminish? Would the United States have more influence on Canadian affairs as the central government is diminished in influence? A decentralized federation appears to be as unwieldy as an asymmetric one.

Ultimately, the EU model will not be the panacea that many Québécois think it is. It has some applicability, but its provisions are specific to the European situation. An independent Quebec, or one that is part of a 'superstructure,' will have to pass legislation that is specific to its own circumstances.[47]

Ontario Premier Bob Rae has suggested that one possible reform might be a constituent assembly. Such an institution would include seventy or eighty politicians and members of the public. Working together, these people would make constitutional reform suggestions to the Canadian parliament and the ten provincial legislatures. According to at least one poll, two-thirds of Canadians, including a majority of Quebecers, would support the creation of a constituent assembly to help chart a constitutional course for the nation.[48] This reflects, in large part, Canadians' distrust of politicians and willingness to let ordinary Canadians into the decision-making process. As will be noted, the Charlottetown Agreement's failure also appeared to represent a rejection of élite-driven politics. Not surprisingly, most politicians have downplayed this suggestion thus far, likely seeing a constituent assembly as a threat to their political turf or, in the case of Quebec, being determined to decide its own fate.

This leaves Canada with a series of difficult choices. If Quebec alone has special powers, then it is possible that the rest of Canada might remain strongly united. Alternatively, Quebec's greater powers might encourage other provinces to demand the same. If all or most of the provinces get the same powers as Quebec, then the central government will be weak and the federation may become unstable. Federal dissolution, annexation by the United States, or conversion into a unitary state all become possibilities.[49] It is unlikely that the other provinces would get the same powers of course, and if they do not then Canada would remain intact for a time following Quebec's leaving.

3

Sovereignty-Association –
A Viable Alternative?

A more dramatic step than a restructured federation is sovereignty-association.[1] The distinction between sovereignty-association and a restructured federation, or between the sovereignty-association and independence, is vague and often misunderstood. For some Quebecers, sovereignty-association is more an affirmation of self-respect than a program with definite content. It is usually assumed to include political sovereignty for Quebec as well as with a monetary and customs union with Canada.

To achieve sovereignty, sovereigntists in Quebec would support a declaration of independence followed by negotiations on both sides to decide future mutual arrangements. Alternatively, the position might be taken that the laws of Canada would be subordinate to those of Quebec if they conflicted. This would probably be a source of ongoing challenges in the Canadian Supreme Court.

With sovereignty-association, Quebec would claim equal partnership or a veto in monetary policy and tariffs against the rest of the world. It would pursue a free trade agreement with the United States and have its own fiscal and taxation policy. In short, Quebec would possess a veto over economic areas that are now exclusively federal.

Sovereignty-association would allow Quebec sovereigntists to have their cake and to eat it too. It would allow for Quebec's representation in the United Nations, NATO, NORAD, the Organization of American States, La Francophonie, and many other international organizations. It would allow for much greater latitude in passing legislation in all sorts in areas formerly under federal jurisdiction. It would require a restructuring of the statute books, or the system of criminal laws, to better reflect the Quebec reality.

Quebec would support these changes while retaining the economic advantages that come with economic association to Canada. From a Quebec perspective, this would mean a common currency, access to the Bank of Canada, ties to Ontario's manufacturing base, and so on. Until late 1992, the sovereigntist Parti Québécois seemed convinced that the rest of Canada, or at least Ontario, would realize that it would be in their economic interest to retain close ties with Quebec as well. This remains to be seen, of course. Ontario residents might be very angry at Quebec, or they might first insist that Quebec pay off its share of the national debt. It could be an acrimonious period.

It is true that most members of the PQ are willing to accept sovereignty-association as a step towards more complete sovereignty. This is not, however, the position of Parti Québécois leader Jacques Parizeau. Since the failure of the October 1992 Charlottetown Agreement, Parizeau has insisted that sovereignty-association is dead.[2] He asserts that the only choices for Quebec will be sovereignty or the status quo. It should be stressed that this is not yet a generally held position with the PQ, but it is a view that should be taken seriously. Parizeau predicts that, if Quebecers choose sovereignty following a referendum, they will focus immediately on several priorities including:

• drafting a new constitution,
• eliminating governmental duplication,
• decentralizing governmental functions so that municipalities have more power,
• devising strategies to share debts and assets with Canada,
• resolving the issue of which currency to use – presumably it would be the Canadian one,
• ensuring a free exchange of goods, services, and people, and
• demonstrating clear support for the North American Free Trade Agreement (NAFTA).[3]

Again it should be stressed that these may be only the priorities of the PQ leader, and not the majority of its members.

No matter what the powers of Quebec under a sovereignty-association, many Quebecers believe it remains a viable option because of the failure of the Charlottetown and Meech Lake accords and other earlier constitutional reform attempts, the patriation of the 1982 constitution without Quebec's consent, the strength of Quebec's business class, and the political legitimacy of the Parti Québécois. The movement to sovereignty reflects the frustration that many Quebecers feel with the constitution, which they regard as a pact between two founding peoples, but which English Canadians see as a series of laws and regulations governing ten provinces, equal in rights and powers. It demonstrates the rift between Quebec's focus on the importance of collective rights to protect language versus English Canada's emphasis on individual rights.

To negotiate 'sovereignty' might be easier than 'association.' The former would require a unilateral declaration of independence, at the least. But association might be harder if the rest of Canada is bitter or decides that economic ties would not serve its best interests. (This is incomprehensible in the long run.) Also, there is no 'rest of Canada' with a legal existence or mandate to negotiate the terms of association. It is not even clear if the remaining provinces together can negotiate as a legitimate political union, particularly if Ontario, by virtue of its population and wealth, dominates what remains of Canada.

There is also the vital question of whether Quebec can legally seek sovereignty.[4] Much of its territory was only added in 1912, well after the 1867 union. The Canadian constitution has no provision for secession. Furthermore, the federal government would be within its legal right to put down any unilateral secession effort, although it would probably not exercise that right. But the legal arguments for and against sovereignty will matter because public opinion will be sought over the legitimacy of the sovereignty movement. If a successful case is made for sovereignty's legality, then public acceptance of sovereignty will be facilitated. Sovereigntists must make a legal claim for sovereignty on the basis of Quebec's status as a 'nation,' the length of time their ancestors have resided in Quebec, the risk to the French fact in Canada, Quebec's and Canada's right to territory, and the disruption that may or may not be caused in the rest of Canada. All of these claims would be challenged by federalists, of course, with persuasive claims of their own.[5]

One study presented to the Bélanger-Campeau Commission maintained that a clear, democratically expressed will by Quebecers for independence could form the basis of Quebec sovereignty. Professor José Woehrling of the Université de Montréal acknowledged that provincial secession was not permitted in the constitution, but he insisted that the amending formula under section 38 could be used to allow for Quebec independence.[6] That formula provides for amendments that are approved by the two Houses of Parliament and at least two-thirds of the provinces comprising 50 per cent of the population. Woehrling noted that it would be simpler to change the constitution to allow Quebec to separate than to change it so that some of its demands can be met within the federal structure. This is because, he argued, secession would call for a constitutional amendment requiring the approval of just the federal government and six provinces, while constitutional reforms, like the failed Meech Lake Accord, require unanimous consent. Other scholars disagree, however, and argue that secession would require unanimous approval.

If the sovereignty process closely adheres to existing legal norms, then it would be much less likely to produce the instability and violence (often unintentional) with which unilateral secession is so often associated. Moreover, if the rest of Canada perceives that Quebec is not committing an 'illegal' act by virtue of seceding, a more constructive environment would result in which negotiations on an economic union based on mutual benefit could proceed. Although no polling evidence on this issue is yet available, it is likely that a majority of Canadians outside Quebec do regard the act of sovereignty as illegal, and this perception would likely have negative consequences in the event that Quebec secedes.

This said, many Quebecers maintain there must be a dramatic change in Quebec's relations with the rest of Canada.

SOVEREIGNTY-ASSOCIATION ELSEWHERE

There are few historical precedents for 'sovereignty-association' in any form. The Austro-Hungarian Empire lasted from 1867 to 1918, but fell apart after its World War I defeat. A variety of customs unions and confederal arrangements have been attempted in several countries with few successes.[7] One exception is Switzerland which is a federal state with some confederal constitutional provisions.[8] The vast majority of loosely integrated nation-states calling themselves confederations, monetary or customs unions, or variations on this theme have either fallen apart or become unitary states. This does not preclude further attempts, however. Candidates for some form of sovereignty-association might include Catalonia, Galicia, or the Basque regions of Spain, Corsica and Brittany in France, Scotland, the occupied territories of Israel, and elsewhere. European economic union in 1992 has strengthened the drive for regional autonomy in many parts of the world. Its model will spur similar experiments in many nations – possibly including Canada. North American free trade has been extremely popular in Quebec – both for its economic benefits and for the legitimacy that it might grant an independent Quebec seeking to be regarded as an equal trading partner with Canada and the United States. In the same way, a single market has been a gift of legitimacy to those who promote regional autonomy in Europe.

It is worth noting that France is experiencing a situation in its Mediterranean island of Corsica that has some similarities to the Canada-Quebec relationship. The inhabitants of Corsica are legally French. Unlike in Canada, however, where the distinct society clause is not yet a part of the Canadian constitution, the French government in November 1990 accepted the existence of a 'Corsican people' within the Fifth Republic and passed legislation to that effect. The law was a concession to put an end to fifteen years of *indépendantiste* bombings. It remains controversial as opposition legislators and even some members of the governing Socialist party oppose granting special status to the mountainous, impoverished island. Since coming under French rule in 1768, the Corsicans have steadfastly refused to give up their language and culture, despite the centralizing forces of the French state.

What is interesting for observers of the Canadian situation is the hostility in France to the Corsicans' national aspirations. Corsica has but 250,000 inhabitants, a tiny fraction of France's 55 million population, and yet most French citizens have little patience for any threat to national unity. Every school-age child in France learns that 'la Nation' is indivisible. The founding Jacobin principle of a 'united and indivisible' republic is fundamental to the concept of French nationhood.

With the concession to the 'Corsican people,' one cultured and linguistic minority has achieved something that the Bretons, the Alsatians, and the Basques have been denied. In Paris, some critics of the government's policy of awarding Corsica special status warn that the 'Corsican people' will soon be demanding total independence and the republic will thus be 'dismembered.' Others warn of the dangers of 'federalism.' These concerns are obviously reminiscent of Canada's situation.

There are important differences, of course. France is a unitary system with less of a constitutional obligation to grant special rights and privileges than a federal state. The Corsicans were not a founding people of France, unlike French Canadians. The Corsicans are a tiny minority, while the Québécois number one-quarter of the national population. Corsica is impoverished, and Quebec is relatively wealthy.

Nevertheless, the similarities are instructive for they make clear that Canada's situation is not unique and similar demands for autonomy can occur in near-homogeneous and prosperous nation-states like France. One final lesson is that a nation's constitutional structure is less important than the necessary political will required to ensure that national unity should be preserved. In any nation, and particularly in a democracy, the constitutional structure must adapt to reflect changing political forces. Otherwise it rapidly loses its legitimacy.

There is another important point to be made, however, and that is that the Canadian constitution does not address the question of whether a province can legally secede. The old Soviet constitution expressly permits its republics to secede,[9] and the Australian constitution expressly prohibits its states to secede.[10] Canada's British North America (BNA) Act of 1867 provides for the admission but not for the secession of provinces. The Constitution Act, 1982, includes no provisions for secession. The American constitution is similarly silent on the issue of secession.[11] Unlike the case of the United States, however, no Canadian court has considered the issue of whether a right of secession exists.[12]

SOVEREIGNTY-ASSOCIATION: AN APPRAISAL

As noted, many Quebec sovereigntists assert that sovereignty-association would be the best of two worlds. It would allow Quebecers to have their own nation, political structures, laws, and public policy-making capability. At the same time, economic association would allow them to enjoy the benefits of a common currency, a common market, and the convenience of shared assets and debts. Quebec would be able to maintain its own military and diplomatic corps to reflect its own interests. Quebec's foreign policy strategies and goals might differ from those of Canada. For example, with regard to relations with the United States in Washington, Quebec representatives would not have to work through the Canadian ambassador, but could use their own diplomats and could, just as effectively, initiate legal action to settle disputes. Quebec officials in Washington are not averse to working within the American legal system to achieve certain goals, a strategy that Canadian officials are noticeably reluctant to pursue.

It should be noted, however, that the meaning of sovereignty-association remains as unclear to many Quebecers as it did at the time of the 1980 referendum. At that time, survey data revealed that a significant segment of the electorate thought that Quebec would continue to send members of parliament to Ottawa under sovereignty-association. At present, the differences between sovereignty-association and complete independence are unclear to many. Analysts ascribe similar costs and benefits to both, for reasons that include their confusion, the sense that the two are not that different, and the view that sovereignty-association will lead inevitably to independence.

Also, the economic costs of sovereignty or sovereignty-association might be prohibitive. The rest of Canada is not as monolithic as some Quebecers would assert. Rather it consists of nine diverse provinces and two territories with frequently competing interests. This implies that Quebec may not have a bargaining partner with a consistent series of concessions and goals. The Spicer Commission and similar groups tried to arrive at certain near-universally held concerns of Canada. They came up with few practical suggestions, however. Constitutional Affairs Minister Joe Clark faced an enormous task in trying to synthesize Canadian views and offer a mutually beneficial deal to Quebec that would entice it to remain within the federation. Of course, the Charlottetown Agreement was defeated.

There might be possible costs other than economic ones to bear as well. Canadian native groups in Quebec might demand secession from a sovereign Quebec or a continued link to the rest of Canada. National bilingualism might not remain a federal government policy, thereby diminishing francophone rights outside Quebec. Many English-speaking Quebecers would leave the province. An April 1991 poll revealed that only 35 per cent of English-speakers would stay if Quebec became sovereign. Unlike the anglophone exodus in 1976, this time francophones might not be able to fill the economic void.

There would be other problems to solve as well. What would be the mechanisms whereby federal civil servants and diplomats from Quebec, federal politicians, or Canadian soldiers from Quebec decide their allegiance? If they became Quebecers, they would become foreigners and probably lose their jobs. Presumably there would be no dual citizenship, although the Parti Québécois claims that it would not stop Quebecers from holding dual citizenship since it supports the free flow of goods, services, money, and people between Quebec and Canada. The terms of sovereignty would decide this point, of course. Montreal lawyer Julius Grey has noted that when Algeria left France, the Algerians were denied French passports. However, when Ireland seceded from Great Britain, the British allowed any Irish citizen to have a British passport.[14]

Quebec sovereigntist leaders insist that these public servants would work for Quebec, but it is not clear if Quebec needs or could absorb all of these people. If these jobs were forfeited, what compensation would be offered and who would pay for it? How would regional disputes be resolved? In the national capital region of Ottawa-Hull, the Treasury Board of Canada reported that 11,582 Quebec residents hold government jobs in Ottawa, while 11,141 Ontario residents work in federal offices in Hull.[15] These figures do not include government-employed consultants or the thousands of spinoff jobs. What would happen to these people and jobs and the cross-border movement if Quebec became independent?

In one poll, a plurality of civil servant respondents in Quebec (42 per cent) revealed that they would prefer to remain federal employees if Quebec became sovereign. Twenty-five per cent would transfer allegiance, and 32 per cent had no answer. Not surprisingly, those living in Hull and western Quebec were most willing to work for Canada. Federal civil servants in Montreal were evenly divided between the two choices of allegiance.[16]

There are those who maintain that if Quebec goes, the rest of Canada might support a stronger federal presence in Ottawa. Others speculate, however, that Quebec's sovereignty would result in a net loss of jobs in Ottawa. Lobbyists, lawyers, consultants, and others would move to the provincial capitals of a more decentralized Canada. Federal operations would be cut, employment would diminish, and Ottawa decline in importance. It is an uncertain future for the national capital area.

What of federal laws in a sovereign Quebec? The Parti Québécois insists that the legal system in an independent Quebec would remain much the same, except that federal laws would be amended where necessary. All existing federal legislation, including the criminal code, judicial tenure, and British common law traditions, would remain. The Canadian legal system is seen by the PQ as a satisfactory combination of the British and U.S. systems. However, this is clearly an area that has received scant attention. There have been few, if any, studies of a judiciary and legal system for a sovereign Quebec. Here, as in so many policy areas, the real implications of a sovereign Quebec have been underexplored.

Most scholars agree that Quebecers have a right to greater autonomy and possibly sovereignty, if this is their desired option. They should enjoy the internationally recognized right to self-determination for a people that is culturally distinct, sufficiently numerous, and historically well established in a particular territory. However, if Quebec becomes a sovereign state, what would its boundaries be? Would they necessarily remain the same as at present?

Quebec's boundaries were extended north in 1912, an extension that went well beyond the territory traditionally occupied by the Québécois. If the Inuit people, for example, choose to remain within Canada, it is not clear that Quebec would have the legal or moral right to force them to assign their land to a sovereign Quebec. It might be the case, then, that Quebec's current territory might diminish with independence, a possibility that sovereigntist leaders have not acknowledged.

Nevertheless, if Quebec can separate from Canada, could not portions of the existing province be allowed to separate from the future independent country?[17] If Quebecers have a right to determine their own political future as a people, perhaps other provincial groups like the anglophone and aboriginal minorities have the same right. If they want to remain Canadians living in a Canadian territory, should they not be allowed to do so? Would the boundaries of an independent Quebec be negotiable?

History is replete with examples of states whose boundaries changed with their political status. What is now West Virginia seceded from Virginia in 1861 to remain in the union after Virginia voted to secede. Western Quebec and West Island Montreal have a substantial English-speaking population which might support their own secession into some new political structure allied with Canada. Equality party representatives who represent predominately nonfrancophone areas of Montreal and its suburbs insist that an independent Quebec could be carved up and have created a partition policy proposal. Indeed a small group in Quebec called Option Canada has investigated this option. Former Prime Minister Trudeau once stated that, 'if Canada is divisible, Quebec is divisible.' In fact, at least one survey by pollster Angus Reid revealed that a majority of Canadians desire that the territorial boundaries of a sovereign Quebec should be altered if regional groupings – such as native peoples or other Quebecers – indicate a preference to remain in Canada.[18]

Realistically, of course, one should acknowledge that if a sovereign Quebec insists that its borders remain intact, that is how it would stay unless the federal government is prepared to use military force. A Canadian government eager to divide a $400 billion debt would likely be averse to sending in troops for what would be an ugly battle.[19]

Nevertheless, some critics of the sovereignty movement question Quebec's legal right to its territory after independence. McGill law professor Stephen Scott argues that the federal government granted territory in the north of Quebec to the province in 1898 and 1912 that had not been a part of New France, the French territory in North America. Hydro-Québec draws its electricity from this region. Without Northern Quebec, the new sovereign nation might not be economically viable.[20] Few analysts believe that Canada would use this issue as more than a bargaining point with a sovereign Quebec, however, since popular sentiment in Quebec is that Northern Quebec is an integral part of the province. Federal authorities have been silent on the issue. Nevertheless, some historians and constitutional experts agree that, legally, Quebec can leave Canada only with the same territory with which it entered Confederation in 1867 – essentially the St Lawrence River Valley. Even this, according to some experts, might exclude a strip of land along the St Lawrence River which links the Atlantic provinces with the rest of Canada west of Quebec. In fact, the federal government claims the area of the St Lawrence east of Anticosti Island.[21]

Related to this point is the issue of native land claims in Northern Quebec. The Indians of Northern Quebec speak English for the most part and would likely oppose Quebec's secession. They could argue that they constitute a 'people' with a claim on Northern Quebec. They might have as much legal standing as those who claim that francophone Quebecers are a 'people.' In fact, in July 1993 Quebec natives banded together and called for a national resolution supporting their fight to get separatism off the Canadian political agenda. Legally and constitutionally, their wishes could not be ignored. They make up the majority of the population of the north, and their political clout continues to grow. Native leaders threaten that if Quebec separates, they will secede from Quebec. Natives claim title to virtually all of Quebec, and they argue that the province cannot take their land out of the federation without their consent. Lawyers familiar with native land claims say that the courts might agree, and the Supreme Court has ruled that the federal government has a fiduciary responsibility for native people.

The most worrisome native claim for the Quebec government is that of the Cree and Inuit to a vast area encompassing the site of the James Bay hydro-electric project. A negotiated settlement of that claim was reached in the 1975 James Bay Agreement. A 1992 $50 million agreement for the further development of Phase II of the Grande Baie James project has been reached. But these are contracts between Canada, Quebec, the Cree, and the Inuit. If Quebec becomes sovereign, the natives might argue successfully that the contract would be null and void. The contract would then have to be renegotiated. In fact, Ovide Mercredi, grand chief of the Assembly of First Nations, has suggested that the Cree might withdraw from Quebec should the province attain sovereignty. However, the Parti Québécois asserts that in the 1975 agreement the Cree ceded their territorial claims. This is a most contentious issue.[22] So is the potential problem of the Mohawks on the St Lawrence River. They have never ceded their claims and they are a fiduciary responsibility of the federal government.

The native people also worry that a sovereign Quebec would ignore native fears concerning the negative environmental implications of hydroelectricity generation without the federal regulations. Native leaders have related these points to a United Nations commission and argued that the North belongs not to the governments of Quebec or Canada, but to the native people. Two United Nations agencies, the UN Center on Transnational Corporations and the UN Center for Human Rights, then issued staff reports attacking Quebec for disregarding indigenous peoples in its James Bay plans. In these reports, Quebec was lumped with Brazil and India in its disregard for indigenous peoples whose lives were disrupted by hydroelectric projects.

The Quebec government insists that the facts were misrepresented and that development has produced, on balance, positive effects for the native population. The government points, in particular, to a doubling of the Cree population and an increase in the average life span since the first phase of the James Bay project was implemented. The dispute remains a hotly contested one, particularly since the New York Power Authority has cancelled a contract worth U.S.$12–$14 billion to buy Quebec hydroelectricity and cited the environment impact on the native peoples as one of the reasons. In September 1991, a Canadian federal court ruled that the Canadian government must conduct an environmental review of any new power projects on Cree ancestral land.

There are signs of some reconciliation between the Cree and the Quebec government however. On 17 October 1993 the Supreme Court of Canada confirmed the legality of the Eastmain River portion of the James Bay and Northern Quebec agreement of 1975. The court concluded that the agreement was negotiated in good faith by the Cree and the Quebec government.

There is another territorial issue as well. In 1927 the British Judicial Committee of the Privy Council ruled that Labrador was a part of Newfoundland and not Quebec. Quebec has never acknowledged this decision, but it has not challenged it strenuously in recent years. However, a sovereign Quebec might claim Labrador under international law, and the people of Labrador would probably oppose the claim. Since Quebec governments have de facto recognized the decision, this issue would probably be resolved without much difficulty.

In reality, neither Quebec nor the rest of Canada really wants to discuss these boundary issues in any detail, for they could lead to demands for greater autonomy from native people throughout the country. In addition, boundaries cannot be legally changed without the permission of the relevant provincial governments. In addition, further discussions about boundaries could arouse anger sufficient enough to poison negotiations. Finally, Quebecers insist that it was the British crown on behalf of the Canadian people which gave Quebec the north. The crown includes Quebecers, of course.

Should Quebec become sovereign, a corridor might be created south of the St Lawrence River to provide a link between Ontario and the Maritimes. Of course, a sovereign Quebec would have no interest in making life more difficult for its neighbours than sovereignty would inevitably cause. It is a fact that not one of the relevant political élites wishes to discuss the boundary question, but the issue is important and is repeatedly brought up.

QUEBEC SOVEREIGNTY: THE PUBLIC'S VIEW

The Bélanger-Campeau Commission report called for a Quebec referendum on outright sovereignty no later than October 1992 unless the federal government could come up with an acceptable counterproposal on increased autonomy and power-sharing. This became the referendum on the Charlottetown Agreement. At the same time, the commission created two committees to pursue the issue further. One would study any offers from the federal government and the other provinces towards making the current federal system more acceptable to Quebec. The other committee would examine the economic consequences of Quebec's sovereignty.

At the time of the commission report in March 1991, Quebec sovereigntists hailed it as a victory and predicted that English Canada would fail to come up with alternate proposals that would satisfy the rest of Quebecers. However,

Quebec's minister of justice and intergovernmental affairs, Gil Rémillard, said that he believed the referendum might never be held if acceptable concessions were made by Canada.

This was not the first referendum that Quebecers have been asked to respond to, of course. In May 1980, Quebecers were asked to vote on a plebiscite concerning the extent to which they would support negotiations leading to sovereignty-association. The referendum question was worded as follows:

The government of Quebec has made public its proposal to negotiate a new agreement with the rest of Canada, based on the equality of nations; this agreement would enable Quebec to acquire the exclusive power to make its laws, levy its taxes and establish relations abroad – in other words, sovereignty – and at the same time, to maintain with Canada an economic association, including a common currency; any change in political status resulting from these negotiations will be submitted to the people through a referendum; on these terms, do you give the government of Quebec the mandate to negotiate the proposed agreement between Quebec and Canada? Yes. No.

By a margin of 60 per cent to 40 per cent, Quebecers failed to support such negotiations. Non-francophones overwhelmingly voted 'no.' But even French-speaking Quebecers, by a slim majority, opposed the sovereignty-association initiative. In June 1991, Bill 150 was introduced in Quebec's National Assembly to implement the Bélanger-Campeau Commission recommendations.[23] Bill 150's provisions called for the institutionalization of two parliamentary committees, one to study various facets of sovereignty and the other to analyse the proposals of the federal government and other provinces. It also called for a sovereignty referendum between 8 and 22 June or 12 and 26 October 1992. The date finally chosen was 26 October. Of course, the Quebec National Assembly could decide not to allow the government to hold a referendum prior to the deadline. Robert Bourassa had, in fact, intimated that a referendum might not be held at all. The sovereignty movement appeared to be slowing down. The francophone business class had been very quiet as the recession deepened in Quebec. If a referendum on sovereignty were to be held in the current business climate, it was not at all clear that it would pass.

In May 1991, Constitutional Affairs Minister Joe Clark told the House of Commons: 'It is not our preference nor is it our intention to seek to resolve complex constitutional questions by way of referendum, but we believe it is prudent for the federal government to have the full authority to conduct a Canadian referendum should that become the best way to achieve consensus on defining our future together.'[24] Prime Minister Mulroney also voiced support for the referendum device under certain conditions. The federal Liberals had advocated some form of Canada-wide referendum to endorse constitutional change. In June 1992, the referendum legislation was passed in the House of Commons.

Some analysts have argued that no province can secede unless the majority of Canadians agree, presumably as revealed in a referendum.[25] Unless such agreement was forthcoming, Quebec's secession would be illegal and illegitimate, they insist. A case can be made, of course, that in practice a majority of Quebecers supporting a form of independence can realize this goal no matter what Canada's response is. Quebec Premier Bourassa, in fact, had once stated that a national Canadian referendum might not have any legal value. He questioned whether the Canadian Supreme Court would accept the notion that a referendum could amend the constitution when the Constitution Act clearly states that it can only be amended by resolutions adopted by the ten legislatures and the federal parliament.'[26]

Furthermore, referendums carry certain risks. If Quebec had supported one option but Canada supported another, it could have aggravated tensions.

SUPPORT FOR SOVEREIGNTY: WHAT CAN THE POLL DATA TELL US?

There have been any number of polls conducted since the failure of the Meech Lake Accord, each endeavouring to help us understand how much support complete independence, sovereignty-association, restructured federalism, or the status quo would attract in Quebec. The results are simultaneously puzzling and fascinating. This section reviews many of the more prominent recent surveys. First, it is worth noting that the choice of wording for a survey question in Quebec can be a sensitive issue. In the course of this study, I have consciously tried to avoid using the term 'separatism,' as Quebecers avoid it, preferring instead the more innocuous terms 'sovereignty' or 'sovereignty-association.' The term separatism is likely to attract an emotional response. By contrast, sovereignty is less value-laden. Of course, in 1994 Jacques Parizeau and Lucien Bouchard began calling themselves 'separatists.' Attitudes to the word may change among sovereigntists, or this could be a strategic error by these leaders if their supporters are not ready for it. It is also worth noting that public attitudes in Quebec are extremely volatile. Up to 25 per cent of the public can change its opinions in a one-month period.

Professor Édouard Cloutier and his colleagues have aggregated the results of 134 polls testing support for sovereignty in Quebec between 1960 and 1990.[27] Their survey results reveal a remarkable increase in support for various forms of sovereignty (see table 6). This is best demonstrated by the 20 per cent support for independence in the early 1980s, versus the 50 per cent support in 1990.

TABLE 6
Support in Quebec for the secessionist idea, 1960–90 (percentage)

Proposal	1960–4	1965–9	1970–4	1975–9	1980–5	1986–9	1990
Separatism	8	10	13	19	–	37	44
	(n=1)*	(n=4)	(n=5)	(n=5)		(n=4)	(n=5)
Independence	–	–	27	20	20	32	50
			(n=1)	(n=2)	(n=4)	(n=3)	(n=3)
Sovereignty	–	–	–	–	18	41	55
					(n=4)	(n=3)	(n=7)
Sovereignty-association	–	–	32	31	39	46	58
			(n=2)	(n=25)	(n=8)	(n=2)	(n=9)
Mandate to negotiate sovereignty-association	–	–	–	49	40	–	68
				(n=17)	(n=19)		(n=1)

* The "n" refers to the number of polls that have been used to compute the rate of support during the period.

Reprinted with permission from Édouard Cloutier, Jean Guay, and Daniel Latouche, *Le Virage* (Montréal: Québec-Amérique 1992)

This trend continued until mid-1991. In fact support for sovereignty grew particularly strong after September 1989, nine months before Meech Lake's failure. In another poll commissioned by the Quebec City daily newspaper *Le Soleil* prior to Meech's defeat, it was revealed that 58 per cent of all Quebecers would back a move towards 'sovereignty-association' with Canada, while 42 per cent would support 'complete independence' if Meech was not ratified. Of the francophone population alone, 67 per cent backed sovereignty-association, and 48 per cent supported complete independence. Not surprisingly, 82 per cent of anglophones and 66 per cent of allophones rejected the option of sovereignty-association.[28] By May 1990, a month before Meech's collapse, the proportion of Quebecers favouring sovereignty reached 60 per cent.

By mid-July 1990, a plurality of Quebecers believed that sovereignty-association would be to Quebec's economic benefit.[29] Interestingly, most polls in 1990 revealed that support for sovereignty or sovereignty-association in Quebec increased with education and income levels.[30] The wealthier, better-educated Quebecers were the risk takers.

By late November 1990, francophone support for political autonomy had grown further. One poll revealed that 73 per cent of French-speaking Quebecers favoured sovereignty-association. When non-francophone Quebecers were included, the support figure diminished to a still-definitive 62 per cent of the province. Almost half of the members of the supposedly federalist Liberal party (49 per cent) backed sovereignty-association. Seventy-three per cent of Liberal party members wanted a referendum on Quebec's future.[31] A subsequent poll in late November reported similar findings and revealed that 50 per cent of all Quebecers supported not just sovereignty-association, but outright independence for the province.[32]

This was reinforced in a January 1991 poll by the Centre de recherches sur l'opinion publique (CROP) in which the respondents were asked, 'Do you think it is possible to reach an agreement with the rest of Canada, or will Quebec have to decide its political future unilaterally?'[33] Only 39 per cent thought an agreement with the rest of Canada was possible. Fifty-four per cent chose the unilateral option.

Some of the poll results were quite puzzling. For example, in a *Le Devoir* poll in February 1991, 54 per cent of Quebecers favoured independence, 58 per cent favoured sovereignty-association, but 60 per cent favoured giving a last chance to constitutional negotiations with Canada.[34] Further probing revealed that only about 35 per cent of Quebecers were unconditional supporters of independence. The rest were moderates who wanted to give Canada a last chance before taking the extreme step.

What this tells us is that Quebecers may or may not want sovereignty, but as of early 1991 they were less afraid of it. Soon after, another poll indicated that Quebec was split. Forty-two per cent favoured sovereignty, and 42 per cent were opposed.[35] By April 1991, however, support for sovereignty in Quebec began to decline.[36] There are a number of reasons for this diminished support, but the most persuasive appeared to be the deepening recession, forcing Quebecers to consider the economic implications of sovereignty and focus their attention on keeping their jobs rather than imagining a future Quebec nation-state. The responses also revealed that for many Quebecers, sovereignty is a concept that could coexist with the idea of remaining Canadian. In fact, in a CBC poll 83 per cent of Quebec respondents agreed with the statement 'Canada is the best country in the world to live in.'[37] This causes one to be suspicious of the chances for sovereignty, at least in the near term.

Similar results emerged in May 1991. A majority of Quebecers surveyed preferred that Quebec remain a Canadian province.[38] Another poll published one week later also showed declining support for sovereignty.[39] A September 1991 poll revealed renewed support for sovereignty in Quebec,[40] but October and December polls saw it diminishing again.[41] Clearly, support for sovereignty remains extensive in Quebec, although it is hard to gauge its precise level.

In fact, the polls were puzzling at times. Two leading polling firms based in the rest of Canada, Gallup and Angus Reid Group, detected a sharp drop in support for sovereignty in Quebec in December 1991/January 1992, while most of the major Quebec polling firms had sovereignty support holding steady or rising. 'Are polls now afflicted by the virus of the distinct society with the result depending on whether the head office of the polling firm is in Winnipeg or Montreal?' asked the *Journal de Québec* after reviewing some of the recent contradictions.[42] One explanation for the discrepancy is that survey questions were phrased differently. Sample size might have also been a factor. Gallup produced Quebec results from samples of fewer than 300 people, with a margin of error of 6 or 7 per cent. Some Angus Reid polls have Quebec samples of fewer than 400 with a margin of error of 5 per cent. Environics had a sample of 500 Quebecers for its latest poll – margin of error 4.5 per cent – while the Quebec firms invariably have samples of around 1000 or more with a margin of error of around 3 per cent. But these factors are not enough to explain the discrepancy between certain poll results, some Quebec experts say.

They suggest that the polls might be tainted by political bias and that the 60–40 vote in favor of federalism in 1980 is now reversed, 60–40 in favour of sovereignty. Of course, people use polls to send messages to their government. In an election the stakes are obviously much higher.

By February 1992, a Gallup poll revealed that 26 per cent of Canadians favoured replacing the current system with two separate countries – Quebec and Canada – which would be associated in an economic union. Sixty-seven per cent of respondents were opposed to this notion and 8 per cent had no opinion. However, 56 per cent of Quebecers supported the idea. Soon after, polls published in Quebec by the Institut québécois de l'opinion publique and by Multi-Reso revealed that about 58 per cent of Quebecers would support sovereignty.

However, there remained a lot of confusion about what sovereignty would mean. In a survey conducted 19–22 March 1992 for *La Presse* by CROP, a significant minority of respondents didn't give the 'right' answers to questions about the implications of sovereignty in different areas. For example, 20 per cent of respondents erroneously thought a sovereign Quebec would still elect members of the Canadian parliament in Ottawa, while another 21 per cent didn't know or didn't answer. Thirty-one per cent wrongly believed a sovereign Quebec would still be part of Canada with another 14 per cent not sure or not answering. Forty per cent thought Quebecers would keep their Canadian citizenship.

CROP found ignorance about sovereignty to be about as widespread among supporters of the pro-sovereignty PQ, 81 per cent of whom would vote for sovereignty in a referendum, as among Liberal supporters. For example, 30 per cent of PQ supporters believed a sovereign Quebec would remain part of Canada, while 34 per cent of Liberal supporters thought so. CROP found respondents to be evenly divided on sovereignty. Forty-two per cent said they would vote for sovereignty in a referendum, while 39 per cent said they would vote against it and the remaining 20 per cent did not know or did not say how they would vote.

If an actual referendum were that close, then the fates of Quebec and of Canada could be in the hands of people who did not fully understand what they would be voting for (or, for that matter, against).

PQ leader Jacques Parizeau insists that all Quebecers agree on the definition of sovereignty, even if they do not all agree with its objectives. 'Sovereignty means that all taxes levied on Quebecers are adopted by the National Assembly of Quebec, all laws pertaining to the life of Quebecers are adopted by the Quebec National Assembly and all treaties linking Quebec to the outside world are accepted by the Quebec National Assembly.'[43] But in fact the definition of sovereignty is widely misunderstood in Quebec.

Some observers have speculated that Quebec politicians have intentionally never made entirely clear what sovereignty would mean. Others suggest that better-educated Quebecers have a clear understanding of sovereignty. One other reasonable explanation for the confusing polling results is that most Quebecers remain attached to Canada.

By April 1992 a Gallup poll indicated that only 20 per cent of Canadian respondents believed that the Canadian federation would break up, the lowest figure since 1984. Only 35 per cent of Quebecers believed that the federation would disintegrate. By June 1992 Quebec business leaders overwhelmingly opposed sovereignty-association. Only 13 of 324 polled supported sovereignty-association while 80 per cent supported a federal solution to the constitutional problems. In fact, only 1 per cent supported outright sovereignty with no economic association. Fully 84 per cent of these business leaders thought that sovereignty would have a negative effect on the Quebec economy. Their opposition to independence may have been based less on any love of Canada and more on economic fears.

A fall 1992 poll revealed that when it was explained to Quebecers that sovereignty means that Quebec would leave Canada, support for sovereignty among all Quebecers decreased from 47 per cent to 39 per cent and decreased among francophone Quebecers from 52 per cent to 44 per cent.[44]

Through 1993, the polls continued to reveal declining support for sovereignty in Quebec. In mid-April 1993, a SOM poll found 50 per cent of Quebecers opposed to sovereignty and 37 per cent in support of it. Thirteen per cent were undecided. Of particular interest was this clear demonstration that the Charlottetown Agreement's failure did not immediately accelerate support for sovereignty. Since the 'no' side was victorious in six of ten provinces, Quebecers could not legitimately feel rejected by the rest of Canada, unlike the perceived rejection of Quebec following Meech's failure. In a *Financial Post* magazine poll following the 25 October 1993 federal election, 60 per cent of Quebec respondents revealed that they would vote to remain part of Canada in a referendum. Quebec francophones opposed the sovereignty option by a 47-to-43 per cent margin. Ninety-three per cent of English-speaking Quebecers would support the federalist option. According to this poll support for the sovereignty option has not grown since the Quebec referendum on the issue in 1980. In fact, it may be declining. In a survey conducted on 18–22 March 1994 by the CROP polling firm, only 14 per cent of Quebecers said the main issue in the 1994 provincial elections should be political independence, while 76 per cent said it should be the election of a 'good government.' Of those intending to vote for the PQ, 68 per cent said good government, not independence, should be the main issue. In addition, of course, Quebec's economic woes dampen support for sovereignty and the economic instability that might be associated with it. In a perverse way, the worse the Quebec economy becomes (within reason), the less Quebecers have a taste for sovereignty. Of course, this could all change if and when the next crisis emerges.

4

Quebec's Economic and
Political Development since 1976

With the election of the nationalist PQ in 1976 came more attempts to bolster Quebec's economic prowess. The original agenda of the PQ was, unlike that of the previous Quebec governments, *socialiste* and *indépendantiste*. It soon became obvious to PQ leaders, however, that their socialist rhetoric would have to be modified in order to give Quebec the economic muscle to become truly independent. Oddly enough, one of the PQ's greatest contributions to the long-term economic benefit of francophones stemmed from its perceived radicalism. The PQ's ascendance to power triggered a mass exodus of businesses headed by anglophones. They fled for the most part to Ontario, hence providing their francophone counterparts with the chance to fill partially the void.

Today, many of these business leaders are playing a major role in the re-awakening of the sovereignty debate in Quebec. Also, non-élites in Quebec are increasingly willing to express their confidence in the economic future of an independent Quebec, although most would not do so without the financial and economic ties that Quebec shares with the rest of Canada.

Under the Régime d'épargne-actions for instance, which was conceived by former PQ finance minister (and now leader) Jacques Parizeau and instituted in 1979, Quebecers were induced through tax incentives to invest more in Quebec-based stocks – thereby not only educating themselves more about business, but also helping to capitalize the provincial corporations. In fact, before the program was instituted, 12 per cent of Canadians outside Quebec but only 8 per cent of Quebecers invested in the stock market. After the program 13 per cent of Quebecers and 12 per cent of other Canadians participated. More importantly, in 1984, the Quebec insurance industry was deregulated through Bill 75. Deregulation meant that Quebec's insurance companies, alone among those of Canada's still-regulated provinces, could offer a wide range of services, or 'one-stop' financial shopping,[1] that greatly increased their revenue-generating capabilities. There have been no such dramatic measures instituted since – in part because the Bourassa government was not committed to a goal of complete economic sovereignty for Quebec, and in part because state intervention was no longer viewed as essential to either Quebec business or the Quebec economy. As Bourassa's Advisory Committee on Privatization put it in 1986: 'The Quiet Revolution has done its job: it has bequeathed us a strong and dynamic private sector. Now it is time to turn the page.'[2]

Nevertheless, the extraordinary degree of cooperation between business and government, popularly referred to as 'Quebec, Inc.,' is still quite evident in, to name just two examples, the tax incentives extended to businesses (write-offs for research and development, low taxes on profits), and in joint business-government efforts such as the new $20 million venture capital fund, Capiteq. (Established to assist small and medium-sized businesses, Capiteq has received contributions from the Caisse, the Order of Engineers of Quebec, the Quebec Federation of Labour, Hydro-Québec, and the pension funds of Bombardier and the École polytechnique.)

The rewards of such cooperation have been substantial. In 1990, Quebec enjoyed a GDP larger than that of Denmark or Norway.[3] Its share of Canada's GDP is 23.6 per cent, it accounts for some 17 per cent of Canada's total exports,[4] and it is home to more than half of the 50 fastest growing companies in Canada. In addition, francophone entrepreneurs have become the major actors in the private sector; they own or control businesses that employ 61 per cent of Quebec's workers, as opposed to less than 50 per cent in the early 1970s.[5]

Such economic figures have generated a new confidence in Quebec's ability to go it alone in a number of sectors, although the recession has hit Montreal particularly cruelly. There is also an increased cynicism about the federal government's capacity to generate economic growth. Given the effort that has gone into building up the province's economy, it is particularly irritating to many Quebecers that, in 1990, they should suffer as a result of the federal government's current economic woes – especially since Quebec has balanced its spending budgets and has a deficit that finances only capital expenses.[6] Few Quebec business leaders have much respect for the way Ottawa has managed the national finances, especially its massive deficit. One consequence is that the proportion of federal funds making up Quebec's provincial revenues declined to 18 per cent by 1992 from 30 per cent in 1980.[7]

Quebec's frustration with federal government economic policies is substantial. Furthermore, most observers would now agree that Quebec would be a viable nation-state if it attained independence. By world standards it is ethnically, linguistically, and culturally homogeneous. An independent Quebec would have a population of 6.5 million with a gross national product of about $145 billion. Quebec has no identifiable external enemies and was an avid supporter of the continental free trade pact including Mexico, much as it was a staunch supporter of the Canada–U.S. deal. A sovereign Quebec would want to retain and expand its privileged markets in the United States and the rest of Canada although, at the same time, Quebec has been reluctant to dismantle a number of interprovincial trade barriers. In addition, it would look more to a unified Europe and the huge Asian market for future trade possibilities. Quebec sovereigntists assert that an independent Quebec would still be based on a market economy and would be firmly positioned in the currents of international trade.

One great advantage Quebec enjoys is that, unlike English Canada, which has relatively small capital pools, it works closely with such giant sources of provincially run investment funds as the Desjardins credit union group (assets of $45 billion) and the Caisse de dépôt et placement du Québec (assets of $38 billion). Although the interests of the Mouvement Desjardins or the Caisse de dépôt may differ at times, most often they work together quite amicably.

The Desjardins credit union group is a particularly fascinating case. It holds 35 per cent of all savings deposits in Quebec, 23 per cent of the commercial lending market, 31 per cent of personal loans and 38 per cent of all mortgages. It has become a financial supermarket for Quebecers, offering everything from trust banking to insurance. But perhaps the most important single resource, which is controlled by the government of Quebec and which first promoted the sense that Quebecers could control their own destiny, is the hydroelectric power developed in Northern Quebec. It was accompanied by the development of a reasonably diversified export sector in the 1970s and 1980s. Although hydro-electricity is only the eighth most important Quebec export as of 1987, following paper products, aluminium, and automobiles, its symbolic importance cannot be overstated.

So, the financial sector of Quebec is fairly strong. Its financial laws have always been more liberal than those in the other provinces or those of the federal government, with the result that Canadian financial institutions have incorporated in Quebec to a disproportionate degree. The financial industry has prospered as banks, trusts, insurance companies, and investment dealers often overlap. Financial institutions like the caisses populaires of the Mouvement Desjardins are flexible and diversified. They have not invested in Third World countries or in troubled big businesses (with the now-bankrupt engineering firm Lavalin a notable exception). They remain highly profitable at a time when many of Canada's national banks' investments have soured.

Interestingly, Quebec's business community, which had been solidly against sovereignty in the past, indicated in early 1991 its support for some form of independence by a substantial margin. Various polls revealed that 57 per cent of Quebec businessmen would welcome some form of sovereignty. In a *Globe and Mail* survey in February 1991, almost 72 per cent of the senior business respondents said they would prefer a sovereign Quebec with economic ties to the rest of Canada.[8] Most of the Quebec business leaders concluded that their companies' interests would be best protected within a sovereign Quebec.[9] It is interesting to note that supporters of independence were usually small and medium-sized businesses. Large businesses tended to favour some form of federalism since they were likely to have commercial links to the rest of Canada and other countries. However, surveys published more recently revealed diminishing business support for sovereignty.[10]

There is an important point to note, however. Francophone Quebec business leaders, and in fact most Quebecers, are nationalists. But this does not necessarily make them sovereigntists. The two are quite different, and at a time of major recession in Quebec uncertainties over the economy may compel many nationalists to support reluctantly the federal tie. In time of economic trouble, economic priorities overshadow constitutional ones.

Nevertheless, in March 1990, a Merrill Lynch report suggested that foreign investors should be confident about buying government bonds or offering loans in the long term in a sovereign Quebec. The Merrill Lynch report stressed that an independent Quebec would collect the same amount of taxes that are now paid to Ottawa and would use that money to provide the same level of services to its population. The Toronto Dominion Bank has also concluded that the Quebec economy could survive as an independent state. The Conseil du patronat, the province's largest business group, disagreed and argued that in an independent Quebec, investor confidence would be shaken and Quebec's economic situation would be undermined.

In fact, uncertainty over Canada's political stability, as well as certain economic considerations, caused a modest flight of foreign capital from Canada in 1990. Over $1 billion in Canadian government bonds were unloaded and some multinational firms quietly diverted a portion of their holdings into other countries. Concern over sovereignty added to the usual yield spread of Quebec bonds over comparable Canadian and U.S. Treasury issues. However, most American observers see Canada and Quebec as sound investment settings for the long term. After Meech Lake's failure, there was no economic panic, virtually no changed investor pattern, and Moody's investor service reaffirmed Quebec's favourable credit rating.

Some analysts maintain that if foreign investment in Quebec is reduced only slightly, it will have a deleterious effect on Quebec's economy when combined with the slowdown in domestic investment, high interest rates and surging unemployment figures. On the other hand, the Canada–U.S. Free Trade Agreement freed Quebec's economy from its dependence on the rest of Canada as its prime market – 35 per cent of the province's exports already move to the United States and only 25 per cent to Ontario.

Furthermore, Quebec's geography, markets, resources, and cheap power will continue to provide strong incentives for foreign investors. As noted, many observers maintain that Quebec's economy could withstand the shock of sovereignty, thanks to its own strength and to a decreasing dependency on Ottawa's transfer payments. In fact, a declassified 1977 study conducted jointly by the U.S. State Department, the Central Intelligence Agency (CIA), the National Security Council, and the Treasury Department revealed that 'there is no question regarding the basic long-term viability of an independent Quebec in the economic sense or in regard to its ability to be a responsible member of the family of nations.'[11] Of course, the interesting question is not whether Quebec will survive, but whether it will do as well as at present. There are serious doubts about this, as will be discussed below.

Nevertheless, the surge of capitalist enthusiasm in Quebec over the past thirty years has been remarkable. Where ambitious young Quebecois once shunned commerce for the professions or public service, they now enrol in business schools. Large French Canadian companies have emerged in recent years, and as of 1992 account for half of Canada's new manufacturing jobs. The share of the province's economy controlled by French Canadians – as measured by total employment in francophone-owned companies – was more than 65 per cent at the end of 1991 compared with 47 per cent in 1961.

The gain cuts across all sectors of the economy and comes at the expense of anglophone and foreign-owned companies. Internationally, Quebec firms have moved far beyond the traditional Canadian expertise in resource and agricultural industries to become competitive in machinery, services, energy, and food distribution. Bombardier, for example, which started as a snowmobile producer, has become a leading manufacturer of transportation equipment. The emergence of the French-speaking Quebec business class has been decisive in giving the province the confidence to redefine its relations with Canada. Marc Levine has called this period 'an unabashed celebration of francophone capitalism and capitalists.'[12]

ECONOMIC CONDITIONS IN QUEBEC AND THE REST OF CANADA

The federal government is strapped for cash and burdened by huge deficits. On an operating basis, Ottawa is running in the black, but the costs of servicing the huge national debt push the yearly accounts into the red. This fiscal predicament ties Ottawa's hands, forcing cutbacks and budgetary constraints and preventing Ottawa from offering generous grants to the provinces.

As noted, Quebec sovereigntists assert that federal finances are in disarray, and its policies in the fields of manpower, research and development, and financial institutions are inefficient. Some advocates of Quebec sovereignty maintain that an independent Quebec would no longer be tied down by Ottawa's fiscal problems. They insist that the expense of duplicating government services would be less if Ottawa handed over responsibility and tax sources to the provinces. This is a debatable point, of course.[13]

However, it is not necessarily the case that an independent Quebec could escape Ottawa's fiscal problems. An independent Quebec would still have to pay its share of Canada's national debt, once its debt share was determined. If it did not, it would forfeit its solid reputation in world financial markets. Reneging on past debts is no way to raise more money.

Since mid-1990 economic activity in Quebec has diminished. This drop in activity could be exacerbated if the federal government is unable to significantly decrease the budget deficit in the near future. In addition, perceptions of federal instability could damage Quebec's credit standing. According to the Canadian Bond Rating Service of Montreal, the federal government could endanger its current triple-A credit rating if the government's attempt to reduce the deficit – the latest in a series of six – fails.[14] If the federal government were to lose this rating, it would have to generate more tax revenue in order to be considered a 'good' borrower. This would, in turn, diminish the tax base upon which the provinces could draw in order to garner their own revenues – which might, in turn, endanger the provinces' own ratings. As noted, Quebec currently enjoys a double-A credit rating, which it might then lose owing to the federal government's economic problems.

Another cause of decreasing economic activity in Quebec, and in Canada as a whole, has been the Bank of Canada's tight monetary policy. Since the mid-1980s, the aim of the Bank of Canada has been to keep potentially crippling inflation rates at bay by fostering high interest rates. This policy has, in a narrow sense, succeeded: Canada's inflation rate from 1991 to 1994 has hovered around 5 per cent. But the cost of controlled inflation is generally unemployment – and Quebec has historically suffered from higher unemployment rates relative to all provinces except those in Atlantic Canada. For 1989, Quebec's unemployment rate was 9.3 per cent.[15] As of September 1990, unemployment in Quebec had moved up to 10.5 per cent, and by June 1993, it was 12.5 per cent – well above the national rate of 11.1 per cent.[16]

The unemployment rate in metropolitan Montreal was 14.6 per cent. Large industry in Quebec is suffering. Many large retail chains have gone bankrupt in the 1990s, throwing thousands of people out of work. Lavalin and Les Co-opérants have closed. Hydro-Québec has lost several billion dollars worth of contracts.

Another casualty of high interest rates is the small business sector, a fact that again has greater significance for Quebec than for many other parts of Canada. The creation and support of small and medium-sized businesses has been a keystone of Quebec economic policy since the Quiet Revolution. In the past, such businesses have accounted for nearly half the income earned by corporations based in Quebec. Yet such businesses lack the resources that larger ones have to borrow money except at exceptionally high interest rates. As a result, coupled with the federal governments policy of highly restricted business loans, high interest rates have put a significant portion of the Quebec economy at risk.

A final and powerful problem in Quebec's economic relationship with Ottawa lies in the simple fact that the federal government is perceived to be making unsound economic policy. In a brief submitted to the Bélanger-Campeau Commission in November 1990, the Quebec Chamber of Commerce chided Ottawa for its 'apparent inability to deal with the impending [economic] crisis.'[17] Its criticism is, in fact, supported by David R. Johnson, who observes that the zero inflation-rate goal set by the Bank of Canada is inconsistent with the Ministry of Finance's aim of accumulating new revenues by partial indexation of personal revenues and transfer payments. 'Partial indexation,' Johnson observes, 'means that inflation, up to [a] 3 per cent threshold, increases tax rates and reduces real transfers. Some inflation ... is extremely helpful in allowing the Minister of Finance to achieve his fiscal goals ... If the Bank of Canada defies the implicit wishes of the Minister and reduces the inflation rate to zero, a serious recession ... is likely.'[18] In other words, financially speaking, the right hand in Ottawa does not seem to know what the left hand is doing. This is hardly the sort of financial management that encourages confidence in an already alienated Quebec. Of course, it should be acknowledged that it is not uncommon for monetary and fiscal analysts to diverge in opinion.

Quebec's largest city, Montreal, has suffered the adverse effects of economic decline. The Montreal region produces half of Quebec's total output, but its youthful generation is remarkably small. There are 29 per cent fewer children of primary or secondary school age in Montreal than 20 years ago. This could mean a sharply shrunken future economy. Furthermore, from 1988 to 1992 between 36 and 39 per cent of high school students dropped out, an extremely high failure rate. Too many of those who remain in school are poorly educated in math and science, areas vital to a productive economy. In fact, only one in ten Quebec workers is a university graduate. Montreal has lost

Figure 1
Unemployment rates for the city of Montreal and the provinces of Quebec and Ontario, 1985–90

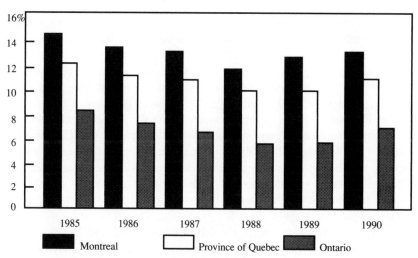

SOURCE: Canada, Department of Finance, *Quarterly Economic Review* (Montreal: CIDEM 1991)

more than 200,000 anglophones since 1976, thereby disrupting many of the old business networks by which the city prospered and diminishing greater Montreal's attractiveness to business communities in other countries. Quebec lost more than $10 billion in personal income tax revenue between 1976 and 1986.[19] The new francophone élites have been unable to reverse three decades of economic decline in the city.

Many of those that Quebec can least afford to lose are going to other provinces or the United States. According to Statistics Canada, Quebec had a net loss of 8515 university graduates between the last two censuses, 2150 people in managerial positions, 1265 with training in the natural sciences, engineering, or mathematics, 2380 teachers or people in related fields and 1380 people in medicine. Among people fifteen years or older with some university education, it lost about 13,000 people more than it gained.

A particularly high percentage of anglophone students plan to leave. One 1992 survey by McGill University sociology professor Uli Locher, for example, found that 62 per cent of English-speaking high school students expect to leave Quebec by 1997, and 73 per cent say they expect to be gone by 2002. Only 5 per cent definitely plan to remain.[20] Montreal has the highest unemployment rate of any major city in North America except New Orleans. It suffers from a disease critics have called chronic underemployment syndrome, offering 200,000 fewer jobs to its residents than its size would justify. The province's unemployment rate over the past fifteen years has averaged more than 11 per cent (see figure 1). It is predicted that the rate of job creation won't increase until 1995. Meanwhile, 400,000 Quebecers are out of work including 180,000 Montrealers.

By the end of 1991, 635,000 Quebecers were on welfare – a 12 per cent increase from the previous year. Of these, more than 330,000 were adults considered employable. In Ontario, 1,131,300 were on short- and long-term welfare in January 1992, a 33 per cent increase from the previous year. (Ontario's estimated population in 1991 was 9.7 million, compared with Quebec's 6.8 million.) On the island of Montreal, 22 per cent of families lived below the poverty line in 1991, according to the most recent statistics. Since then, the situation has deteriorated further. As of January 1994, 469,000 Quebec households were dependent on welfare.

• Nearly one in five adults on the island of Montreal and Laval lives on government handouts – either on unemployment insurance or on welfare. The population for the region is 1,707,000. There are 148,300 people on unemployment insurance not counting people who draw unemployment insurance for parental leave. There are also 166,404 welfare recipients in the region. The total – 314,704 – represents 18.4 per cent of the region's adults.

• Quebec has a higher percentage of families living below the poverty line than Newfoundland, the province often cited as Canada's poorest, according to the latest statistics. In 1990, 14.5 per cent of Quebec families lived below the poverty line. Statistics Canada sets the poverty or low-income line according to the size of the city and size of the family. For example, it's $28,081 for a family of four in a big city. In Newfoundland, 14.3 per cent of families lived below the poverty line in 1990. In Ontario, 9.8 per cent of families did. In fact, Quebec has the largest number of low-income people in Canada – one million, which is more than the combined total population of all four Atlantic provinces. With only 25 per cent of Canada's total population, it has 32 per cent of its poor families.

• In February 1991, 20 per cent of Quebecers aged 15 to 24 were without jobs. In Ontario, 18.7 per cent of young people were unemployed that month. The Conseil du patronat, which represents firms that employ 70 per cent of Quebec workers, estimates that 80,000 jobs are going begging because of a lack of skilled workers. The forestry industry – Quebec's largest, accounting for 22 per cent of the province's exports – laid off 10 per cent of its 65,000 workers in 1991.

Decisions to modernize the Montreal economy should have been taken in the 1970s but were never made, partly because Montreal quickly moved from being a national business centre to a purely regional one. As a result, there has been a significant lack of new investment in the city. Private investment in 1991 was estimated at $27.5 billion, $1.2 billion less than 1990. Montreal's industrial structure has changed little since the 1950s, with a heavy concentration in uncompetitive industries.[21] The few exceptions would include Montreal's dynamic pharmaceutical and aluminium industries, its thriving advertising and fashion sectors, and its stable transportation (Spar Aerospace, Bombardier) and data processing sector.

In addition, Quebec's manufacturing output has lagged behind Ontario's by about 25 per cent since 1980, and personal taxes are among the highest in the country. Provincial public debt, at $13,130 per person, rivals the federal debt in proportionate terms. On the other hand, the trend in Quebec since 1989 has been towards diversification of industrial capacity. Quebec may now be more diversified industrially than Ontario which is so dependent on its automobile sector.

Quebec's and Canada's economic problems are severe. The recession there has been more pervasive than in the United States. Most Canadians, both inside and outside Quebec, are much less interested in federal-provincial constitutional squabbling than they are in their own economic plight. Various polls in 1990, 1991, and 1992 support this view. A *Maclean's* survey taken in November 1990 demonstrated that national unity was only fifth on a list of issues important to Canadians. Indeed, only 8 per cent of Canadians considered it the most important issue. Taxes, the recession, the environment, and unemployment were considered more important issues in that order by Canadians.[22] A subsequent Gallup survey in January 1991 revealed similar results.[23] Poll respondents were asked whether national unity or economic recession was a more serious problem facing Canada. Only 23 per cent considered national unity more important. Economic recession was the choice of 73 per cent, and 4 per cent had no opinion. Notwithstanding the economic priorities of Canadians, the news media and the federal government are perceived as devoting more attention to national unity issues. In turn, many Canadians perceive the federal government as out of touch with their interests.

One cannot divorce economic concerns from constitutional or political ones, however. The unstable political situation could pose a financial risk to the economy. The confidence of foreign investors could be shaken. Canadians seem to understand that the constitutional problems are hurting the economy, although most are unwilling to act upon this situation.[24] This demonstrates a cynical population lacking confidence in its political leaders and growing inward in its priorities. Indeed, since Canada was founded in 1867, political thinkers have focused on national unity – on how to contain Quebec nationalism within the bounds of a federation and how to balance the power of the central government and the regions. That obsession has often overridden other issues, like poverty. It has also distorted politics in Canada. The difference between major political parties has been based more on national-unity issues than on a conservative or socialist view of how to run the economy.

Poverty is one of the most serious issues in Canada today. Some politicians respond by saying that you cannot have a viable economy until national stability is ensured. This may be true. But in the meantime, hundreds of thousands are suffering.

5

Political Sovereignty for Quebec –
The Economic Costs and Benefits

Since the failure of the Meech Lake Accord, there has been much educated speculation about the relative economic costs and benefits of political sovereignty for Quebec. It should be stressed that this is just speculation. It is impossible to calculate the true costs of Quebec's sovereignty, because we know little about the complex economic, political, and emotional factors that would affect everything from Quebec's links with its trading partners to foreign investors' willingness to keep putting billions of dollars into factories, hydroelectric dams, and government spending in Quebec. Much of the uncertainty stems from the fact that no one has any idea of just how independent an independent Quebec would be. The distinction between separatism, sovereignty and sovereignty-association is not entirely clear. Canada's response to these options is not yet known. How much power, and what concessions, Canada and Quebec can afford to yield are yet to be determined. This makes the task of evaluating the economic costs and benefits of sovereignty a particularly difficult one.

Most analysts agree that the Quebec economy is viable. It is less clear if Quebec would be better off economically with sovereignty. What would be the reaction of foreign and domestic capital to Quebec's sovereignty, with all of the associated fears of putting one's capital at risk abroad? Investment in resource industries is likely to continue unabated. But what of the import-competing industries that must now contemplate serving a much more restricted primary market? What of the export industries that may instead choose the larger and safer locales of English Canada or of the United States?

There are many questions about the economic implications of sovereignty that must go unanswered at present, but two points seem clear. First, in the short run there will be trade uncertainty, monetary uncertainty, and capital uncertainty. Capital uncertainty would affect production sharing, economics of scale, investment, fear of decline, and accelerated out-migration of capital and people. Second, again in the short run at least, the available evidence strongly suggests that Quebec stands to lose a great deal following sovereignty. There are several arguments that support this view.

One of the first post-Meech studies exploring the costs of sovereignty was an October 1990 investigation by the leading Quebec business association, the Conseil du patronat. This report made clear that the federal system would have to be renegotiated, but that federalism remained the best option for Quebec and that sovereignty would cost Quebec in prosperity and jobs. The main thesis of the council's report was that only a federal system could give Quebec the full benefit of participating in the bigger, more diverse Canadian economy at the same time that it leaves the Quebec government in control of sensitive areas such as culture, language, and education. By remaining in Canada, for example, Quebec could retain easy and cheap access to western Canadian oil fields. There is no guarantee of this access for a sovereign Quebec. In addition, Quebec companies have a large domestic market they can exploit without having to deal with trade barriers or the complexities of international trade. This is particularly significant for Quebec, which is more dependent on interprovincial trade and the national market than is any other province. Quebec sells 55 per cent of its finished products and 26.5 per cent of its manufactured goods within Canada.[1] In fact, 25 per cent of its exports go to Ontario. Quebec sovereignty would not necessarily mean that these benefits would disappear, but some would inevitably be lost because it is not likely that English Canada would be willing to negotiate the same freedom of movement for people, capital, and trade to an independent Quebec, at least in the short run.

How would sovereignty affect the rest of Canada? Ontario would be most affected because of its geographic proximity and substantial economic integration with Quebec. In 1989, Ontario exported $16 billion worth of goods to Quebec and imported $13 billion, a trade flow equivalent to that of many medium-sized countries. About 80 per cent of the interprovincial trade in Canada is between Quebec and Ontario. Of manufactured goods alone, 17 per cent of Quebec's total went to Ontario versus 8 per cent of Ontario's to Quebec. In 1990, Quebec generated more revenue from sales to Ontario ($18 billion) than to any other destination.[2] The two provinces are closely integrated, but Quebec is more dependent on Ontario than the reverse. The United States and even western Canada are more important markets for Ontario's manufactured goods than is Quebec. In fact, some analysts argue that Ontario would have a better chance of making it on its own than would Quebec in the international trading arena. Statistics from Statistics Canada demonstrate this point as shown in table 7. Ontario's relative importance in Canadian manufacturing has increased, while Quebec's has declined (see tables 8 and 9). The personal income per capita of Ontarians is increasing more rapidly than is Quebecers' income (see figure 2). In addition, the value of Ontario's international trade in goods with the rest of the world was $60.2 billion, the most of all provinces and almost three times the value of Quebec's international trade at $22.7 billion. Based on 1989 statistics, Ontario would rank twelfth among the nations of the world in gross national product. And its standard of living, as measured by GNP per capita, would be second only to Switzerland's. While the recession may have lowered those rankings, there is no question that Ontario has the kind of manufacturing, resource, and service industries to thrive as one of the world's more diversified and powerful economies.

However, another story released by the Economic Council of Canada concluded that Quebec would be a big loser and Ontario would be a winner if Quebec broke all fiscal ties with Canada. Breaking up the country would permanently cut the size of Quebec's economy by 1.4 per cent to 3.5 per cent while Ontario's economy would gain up to 0.4 per cent, according to a computer analysis that assumes a peaceful and relatively harmonious divorce. A messy breakup would almost certainly cost Quebec much more. If Quebec left Canada, the federal government would save $4.38 billion because it spends more on transfer payments, goods, and services in that province than it receives in tax revenues, the study concludes. Under separation, the study's computer simulation also showed the economy would:

- Grow 0.2 per cent to 0.4 per cent in Atlantic Canada.
- Shrink about 0.1 per cent in Manitoba and Saskatchewan.
- Either shrink 0.2 per cent or grow up to 0.4 per cent in Alberta (depending on different economic assumptions).
- Shrink 0.1 per cent to 0.3 per cent in British Columbia and the territories.

It should be stressed that this study assumes that all fiscal ties would be cut. A less-than-clear fiscal break would undoubtedly find different results.[3]

In Canada as a whole, the costs of Quebec's sovereignty might be substantial. According to the Business Council on National Issues (BCNI), which is composed of the heads of 150 of Canada's biggest corporations, Canada's partial dismemberment would cost Canadians $1100 each in lost incomes but the price tag would run much higher. Separation would add billions of dollars to interest payments on mortgages, consumer and business loans, and government debts. Economic growth would diminish. There would be a loss of $30 billion in national income. The BCNI assumed that interest rates would be pushed up by two per centage points during the period of uncertainty and

TABLE 7
Comparison of Quebec's and Ontario's relative importance in the Canadian manufacturing sector using three criteria (percentage of total)

Year	Number of establishments			Number of employees			Value of shipments to the rest		
	Que	Ont	Q/O	Que	Ont	Q/O	Que	Ont	Q/O
1960	33.8	36.8	0.9	33.7	46.6	0.7	30.4	49.3	0.6
1965	32.9	38.3	0.9	31.8	49.3	0.6	28.0	52.1	0.5
1970	31.9	39.9	0.8	31.4	49.3	0.6	28.2	51.8	0.5
1975	31.1	40.7	0.8	30.6	48.8	0.6	27.1	50.2	0.5
1978	30.3	40.9	0.7	29.2	49.2	0.6	25.8	50.5	0.5
1980	30.3	40.7	0.7	29.0	48.2	0.6	26.6	48.9	0.5
1981	30.5	40.7	0.7	28.9	48.1	0.6	26.3	49.3	0.5
1982	30.0	41.4	0.7	28.7	48.6	0.6	26.2	50.0	0.5
1983	29.3	41.8	0.7	28.4	50.2	0.6	25.6	51.1	0.5
1984	29.2	41.8	0.7	28.1	51.5	0.5	23.2	55.6	0.4
1985	27.4	42.2	0.6	27.7	51.5	0.5	23.0	55.9	0.4
1986	28.8	42.0	0.7	27.8	51.6	0.5	24.1	54.0	0.4
1987	30.3	41.1	0.7	27.9	51.3	0.5	23.1	56.0	0.4

I am grateful to Gérard Bernier of the Université de Montréal for alerting me to this table.

SOURCES: G. Bernier, *Le Québec en chiffres de 1850 à nos jours* (Montreal: ACFAS 1986), 181; Statistics Canada, Manufacturing Industries of Canada (31–201); Statistics Canada, *Manufacturing Industries of Canada, National and Provincial Areas*, Catalogue 31–203; Statistics Canada, *Manufacturing Industries of Canada, Subprovincial Areas*, Catalogue 31–209, Annual

calculated that homeowners would pay $2.5 billion more a year in mortgage payments.

The higher rates would also cost consumers $1.7 billion more a year in charges on their other debts, businesses $4 billion more, and governments $3.3 billion extra. Those costs would rise if the period of uncertainty was extended and more long-term debt, which would have to be rolled over at the higher

TABLE 8
Ontario's manufacturing shipments, 1974 and 1989

	Value of shipments	Share distribution of Ontario's shipments			
	1989 *(e)*	Quebec %	Ontario %	Other provinces %	Int'l exports %
All manufacturing	$166.3 B	5.87	46.63	13.22	34.28
Food & beverage	18.1	9.41	64.75	20.37	5.47
Clothing	2.0	13.32	53.16	31.02	2.50
Paper & allied	7.7	10.53	42.29	12.54	34.64
Trans. equip.	44.0	1.79	12.89	2.56	82.76
	1974				
All manufacturing	$40.6 B	11.45	51.31	16.51	20.73
Food and beverage	5.9	10.42	69.21	15.28	5.09
Clothing	0.4	14.53	50.77	33.5	1.20
Paper & allied	2.4	11.94	53.86	6.52	27.68
Trans. equip.	7.8	6.37	25.25	9.67	59.71

(e) = estimate
SOURCE: Statistics Canada (31-522/30)

TABLE 9
Quebec's manufacturing shipments, 1974 and 1989

	Value of shipments	Share distribution of Quebec shipments			
	1989 *(e)*	Quebec %	Ontario %	Other provinces %	Int'l exports %
All manufacturing	$80.7 B	49.22	14.51	10.33	25.94
Food & beverage	10.8	74.04	10.31	7.41	8.24
Clothing	4.3	57.26	23.89	15.61	3.24
Paper & allied	8.1	24.69	16.78	2.55	55.98
Trans equip.	7.5	20.77	8.82	4.85	65.56
	1974				
All manufacturing	$22.6 B	49.11	19.17	18.13	13.59
Food & beverage	3.9	70.96	12.29	12.2	4.55
Clothing	1.4	41.05	22.75	32.51	3.69
Paper & allied	2.4	39.32	18.67	6.62	35.39
Trans. equip.	1.4	19.84	11.33	23.45	45.38

(e) = estimate

SOURCE: Statistics Canada (31-522/30)

Figure 2
Personal income per capita, Quebec and Ontario, 1979–89

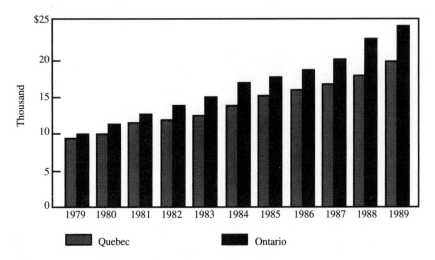

SOURCE: Canada, Department of Finance, *Quarterly Economic Report* (June 1991)

interest rates, was affected. And there would be other costs, it added. 'Slower economic growth, higher interest rates and deferred business investment would slow job creation and contribute to higher unemployment.' If separation resulted in 1 per cent of the workforce's becoming unemployed it would mean the loss of 137,000 more jobs, reduce employment income by $3.8 billion, and cut tax revenues by $1.2 billion. The cost in extra unemployment insurance payments would be almost $2 billion a year. Investor fears could push down the value of the dollar by 3 per cent. The devaluation would boost inflation by about 1 per cent, the council said.[4]

Of course, if Quebec attained sovereignty, many of its commercial ties to the rest of Canada would remain. There would still be trade, investment, the movement of goods and services, tourism, transportation links, and so on. But these activities would be on a lesser scale in the short run.

As matters now stand, the province can benefit from reasonably secure access to this market, even though it is hindered by an arcane array of provincial trade barriers. Further, as David Laidler has observed, Quebec also benefits from the 'concentration of the Canadian financial system – along with the existence of widespread branching of financial institutions across the country – [which] does much to promote capital mobility within Canada and gives the system considerable stability.'⁵ In short, access to goods and services to the rest of Canada might well be hindered in the transition period, usually thought likely to be seven to ten years, following sovereignty.

Should Quebec attain sovereignty, Ottawa's transfer payments to the new nation would cease. At present, transfer payments account for about one dollar of every three that come from Ottawa to Quebec. They help pay for health care, post-secondary education, welfare provisions, and other services. However, transfer payments have been frozen, and Quebec is essentially bound to provide the federal government with the same per centage of tax revenues while receiving less in return. Not that this is anything new: the Conseil du patronat has noted that, although Quebec once received an average of $2.3 billion more from the federal government in annual revenues than it paid in, that figure has declined over the past three years due to Quebec's increased economic power.⁶ Further, Parti Québécois leader Jacques Parizeau has observed that Ottawa's budgetary problems effectively 'prevent it from proposing financial "sweeteners" that might harmonize its relations with Quebec.'⁷ In addition, as accusations of fiscal mismanagement grow in Ottawa, Quebecers are more likely to believe they can better administer their own budget.

Pierre Fortin of the Université du Québec à Montréal insists that Canadian federalism is such an economic mess that Quebec would have little to lose as a sovereign nation. He cites examples of Canadian problems such as its large national debt, high interest rates, wasteful duplication of government services, and the failure of federal policies on training and industrial research to make his case.⁸ Fortin stresses that problems arising from investor uncertainty, the division of Canada's national debt, and negotiation of a new economic link with Canada would be 'manageable.' The adjustment costs would be minimized, Fortin says, by Quebec's continued use of the Canadian dollar, by an economic common market with Canada, and by its continued access to the U.S. market through an extension of the Canada–U.S. Free Trade Agreement to include Quebec.

This might be, but the economic costs to Quebec could still be substantial. For example, according to one study by Infometrica, a sovereign Quebec would lose more than $1 billion a year in unemployment insurance funding now provided by the rest of Canada.⁹ This could lead to tax increases averaging $700 for a Quebec family of four. According to Infometrica, the only way to escape such a jump in taxes would be for a sovereign Quebec to make unemployment insurance payments smaller or harder to get, unless the new sovereign state could find a cure for its high unemployment. As noted, a central argument in support of sovereignty for Quebec is that the Quebec economy is stronger and more dynamic than in the past. It is less dependent on Canadian markets as its foreign trade has grown. But the federal system hinders this growth and drains Quebec's resources. Ottawa has been unable to reduce its deficit and consequently lower its interest payments. Its monetary policy has been problematic. Its development policies have failed, as competitive federalism has resulted in duplication, federal-provincial friction, incorrect policy, and waste.[10]

But what of the transfer costs associated with sovereignty? There will be the substantial costs of negotiating transfers of assets, debts, public employees, programs, and resource sources. There might be a labour exodus and increased investor concern. Finally, there is little tangible evidence that a sovereign Quebec's economic policies would be any more efficient than are Canada's. In fact, in no area does the federal and Quebec government deliver exactly the same services. Furthermore, centralized national programs can keep regions from undercutting each other to attract investors through lower taxes, resulting in fewer social services.[11]

Stéphane Dion credibly argues that most Quebecers are less interested in a massive transfer of powers than they want 'symbolic atonement' for the failure of the Meech Lake Accord. Greater power sharing would be a Canadian demonstration of good will to Quebec. It would be a recognition of Quebec's distinct society status.[12]

Many sovereigntists also insist that the English-speaking people, and their capital and resources, who fled the province in the late 1970s have been replaced by francophone entrepreneurs. With more francophone control of management positions, a new anglophone flight will not be disastrous, or so sovereigntists argue. On the other hand, Reuven Brenner of the Université de Montréal notes that all Quebecers in a sovereign Quebec would have to pay more for social problems and the inherited debt because of the impact of the outmigration of many of the most talented and prosperous Quebecers.[13] These people would leave, he asserts, for countries with what he regards as having better records of protecting individual rights and with less danger of unpredictable political and economic problems.

In fact, in the early 1980s, tens of thousands of young Quebecers left to seek jobs elsewhere. As noted, over 200,000 anglophones have left since 1976 for reasons including political and economic uncertainty.[14]

The report by the Task Force on Job Opportunities for English-speaking Youth found that most young anglophones express a sense of malaise and frustration about the language situation. 'They believe that their language rights are violated by the imposition of French, especially in connection with commercial signs, language of work, and public services ... The task force repeatedly heard that having an English name excluded a candidate from being hired by some firms.'

Those impressions may be overstated, but the malaise is real. It translates into expectations among young anglophones that there is no future for them in Quebec. This is not new. Between 1971 and 1986, the per centage of anglophone Quebecers under 15 declined from 26 to 18. That was much greater than the decline in the French population under 15, as the aging English community as a whole shrank in real numbers and in proportion to the total population.

Jacques Parizeau asserts that this is regrettable, but that economic instability is not a serious threat in a sovereign Quebec. He insists that a sovereign Quebec would want to negotiate a common monetary policy with Canada so as to avoid financial uncertainty. It would also be willing to pay its share of the Canadian national debt, provide solid protections for English institutions in the new country, honour international agreements such as free trade with the United States, and allow easy mobility across the Quebec-Canada border. In fact, a customs union would be a likely scenario for Quebec and Canada. However, retaining a customs union is not a sure thing. Tariffs and other protectionist measures benefit certain industrial sectors at the expense of all Canadian consumers and taxpayers. As we have noted, some of those sectors, like dairy products and textiles, are concentrated in Quebec, and the rest of Canada would probably not accept continuing to subsidize producers concentrated there.

Nevertheless, Parizeau states that a sovereign Quebec would maintain a customs union with Canada in the form of uniform tariffs and rules of entry. This would facilitate the transshipment of overseas goods with a minimum of paperwork and expense. According to Parizeau, the level of tariff protection in all of Canada is low, and many old, barely competitive industries have moved from Quebec to Ontario, so Quebec does not have a problem of obsolete, high-cost industries. This argument is debatable, since one does not have to look far to discover outmoded industries in Quebec, much of the furniture and textile industries being prime examples.

If sovereignty or sovereignty-association is the course that Quebec ultimately chooses, the province will be administering its own social programs, collecting its own taxes, and maintaining only monetary ties with the rest of Canada. Any overlapping of federal and provincial services would be eliminated. If the Conseil du patronat is correct in reporting that Quebec receives $1 billion more from the federal government than it takes in as of 1988, or $157 per Quebec resident, then the province's 1991 deficit of nearly $4 billion would increase markedly – or substantial budget cuts in social services or business assistance, affecting millions of Quebecers, would have to be made. Businesses such as Lavalin (now bankrupt and operating as SNC-Lavalin) and Bombardier, no longer able to rely on federal help, would be pulling at the provincial purse strings as well. Other financial drains could result from the unemployment of thousands of Quebecers who currently work for the federal government, from Quebec's payments to Ottawa for federal properties within the province and from the possible relocation of key businesses.

Traditionally, Quebec has been overrepresented in federal cabinets and in the senior federal bureaucracy. With sovereignty, these people would have to make the extremely painful choice of first allegiance. As noted, thousands of Quebec residents who work for the federal government in the Ottawa-Hull area would have to move out of Quebec or lose their jobs, since residency in Canada is a condition of employment in federal public service.

In one poll, only three of ten Canadians said that Quebec residents should be permitted to keep their jobs with the federal government if the province gained independence. Furthermore, whereas 62 per cent of Quebecers believed that federal civil servants resident in Quebec could keep their jobs, only 19 per cent of Canadians in the other nine provinces agreed. Former prime minister Mulroney asserted that the 50,000 Quebecers employed in the Canadian public service would lose their jobs if sovereignty was achieved.[15]

In addition, an independent Quebec would have to pay out high expenditures to create foreign diplomatic missions. Quebec would have to expand its offices abroad, upgrade them to embassy or consular status, and pay the substantial costs of training new foreign service officers.

One other consequence of Quebec's sovereignty might be the end of official bilingualism in Canada's federal institutions. Without Quebec, francophones in Canada will number about one million which would not be enough to sustain support for the costly duplication of services that national bilingualism requires. Instead, Canada might adopt a policy of offering bilingual services only where numbers warrant. The office of the Commissioner of Official Languages, the government watchdog on linguistic issues, might be abolished. Assimilation of francophones outside of Quebec into the predominately English-speaking environment would accelerate. French immersion classes would diminish in number. French documentation and labeling would no longer be obligatory for foreign suppliers of goods to Canada, thereby eliminating a non-tariff barrier to trade. According to the PQ, an independent Quebec would no longer be required to run a bilingual legislature or judiciary. It would not have to provide an English education to immigrants who had been educated in English elsewhere in Canada, and it would not retain a federal broadcasting regulator. Quebec would have all of the powers it needed to promote the growth of its culture and language. Presumably, the anti-French feeling existent in parts of the rest of Canada would disappear along with official bilingualism or would become of trivial importance and minority language rights would be protected only where numbers warrant. The result would be a more homogenous English-speaking Canada and a more homogeneous French-speaking Quebec.

This does not mean that the PQ believes that a wholly francophone Quebec is a good thing. The Parti Québécois government of René Lévesque in the late 1970s to early 1980s had been extremely generous in supporting minority parochial schools. More recently, Jacques Parizeau was quoted as stating that he would 'boot the rear end of anyone who can't speak English.'[16] However, the society would function in French. In fact, according to Jean Allaire of the sovereigntist Action démocratique party, immigrants wanting to settle in Quebec should have to sign a social contract committing themselves to becoming part of the francophone majority.

In a sovereign Quebec, Revenue Québec would replace Revenue Canada as the government tax collector. One would file only one tax return for Quebec and pay the present federal plus Quebec tax rate. Old age pensions would come only from Quebec, as would family and children's payments.[17] The average pensioner would receive approximately the same amount that he or she gets from both governments. Quebec insists that whether sovereign or not, it can use its tax base more efficiently than if it must rely on federal transfers. Also, by not having to make these payments to Quebec, Canada would save $4 billion in annual subsidies.

This being said, the transition period following sovereignty could be difficult for both Quebec and Canada. There might be economic uncertainty arising from what could be difficult negotiations of territorial questions, contracts, treaties, and the division of the federal debt. Pierre-Paul Proulx of the Université de Montréal has estimated that the negative transition costs of secession could total 5 to 10 per cent of the GDP in Quebec and Ontario.[18]

Furthermore, between 1965 and 1990, average annual growth in Quebec was 3.5 per cent versus 4.1 per cent in the rest of Canada. Per capita gross domestic product in a sovereign Quebec would be U.S.$12,300 versus U.S.$14,000 in the rest of the country, according to various estimates. In fact, most Quebecers and most Canadians agree that after sovereignty, the standard of living in Quebec would probably diminish or, at the very best, stay the same. In one national poll, 50 per cent of the respondents in Quebec felt that the standard of living in Quebec would diminish if Quebec separated. Fully 75 per cent of the respondents in the rest of Canada thought that Quebec's quality of life would diminish with sovereignty.[19] However, another poll indicated that 48 per cent of Quebecers believe that their income would not change if the province separated. But 71 per cent of respondents in the rest of Canada thought sovereignty would not affect their income.[20]

One observer, Carl Sonnen of Infometrica, estimates that the separation of Quebec would cause a 4 to 8 per cent drop in the standard of living of Quebecers and a 2 to 6 per cent drop for Canada as a whole.[21] A Quebec National Assembly report in September 1992 predicted a decline of between 1.5 to 4 per cent in Quebec's gross domestic product in the short term.

A controversial report issued in September 1992 by the Royal Bank of Canada forecast a post-sovereign Quebec unemployment rate of 15 per cent, increased out-migration, devalued pensions and savings, and an economic cost to each Canadian of $4000. This report predicted various dire consequences and its timing, revised just one month prior to the Charlottetown Agreement referendum, may well have been an act of manipulation, no matter the accuracy of its predictions. Nevertheless, the Royal Bank report concluded that all Canada would suffer from a breakup, recessions would be deeper, interest rates would be higher, a joint currency would be difficult or impossible, and per capita income in Quebec and Canada would be reduced at least until the millennium.[22] Nevertheless, François Vaillancourt of the Université de Montréal has argued that francophones will sacrifice some per centage of their real income to remain French.[23] They are willing to give up some portion of their economic strength to ensure the continued cultural vitality of their distinctive French language and culture. Vaillancourt suggests that the cut could be as much as 20 per cent in their standard of living, or about $4000 to $16,800. This would be similar to that of Canada's poorest province, Newfoundland. Whether this means that most francophone Quebecers would choose a culturally protected but economically uncertain future in a sovereign Quebec over the problematic federal structure is not clear.

Supporters of Quebec sovereignty insist that the economic costs of Quebec independence would be minimal. However, no one can foresee all the effects that political instability may have on economic activity in the province, nor can one predict the kinds of economic arrangements that may be worked out. Also, there is no guarantee that Quebec-Canada economic relations will be entirely civil, at least in the short run. It should be stressed that Quebec's place within the Canadian federation has been a relatively successful one. Quebec has been democratic, stable, and prosperous. It has retained its French language and character and expanded its economic opportunities within the Canadian federation. Quebec's sovereignty or sovereignty-association might adversely affect all of these gains.

There are other economic advantages to federalism as well. Quebec already has sovereignty in certain areas of jurisdiction, such as education, health care, tourism. It benefits from the federal government's role as arbiter of regional interests. Federalism offers unemployment insurance benefits for the eastern half of the country and agricultural subsidies for the west. In fact, Quebec farmers received a disproportionate amount of agricultural production quotas. In the absence of the federal role, it is not clear how Quebec would manage its economic relations with its neighbours. Without an arbiter, Quebec would have to deal one-on-one or collectively with the provinces and the bargaining would be much tougher. Also, as part of a diversified economy, Quebec could be isolated from economic shocks, particularly energy-cost hikes.

There are many economic advantages for Quebec in the federation. At present, Quebec can take advantage of national laws governing import regulation, competition policy, banking, intellectual property, and consumer product safety. All this would be lost with sovereignty. Quebec plays a vital role in the economic union and can take advantage of greater national market integration, mutual cost-sharing, risk-pooling across provinces, and increased bargaining power internationally. A sovereign Quebec would be vulnerable to all sorts of unpredictable economic shocks if economic cooperation with Canada was substantially reduced.

It is worth noting that Pierre-Marc Johnson, a former Parti Québécois premier, has admitted that he is no longer convinced that Quebec independence could be justified. He stated that there are several reasons for a nation to become independent. The first is that it is oppressed, but Quebec has not been oppressed for some time. The second reason is a desire for cultural affirmation through specific political proposals, but for Quebec this desire can be accommodated within the existing federation. A third reason is the overlapping of certain constitutional jurisdictions, but fewer of these overlaps exist now because governments have tended to withdraw from more programs. Johnson stresses that political and economic stability are necessary conditions to ensure foreign investor confidence.[24]

A sovereign Quebec would have fewer than seven million people, and yet would be forced to compete with a Canada triple its size. Would post-sovereignty negotiations with Canada really give more bargaining power to Quebec? Furthermore, what is the incentive for the rest of Canada to accept Quebec as a legitimate bargaining partner? Canada would be politically fragmented and resentful and unlikely to negotiate important matters with a sovereign Quebec in the short run. Economist Thomas Courchene of Queen's University notes that federalism probably gives Quebec more flexibility than sovereignty-association would. Within federalism, Quebec can use its political power to win economic benefits. Outside, everything would be defined by detailed commercial rules, as in the European common market. As the smaller partner, Quebec would be at a disadvantage, Courchene asserts.[25]

HOW WOULD QUEBEC'S SOVEREIGNTY BE REGARDED BY THE REST OF CANADA?

There have been a number of studies and surveys investigating how the rest of Canada might respond to Quebec's sovereignty, should it occur. Many show that Canadians would be angry and hurt and unlikely to regard a sovereign Quebec favourably, at least at first.

A study commissioned by the Business Council on National Issues speculated that Quebec's independence could produce a negative emotional backlash in the rest of Canada that could undermine future economic relations between the two.[26] This view was reinforced by a submission of the Association of Quebec Economists to the Bélanger-Campeau Commission. This study concluded that, in the short term, the transition period to Quebec independence would be difficult and unfriendly. The brief outlined Canadians' anger regarding Quebec's move and the economic decline and political instability that would surely occur. The economists asserted that it is 'easy to imagine the hostile demands on Quebec – financial, fiscal, political, and territorial – by the rest of Canada.'[27] The authors concluded that the economic advantages of independence over federalism 'tend toward zero,' but they understand that sovereignty is less an economic than a political and social proposition. However, in their view Quebec should not declare independence unilaterally without understanding the consequences of such an action.

As the failure of the Charlottetown Agreement demonstrated, many bitter Canadians in the rest of Canada express indifference to Quebec's constitutional demands. They complain that Quebec has always been favoured by Ottawa and that it is time for a change. They are not sympathetic to Quebec's demand that it be officially recognized as a distinct society[28] and would go so far as to suggest that if Quebec wants to secede, then they can live with that choice.[29] In fact, one essay concluded that it would be in the interests of both Quebec and the rest of Canada if Quebec were to become sovereign.[30] Subsequent polls reinforced this 'let Quebec go' attitude,[31] although at least one study noted that an attempt by Quebec political leaders to secede unilaterally might result in criminal charges, including sedition and treason.[32] It is hard to know how seriously to take this possibility. But it is certainly possible that, without the federal arbiter, Quebec, Ontario and the western provinces might compete for scarce resources amid much hostility.

Not only does the rest of Canada appear to be willing to let Quebec go, but a number of surveys have revealed that Canadians would oppose an economic association with Quebec as well as any relationship that would give Quebec a more favourable status than that given to the other Canadian provinces.[33] Former Alberta premier Don Getty had been particularly explicit in stating that his province would reject any attempt by a sovereign Quebec to form an economic association with the rest of Canada. In fact, one poll revealed that almost 90 per cent of Canadian business leaders oppose sovereignty for Quebec. However, 80 per cent of the sample would maintain their business ties with the province if it chose to be independent.[34]

The sovereigntist Parti Québécois insists that Canada will negotiate with Quebec because Ottawa has four major concerns:

- Quebec's share of the national debt,
- transportation lines between Ontario and the Maritimes,
- economic markets in Quebec for Canadian products, and
- social harmony.

The PQ insists that Canada will negotiate to preserve economic ties. If it does not, however, it insists that Quebec's separation would be a relatively easy event. Indeed an October 1991 study by the Economic Council of Canada speculated that, if relations between both sides were to remain harmonious, then the costs of the transition to sovereignty would be limited. Indeed, the study reported that sovereignty-association would cost the average Quebec family about $1800 a year for a generation.

This is a big 'if,' however, for the transition may be anything but easy. For example, even if the rest of Canada agreed to a new association with Quebec, it would likely balk at demands for the continuation of high duties on textiles and footwear to protect Quebec jobs or a monetary union in which the Bank of Canada took orders from two governments.

Other studies maintained that any attempt by Quebec to leave the federation would lead to complete and lengthy negotiations over critical economic issues, such as how much of the national debt Quebec would be responsible for (the Parti Québécois suggests 25 per cent) and what share of national assets it would receive. How would federal government properties, such as buildings, ports, and air terminals in Quebec, be divided? Many are on the accounting books as being worth one dollar. There would be a prolonged period of uncertainty. The stability of the dollar or of interest rates would also come into question.

One of the most prominent studies looking at this issue was authored by

Patrick Grady of the conservative Fraser Institute. Grady concludes that a bitter breakup would be expensive for Quebec.[35] In fact, Grady predicts that Quebec's economic output would fall by as much as 10 per cent after sovereignty. In addition, Quebec's recession would be as devastating as the 1930s Depression, and industries relying on trade protection and federal subsidies, such as textiles and dairy products, would be particularly hard hit. Emigration from Quebec would accelerate and immigration would diminish. Transfer payments from Ottawa would cease. There would be high pension and health costs, high taxes, diminished public services, and reduced foreign investment. Grady also insists that there would be a flight of capital, higher interest rates, an enormous debt, the loss of markets for Quebec industries, and possibly even a collapse of Quebec stock prices and property values. The rest of Canada could suffer a serious recession and a drop in stock market prices. It might lose international influence and be forced to rewrite treaties, laws, and regulations.[36]

Grady and others have noted that, on issues such as currency, monetary policy, and trade, an economically associated but politically sovereign Quebec would probably want a veto. This would be a recipe for political intransigence. Canada would be paralysed in dealing with the world because of Quebec's veto power. Why would the much larger Canada want to surrender its freedom of action to a poorer, smaller country? Why would Canada want to be constrained by sovereignty-association?

Canadians might well reject sovereignty-association with Quebec. On the other hand, they might welcome a free trade agreement with the nation, particularly if there is a national perception that Canada will be worse off without such a tie. Two polls indicate that Canadians would negotiate, particularly if there would be negative consequences if they did not.[37]

One thing is almost certain. If Quebec becomes sovereign, Ontario will dominate what remains of Canada to an even greater degree than it does now. Almost 50 per cent of Canadians would live in Ontario and they would dominate parliament's representation. Ontario would be a haven for a massive concentration of the nation's wealth. This dominance would aggravate western Canadian tensions and alienation. One likely remedy would be to create a regionally or provincially balanced elected Senate. But this could bring about its own share of problems as well.[38] In short, it would be difficult to reconstruct the federal structure to give the perpheral provinces effective representation in Ottawa.[39]

Provincial anger and fear concerning Quebec's demand for greater powers and its possible secession have been marked. Before he lost his bid for reelection, Ontario premier David Peterson threatened to sue both Quebec and the federal government if they came to an agreement on Quebec's status without consulting the provinces. Also, the provinces might express their resentment towards a sovereign Quebec by looking for new supplier markets, especially in Ontario and the United States. This would obviously be detrimental to an independent Quebec's economy, which would already face an extremely high budget deficit. Deprived of billions of dollars in federal equalization payments, a sovereign Quebec would have to choose between tax increases or cuts in services. In one study, economist André Raynauld revealed that between 1981 and 1988, Ottawa gave $27 billion more to Quebec than it collected in taxes.[40]

Quebec's independence would have less of an economic impact in western Canada. These resource-rich economies are increasingly dependent on the California market for natural gas or on world wheat prices. They are less dependent than in the past on southern Ontario's manufacturing capability. In fact, a post-secession Canada would foster a more powerful West. The conservatism and market-driven perspective found in Alberta, the class-based politics of British Columbia, the western distrust of Ottawa, and the predilection for small parties would all become more dominant features of Canada.

Constitutional changes, should they occur, would better reflect western interests, at least in a broad sense. The House of Commons and Senate could expect substantial reforms. The NDP would grow stronger on the national level, since its support base has always been in Ontario and the West. New parties might also emerge.

Of course, the West is not monolithic by any means. Each province has its agenda for change. British Columbia and Alberta, the two wealthier provinces, want more opportunity to promote their social and economic priorities with little interference from the federal government. Saskatchewan and Manitoba are more sympathetic to federal interests and are reluctant to support more constitutional decentralization. There is no one western position, and the differences between the provinces are growing.

It is possible that the trauma of Quebec leaving might enhance the sense of Canadian identity in the rest of the country. The challenge of creating a new Canada without Quebec might provoke a feeling of shared crisis and enhance Canadian solidarity and promote differences from the United States. The Spicer Commission report certainly demonstrated a substantial depth of nationalism in English Canada, but there would be serious problems for the rest of Canada after sovereignty.

The Atlantic provinces would not be contiguous to the rest of Canada, but the implementation of sophisticated communications and transportation systems and an aggravation-free crossing at the Quebec border might reduce their sense of isolation. But this assumes the best possible circumstances following sovereignty. In the transition period following sovereignty, there might be a diminution of transportation services between Quebec and Atlantic Canada. A sovereign Quebec would own the rail, highway, and part of the St Lawrence rights of way and could impose user or transit fees on goods flowing to the rest of Canada from the Atlantic region.[41] The federal government would be counted on to fill the financial void. Of course, if Quebec were to attain sovereignty, Atlantic Canada would be perceived both inside and outside Canada as remote and an economic 'basket case.'

If federal transfer payments to Atlantic Canada were slashed, the results would be chilling. The region's standard of living would plunge. In Newfoundland particularly, Quebec sovereignty could have dismal implications. Newfoundland is dependent on Quebec as a market for its Canadian-based hydroelectric power. Its iron exports to the world pass through Quebec. Canada's poorest province might find a new emigration of its young professional class to Ontario, British Columbia, and the United States in search of work.

Atlantic Canada is heavily dependent on what little is left of the fishing industry. Post-sovereignty there might be tough bargaining between Atlantic Canada and Quebec over the monitoring and enforcement of stock management practices within the 200-mile fishing limit. National standards for the fishing industry would face pressure from aggressive provincial bureaucrats pursuing their province's perceived best interests. It could be more difficult to impose strict environmental controls in the St Lawrence River and elsewhere.[42] Quebec would also find it expensive to administer its own fisheries and oceans policy. It would also have to create a coast guard. But its problems would pale in comparison to Atlantic Canada which is so much more dependent on one industry. So Atlantic Canada might suffer if Quebec went it alone. There might be a decline in living standards in the short run and a migration of many of their most skilled workers. The province of Ontario might try to revise equalization payments and regional development programs. The entire federal transfer system could be at risk.[43] If this support diminished, then a long-run option for Atlantic Canada might be a political union with their long-time trading partners in New England. This is mere speculation of course. In fact, most Atlantic Canadians oppose an Atlantic economic union.

No matter how the rest of Canada responds, of course, Quebec will set its own course. The sovereignty decision, if it comes to that, will be its own. Nevertheless, how the rest of Canada responds does matter after sovereignty is attained. A close look at the poll results reveals that, although at first glance many Canadians would just write Quebec off, they would not do so if it would hurt them economically. Furthermore, Canadian élites are concerned about Quebec's future, even if the general public resents Quebec's demands for new rights without giving anything to Canada in return. Polls also indicate that the views of Canadians are contradictory and fragmented. There does seem to be a general agreement, however, that any future constitutional deal must accommodate the concerns of all Canadians and not just Quebecers. All provinces demand to be treated equally, and special status for Quebec will be unacceptable. Also, any constitutional agreement must protect the supremacy of the Charter of Rights and minority language guarantees. Otherwise, there will probably be no agreement.

It is certain that Canada has a great deal to lose if Quebec were to go it alone. If Quebec leaves the Canadian federation, then about one-third of the national population with its attendant productivity would also depart. The cost in terms of economies of scale in government would be enormous. Canada would lose the province that is in the forefront of creating successful social programs. It would also lose some of its most successful entrepreneurs. Canada might lose its unified currency, where all the resources of the nation back up the international credit standing of all governments and corporations. Canada would lose a fiscal structure that automatically helps regions facing adversity. It would lose tax and regulatory harmonization that lowers the costs to all Canadians and helps to maintain competitiveness. It might be faced with ten different health care regulatory environments or ten different social policies and labour protection laws. Canada might also forfeit the free movement of capital, people, services, and most goods. Some critics fear that the whole country's economy would be threatened, as jobs are lost and the regions paralysed by huge debts.[44] Taxes in Canada and Quebec might go up and many civil servants would be looking for work. Polls of Canadian economists tend to reveal widespread pessimism about Canada's economy should Quebec leave.[45] They predict weak financial market performance, higher unemployment, and higher interest rates. Atlantic Canada and Ontario would be particularly hard hit. The economies of British Columbia and Alberta might improve slightly if the oil and gas sectors prosper, as expected. This is because Canada now limits export permits for natural gas to ensure future national energy needs. If Quebec leaves, Ottawa might increase export levels.

Economists Richard Harris of Simon Fraser University and the late Douglas Purvis of Queen's University have argued that, without a strong national government, there would be nothing to rein in the provincial special interest groups that already make it difficult to buy wine from one province in another province's liquor stores and that restrict the rights of some workers to work in other provinces.[46] As interprovincial trade barriers multiply, Canada's national unity would be further diminished. As provinces become the main focus of political power, it is likely that interprovincial squabbling over trade would lead to a reluctance by rich provinces to subsidize social programs in poorer ones and, eventually, to restrictions on free movement among provinces.

For example, the Canada Health Act calls on all provinces to provide fully portable health care with no up-front charges. Quebec does not honour an agreement to cover the cost of non-hospital medical care in other provinces. Thus, a Quebecer seeking urgent care in another part of Canada is usually required to pay the physician first and obtain partial reimbursement later from the Quebec government. If Quebec becomes sovereign, it is likely that medical facilities in the rest of Canada would no longer offer free care to Quebecers. Even a partial reimbursement might not be possible. Quebec officials respond by saying that Quebecers would purchase supplemental medical insurance when traveling in Canada. However, at present, this insurance will not cover an initial three-month waiting period, and it is unavailable to people with a serious pre-existing illness. It is not clear that patients could be transferred from Quebec to Canada or vice-versa for more effective treatment. The federal government and the government of Quebec have both called for a free flow of goods and services, but it is not clear how likely this would be if health care throughout Canada and Quebec is difficult to get – particularly if relations between the two are acrimonious after sovereignty is attained.

In addition, should Quebec leave, Canada's influence in the World Trade Agreement (WTA), the North American Free Trade Agreement (NAFTA), the United Nations, and other international organizations might diminish. A truncated Canada would have less influence on the world stage. It is not clear if it would be allowed to remain in the Group of Seven. It might be displaced by Spain. Since its GNP would diminish, Canada would have a reduced vote in the World Bank, the International Monetary Fund, and other international economic organizations.

Atlantic Canada would be cut off geographically and would likely suffer decreased equalization payments. Canada would lose the significant trade diversification brought by Quebec in industries such as aerospace, newsprint, mass transit, electricity, and electronics. The economic turmoil associated with redistributing Ottawa's assets and reorganizing federal bureaucracies would be substantial and would affect Canada's international competitiveness and trade efforts. As was earlier noted, Professor Pierre-Paul Proulx of the Université de Montréal has estimated that the negative transition costs of secession could total 5 to 10 per cent of the gross domestic product in Quebec and Ontario.[47] We should be wary of assigning specific numbers to the costs of sovereignty, however. Predictions of economic collapse are based on assumptions about the unknowable: how assets and liabilities would be split, how angry the rest of Canada would be, and what policies would develop after the split. All we can usefully say, then, is that the economic costs of breaking up could be substantial.

The military implications of sovereignty have played a minor role behind economic, political, and cultural concerns, but they are not trivial. How Canada and Quebec would resolve defence-related interests is not yet completely clear. A divided Canada might have trouble promoting coherent policies. Canadian military officers might resent serving with their Quebec counterparts in the short run. From a U.S. perspective, a fractionalized Canada might be reluctant to take a strong stand in support of its allies over concerns such as sending troops overseas or permitting U.S. military flights over Canadian air space. In addition, the smaller members of NATO contribute disproportionately less funding and other support than the larger members. International security is less important to them. American military analysts who already complain that Canada does not spend a high enough percentage of its gross national product on defence might have even more to complain about.

One-half of Canada's aerospace industry is situated in the Montreal area. The PQ pledges that, if it formed the government of a sovereign Quebec, its military would be non-nuclear, a member of NATO and NORAD, and a participant in UN peacekeeping operations. A Quebec army already has an infrastructure, given the fairly strong presence of the Canadian army in Quebec. The air force is already well established in Quebec. However, a Quebec navy would be weak. The PQ is committed to strengthening its coast guard. This assumes an amicable divorce. The division of military assets between Canada and Quebec could be acrimonious. How many planes or ships would go to Quebec or Canada? Would all military personnel based in Quebec become Quebec soldiers, or would some choose Canada? Also, it is not clear that the United States would support a three-nation membership in NORAD. Quebec might not be permitted to handle air defence, or it could decide of its own violation that Canada would handle this function on Quebec's behalf. In any case, the United States, Canada, and Quebec would have to negotiate joint air defence arrangements and ship passage provisions.

Figures compiled by the Department of National Defence indicate that the armed forces spend $2 billion a year in Quebec. If Canadian soldiers left Quebec, the effect would be equivalent to losing Hydro-Québec, the second largest industrial corporation in Quebec behind Bell Canada. In 1988–9, the 12,000 soldiers and 5000 civilians on the armed forces payroll in Quebec received $701 million in salaries, while defence-related expenditures added another $1.3 billion to Quebec's economy. Military contracts in Quebec include the overhauling of CF-18 jet fighters and the development of a high-tech anti-aircraft weapons system by Oerlikon Aerospace, Inc., in Saint-Jean, Quebec. Other prominent Quebec-based defence contractors include Canadian Marconi and Canadair. Overall, Quebec is the second largest beneficiary of armed forces spending in Canada. It might have a lot to lose after sovereignty.[48] In fact, according to one estimate, the creation of a Quebec army could cost $6 billion to $10 billion plus an annual cost of at least $6 billion.[49]

The extent to which Quebec remains prosperous, should it attain sovereignty, will depend, in part, on whether negotiations with the rest of Canada can proceed in an atmosphere of acrimony or harmony.

6

Investment in Quebec after the Failure of the Meech Lake and Charlottetown Accords

The failure of the Meech Lake and Charlottetown accords has had little discernable long-term impact on U.S. investment in Canada and Quebec thus far, although there have been short-term costs for Quebec. When it first appeared that the Meech Lake Accord would fail, there was speculation that investment in Quebec and the rest of Canada would diminish rapidly and that the Canadian dollar would take a beating in world financial markets. In fact, in May 1990 a record $2.2 billion worth of Canadian bonds was dumped by foreign investors. In December 1990 investors bought only $115 million in government bonds, well below the 1990 monthly average of $1.1 billion.

Quebec and its electric utility Hydro-Québec are major players on Wall Street. They have more than U.S. $10 billion outstanding in U.S. debt (although they have begun to reduce this figure), and investment bankers compete intensely to underwrite that debt. Executives at major firms such as First Boston Corporation, Merrill Lynch and Company, Goldman Sachs and Company, and Salomon Brothers have nurtured strong ties with Quebec's major political parties. These investment bankers have calculated the risk premium that Quebec must pay on its bonds to compensate investors for the uncertainty.

After the Meech and Charlottetown failures, their attitude was one of concern, but, for the most part, it is still business as usual. This is a far cry from the hysteria that followed former premier René Lévesque's New York visit in 1977. At that time, Wall Street was so alarmed by Lévesque's predictions of separation that they bailed out of the province's securities. It was years before Quebec could sell its debt in the United States in any substantial way.

Foreign investors are a skittish lot. When they detect political uncertainty and instability in a country, they do one of two things. They either demand higher interest returns on the bonds they buy from that country, or they take their money elsewhere. As a result, interest rates go up, the Canadian dollar drops in value, efforts to reduce deficits are frustrated, capital costs rise, and growth slows down.[1] Businesses and individual borrowers would see their loan costs rise. The unemployed would have to wait longer for a weaker economic rebound. Taxpayers would have to pay lenders higher interest rates on federal and provincial debts.

Clearly, Quebec has reason to be concerned. It has a large chunk of debt held by foreigners and can ill afford to worry foreign investors. Getting accurate figures for the amount of this debt is near impossible, however, and seems to depend on to whom one talks and how the figure is calculated. The proportion of the federal government debt held by foreigners as of the third quarter of 1991 was $74 billion out of a total of $342 billion or about 21.6 per cent, according to Bank of Canada figures. In any case, if Quebec were to become sovereign, foreign investors would probably sell some of their Quebec bonds, perhaps switching their money to U.S. securities.

At stake is more than just the Quebec government's need for foreign capital to finance its debt. Uncertainty over Quebec's future has probably caused some foreign companies to reconsider plans to build factories or make other investments in the province. In February 1991, major investor First Boston released a report revealing that Quebec's challenge to Canada's constitution represented 'an element of risk for investors.' The report stated that the political uncertainty probably means that at least a 100-150 basis-point premium on Canadian over U.S. long-term bonds would prevail for political reasons, regardless of economic fundamentals. The report also predicted that the impact on investment could be greater on foreign investors unsure how to 'interpret a complex, legal, social and economic process.' Put another way, to sell its long-term bonds, Canada had to pay an interest rate that was one or one and one-half per centage points higher than the rate on American bonds.

Despite this situation, U.S. investors continue to buy Quebec securities in large number. In January 1991 Hydro-Québec raised CDN $900 million in bonds, the largest foreign government debt issue ever in the United States, at a slight premium of about 25 basis points above normal levels. This is quite surprising, given the 'credit watch' that was placed on Quebec's credit rating by the Canadian Bond Rating Service (CBRS) in March 1991, and the early concerns expressed by First Boston, Merrill Lynch, and other firms. Merrill Lynch was particularly quick to calm investors' fears later, however. It should be noted that Merrill Lynch is one of the biggest underwriters of Quebec bonds in the U.S. market, and it is the syndicate manager for loans extended to Hydro-Québec and the provincial government itself. Some have suggested that it was in Merrill Lynch's interest to calm investors' fears about Quebec sovereignty.

A 'credit watch' is not a downgrading of Quebec's rating, but it is a suspension of that rating and a warning to bond buyers of new risks that may lead to downgrading. It was the first time CBRS had ever put a province on credit watch. This was a milder action than the June 1990 move by Standard and Poor's Corporation of New York to lower Quebec's rating from AA– with 'positive' implications to AA– with 'developing' implications. According to analysts at the time, the CBRS report did not disturb markets, mainly because the news was already out, and investors had already received a risk premium for holding Quebec bonds. In November 1992, CBRS removed its credit watch on Quebec, but simultaneously downgraded its credit rating of the province. It attributed the downgrade to Quebec's high debt. The CBRS also warned that continuing political uncertainty could hinder Quebec's economic recovery.

In June 1993, Quebec suffered another financial setback when Standard and Poor's dropped the province's long-term debt outlook to 'negative' and reduced its double A ranking to single A plus. They attributed this downgrading to Quebec's high debt and the unity crisis. British Columbia, Ontario, and Alberta were judged better credit risks. The revised outlook for Quebec pointed to a 'significant probability' that the province's rating would be downgraded in one to three years. Also in June, Moody's Investor Service downgraded Quebec government bonds, citing the constitutional uncertainty and expensive provincial social programs as reasons for their action.

At present, the foreign financial community is not overtly nervous about the political uncertainty, although there is obvious concern that Quebec's economy is not sufficiently diversified. (There are similar concerns about Ontario.) Quebec's single largest export industry, hydroelectrical power, is dominated by a state monopoly, Hydro-Québec. Of course, Canada has a per capita income that is the second highest of all nations in the Organization for Economic Co-operation and Development (OECD) and an economy that grew faster than any other G-7 country except Japan during the 1980s. For that reason, many investors appear to be skeptical that Quebec could break apart such a prosperous country.

On the other hand, foreign investors are not blind to the status, no matter how difficult it is to understand. For example, in March 1991, the U.S. Securities and Exchange Commission sought more information about Quebec's political situation before clearing a prospectus prepared by Montreal's regional government, the Montreal Urban Community, to float a U.S. $135 million bond issue. Other potential investors are becoming similarly cautious.

The Canadian federal government has portrayed Quebec's constitutional challenge as a manageable situation unworthy of too much concern by foreign investors. The former Canadian ambassador to the United States, Derek Burney, had stated in reference to U.S. investors: 'I don't want to exaggerate for a minute that they're standing there trembling at the prospect that something is going on in Canada that should concern them.'[2] The ambassador also suggested that a referendum on sovereignty would not stir up controversy. 'They might react if there were a referendum, but even then they'd probably wait to see what the referendum was, what it said and what was the result.'[3]

This might be wishful thinking, however. It is not clear that foreign investment in Quebec is down significantly because of Meech Lake's failure (the recession may be a more obvious culprit), but there is evidence of foreign concern.

Quebec's business class has noticed. Economic concerns have dwarfed constitutional issues for most Quebecers. In 1993, the province had an unemployment rate of over 12 per cent. As noted, a majority of business leaders in Quebec expect Quebec's economy to suffer after sovereignty. They worry about the possibilities of higher interest rates, lower profits, substantial debt, and reduced investment. Indeed, it is difficult to be a sovereigntist in the midst of layoffs, plant closing, bankruptcies, and a jobless rate that is substantially higher than that of Ontario. The francophone business elite, many of whom had vigorously argued for sovereignty-association immediately after the Meech Lake failure, is now virtually mute. They realize that a sovereign Quebec might lose many of its economic agreements with Ontario to the other provinces. They acknowledge that national companies like Bell Canada, Canadian Pacific, and Air Canada would likely move their head offices from Montreal to Toronto. They understand that the economic upheaval of independence would force a reapportionment of the national debt. Much of Quebec's corporate élite realizes that in a time of recession, the political instability associated with independence can only aggravate an already difficult economic situation. Quebec's independence might be a noble and worthwhile goal, but for many business people it is a luxury to be pursued when economic times are good, not at a time of economic downturn.

In the months following the failure of the Meech Lake Accord, there were those who suggested that it was unclear if Canada's economic problems would promote or hinder the Quebec independence movement. They might hinder it to the extent that Quebec's priorities became focused on enhancing political stability to provide a secure environment for economic development. Alternatively, economic problems might promote the independence forces if there was a perception that Canada's economic advantages are less obvious and there is less to lose. To everyone's surprise, the members of the Quebec business class, for a time, were among the most strident sovereigntists. No experts predicted this, especially since corporate leaders were conservative supporters of the status quo after the 1976 PQ victory and the 1980 referendum.

By February 1991 the views of Quebec's business class on sovereignty were decidedly mixed. Following the release of the Allaire report, a poll of the province's largest employers' group revealed that selected business leaders favoured a renewed federation, acknowledging that sovereignty would result in five difficult economic years. However, they doubted that the rest of Canada would agree to Quebec's demand for more power in time to meet the 1992 referendum deadline. It was clear, however, that these Quebec business people were no longer convinced, as they had appeared to be earlier, that the province's economy would thrive whether Quebec attained sovereignty or not.[4] Indeed, Bertin Nadeau, chairman of the Quebec food chain Provigo, estimated that 98 per cent of his business colleagues were against sovereignty.[5] Nadeau argued that sovereignty would imperil the chances of gaining access to capital at an affordable cost. Nadeau might have been overstating the degree of opposition to sovereignty, however; one week after his statement, another poll of Quebec business leaders revealed that 72 per cent favoured sovereignty-association while only 17.5 per cent supported new constitutional negotiations. By contrast, 12 per cent of business people outside Quebec favoured Quebec's sovereignty, and almost 53 per cent felt that new constitutional negotiations should be started.[6] The poll suggested that business leaders throughout Canada were tired of the constitutional debate.

These competing poll results were confusing. One way of disentangling the contradictory results, however, was to look at the survey samples. Business leaders considered whether their companies' interests were best protected by having Quebec stay in Canada. The first sample was made up primarily of large companies with commercial links to the rest of Canada and other countries. They were likely to oppose sovereignty. The second sample consisted of small and medium-sized businesses, concentrated in Quebec and wary of the consequences of Ottawa's monetary policy. These were the sovereigntists.

Jacques Parizeau insists that business people in Quebec have found the costs of dealing with two levels of government expensive and inefficient. Also, many have had success in exporting to the United States and find development of U.S. export markets to be easier at the margin than expanding already-developed markets in western Canada.[7] By contrast, former premier Robert Bourassa made the case that a sovereign Quebec would be deficit ridden and unable to pay for needed social programs. At present, most Quebec business leaders seem to be in agreement with the latter view, as many as 98 per cent according to one poll.[8] The public statements in support of sovereignty by several of them have diminished. In fact, the only high-profile Quebec business leaders to express public support for sovereignty were Domtar's chairman, Jean Campeau, the Desjardins group's chairman, Claude Béland, and Quebecor's

Pierre Péladeau. The recession is of primary concern to business leaders and most average citizens. The risks of sovereignty may be too great at a time when unemployment and high taxes are the focus of attention.

In fact, trade disruption might occur if tariff barriers, import quotas, 'buy provincial' discriminating measures, or nationalistic regulations interfere with the flow of goods and services and reduce economic efficiency. This being said, one could make the case that these might be short-term problems that, with some effort, could be managed by Quebec and Canadian authorities.

Nevertheless, it would be a tough road to follow. For example, the Japanese are highly sensitive to political instability and the impact of any transfer of federal debt to a less highly rated borrower.[9] In fact, Quebec is, in some ways, becoming less attractive as an area for foreign investment even if one discounts the sovereignty issue. In global terms, Quebec is a subregion within the North American market. It is too small and remote to attract much first-time investment. Moreover, Quebec's cultural distinctiveness often requires a company to spend as much on marketing there as it spends on the rest of North America.

The Quebec government has a greater hand in shaping its economy than any other in North America, making the province more vulnerable to a decline in the activity of the private, tax-paying sector. The province's pension-investment fund has been particularly interventionist. Government regulations add to business costs. Linguistic and cultural estrangement from the rest of North America reduces the mobility of Quebec's labour force, reflected in an unemployment rate traditionally 4 per cent higher than Ontario's. This causes further government spending for social assistance.

Canadian federalists maintain that Canada needs a strong central government to keep the provinces from exerting too much unilateral power. They insist that strong central institutions are best equipped to deal with the continuing array of interprovincial trade barriers. If Quebec were to go it alone, however, there might result still more barriers and greater segmentation of the Canadian market.

Federalists also note that a united Canada ensures the nation more bargaining power on the world economic stage. It provides greater risk diversification and helps to restrain the forces of segmentation. Furthermore, federal advocates point out that Quebec is a net beneficiary of federal spending in the form of goods and services transfers.

Sovereigntists counter these arguments by insisting that the federal government has mismanaged fiscal policy, allowed the national debt to skyrocket, allowed the environment to deteriorate, and forced costly duplication of government services. Sovereigntists note that the world is changing in terms of global capital flows, and small states can adapt successfully to these changes.

'Globalization,' or the internationalization of competition, has become a consistent theme of the sovereigntists' rhetoric. PQ constitutional adviser Daniel Latouche told the Bélanger-Campeau Commission that globalization was the most important factor leading to a redefinition of the current constitutional debate and was the principal challenge facing Quebec.[10] Entire societies are now in competition with one another world-wide, and their success largely depends on their capacity for social compromises and rapid adaptation to changing economic conditions. Yet federal-provincial competition in Canada is reducing Quebec's capacity to adapt to the new global imperatives argue sovereigntists. Canadian federalism is a form of 'political protectionism,' which, like economic protectionism, has had its day in Quebec. Sovereignty would give Quebec a greater range of policy instruments than those of a province.

Former prime minister Mulroney has stated that Quebecers should 'watch out for the dream merchants, those who say it's no problem to destroy a great country and rebuild it later.' He may be right.

The Parti Québécois insists that Quebec will remain a safe habitat for foreign investors. But can a sovereign Quebec compete for capital without employing an industrial policy of subsidies and other assistance that runs counter to the rules of the free trade agreement (FTA)?[11] Also, the free trade agreement between Canada and the United States is a deal between two federal governments. It is not a deal between a federation and a constituent unit of a federation. This is relevant because certain aspects of the agreement, including its procurement and investment review provisions, would apply if Quebec became a nation-state but are less relevant for Quebec as just a province. Quebecers might discover that the United States would enjoy terrific leverage in FTA negotiations with a much smaller partner. In addition, Quebec's subsidies and its intervention in its economy might prove problematic in any free trade discussions with the United States. Quebec's position on the FTA will be returned to.

There are other factors that make one pause about the sovereignty option. Even the most successful Quebec-based companies have been dipping into federal funds to subsidize their deals. For example, Bombardier acquired aircraft manufacturer Canadair only after Ottawa paid Canadair's outstanding $1.2 billion debt load. Bombardier was then granted a CF-18 aircraft maintenance contract for immediate cash flow and ended up paying Ottawa only $120 million for all of Canadair's considerable assets, including the rights to the successful Challenger executive jet. Similarly, Montreal-based Lavalin Inc. reached contract terms with Bangkok Skytrain, but only after Ottawa paid over $1.1 billion in low-interest and interest-free loans. As noted, Lavalin subsequently went bankrupt. Similar deals may be impossible without Ottawa's support.

Should Quebec attain sovereignty, it would have to absorb job losses in industries including textiles, footwear and resource industries. In these sectors, competitiveness, declining tariffs, and value-added considerations pose difficult challenges. Also, Quebec is less export-oriented than Canada as a whole. For example, while it accounts for 26 per cent of all Canadian imports, Quebec accounts for only 16 per cent of all Canadian exports and less than 23 per cent of Canada's exports to western Europe.

In addition, shareholder participation in the Quebec economy is lower than the Canadian average, thereby suggesting that the depth of Quebec's domestic ownership is not as significant as Quebecers may think. Although Quebec has many domestically controlled firms, it also has many foreign-controlled firms which make their major strategic decisions elsewhere.[12] Furthermore, Quebec's unemployment rate exceeds the Canadian average. This means that the province draws higher-than-average benefits of approximately $600 million in net annual benefits accruing to Quebec from its involvement in Canada's unemployment insurance scheme. In addition, Quebecers pay lower-than-average income taxes, or 22 per cent of all personal federal income taxes collected by Ottawa. If Quebec were sovereign and carrying its full load of 26 per cent of taxes, Quebec residents would pay an additional annual amount of $1.6 billion or $500 per taxpayer. In 1986, each Ontario taxpayer paid over $3500 in federal income tax. Their Quebec counterparts paid $2800. Of course, such discrepancies would not exist if Quebec became sovereign.[13] Since Quebecers would no longer pay federal taxes, their tax load might then be heavier.

A sovereign Quebec's problems might also include a difficulty in capital generation. Not one of the fifty most profitable Canadian companies is owned or managed by Quebecers. Of these companies, thirty-two have their head office in Ontario, eight in Quebec. These include Air Canada, Seagram's, Alcan, the Bank of Montreal, Canadian National Railways, the Royal Bank, Bell Canada, and Canadian Pacific. Only Alcan is likely to stay after sovereignty. The savings of most Quebecers go into English Canadian banks and insurance companies or into stocks in American and Canadian companies. The only significant accumulation of Quebec capital is in the provincial government's pension fund and in the *caisse populaire* financial cooperatives. Both of these have to balance the interests of their policyholders and shareholders against Quebec's need to finance its own technological development. Quebec probably has less private wealth available for such development than the western provinces.

The sale of the Montreal Expos baseball team is an example of how scarce these investment resources are. It took a $25 million investment by the city of Montreal and a $50 million loan guarantee from the government of Quebec to raise the $100 million purchase price for a ball club with an uncertain economic future. In other sectors including minerals, pulp and paper (Quebec's largest export), agriculture, pharmaceuticals, automobiles, and shipbuilding, Quebec stands to suffer economically with sovereignty.[14] Interestingly, the Parti Québécois blames Quebec's vulnerability in these sectors on federal government policies.[15] One could also make the credible point, however, that federal policies have enabled these industries to achieve the success that they have.[16]

There are also questions about how an independent Quebec would fare in terms of its weaker sectors. For example, within the Canadian dairy market, Quebec is the dominant producer of industrial milk (milk manufactured into butter, cheese, yoghurt, ice cream). The industrial milk market accounts for 61 per cent of all produced milk. Last year alone, net dairy cash receipts for both fluid and industrial milk totalled $3.1 billion. Shipments of dairy products from processing plants were valued at over $7 billion. The potential loss to Quebec dairy farmers from separation is three-fold: the loss of income derived from no longer qualifying for Canadian Dairy Commission (CDC) subsidies; losses from less industrial milk being sold to processors; and capital losses owing to reduced or devalued quota values.[17] The Canadian dairy industry operates with restrictions on imports and exports of milk and dairy products. Observers say that the exports from an independent Quebec to Canada should be in businesses that rely on debt and not equity. For example, Peter Cook notes that 50 per cent of Quebec farm cash receipts come from marketing boards that are heavily funded by the rest of Canada. Without them, Quebec agriculture could be impoverished.[18] This is a particularly interesting concern. For example, the chairman of the Ontario Milk Marketing Board, John Core, has maintained that if Quebec separates from Canada, Quebec dairy farmers would not be able to preserve their share of the market, 48.5 per cent of Canada's industrial milk. The province's dairy industry wants to keep its share of the market even if Quebec separates.

However, one study concludes that Quebec dairy farmers could lose as much as $1.75 billion in sales to Canadian markets if Quebec becomes sovereign.[19] Almost half of Quebec industrial milk would become surplus, resulting in lower milk sales. As noted, Canadian Dairy Commission subsidies would be eliminated, and devalued dairy quotas would propel capital losses. The report estimates that a Quebec-based dairy subsidy would cost Quebec taxpayers about $67 million. Not replacing it would cost each Quebec farmer $7500 annually. Much depends, of course, on the response of the rest of Canada to sovereignty. The rest of Canada would have to decide whether it would continue some supply-management arrangements with Quebec or not.

Political sovereignty for Quebec might hamper other industries as well. The collapse of Canada's internal customs union could find Quebec's highly protected textile industry facing a major loss of markets in the rest of Canada. The textiles and clothing industries, the largest and most important of Quebec's 'soft' industries employing 8 per cent of the goods-producing workforce, are able to operate only behind high tariff walls and then only after being propped up by voluntary export restraints under the Multi-Fiber Agreement. Effective rates of protection for textiles average 16.6 per cent, and most-favoured-nation customs tariffs for most clothing are 25 per cent. Import penetration in the market for textiles and clothing has been limited to 30 to 33 per cent through restraints on 80 per cent of imports. Import restraints are a much more important source of protection for the textiles and clothing industries than high tariffs.

Quebec's pharmaceutical industry could also be vulnerable if Quebec attains sovereignty. The Montreal-based pharmaceutical industry consists of 48 companies, or one-third of Canada's total. They account for 8500 Quebec jobs, or 39 per cent of all employment in the $4.2 billion national industry. The industry serves the Canadian market, but it is largely shut out of other countries by protectionist structures designed to subsidize their own pharmaceutical concerns. Such companies as Merck and Schering-Plough have received large tax breaks to situate in Quebec.

With sovereignty, Quebec would have trouble selling pharmaceuticals to a protectionist rest of Canada. Quebec would also have to spend a great deal of money to duplicate the drug testing and certification now done in Ottawa. Quebec's small market would probably pay higher drug prices, and attracting future investment in the industry would be challenging. They might be lucky to retain what they have.

In addition, in a sovereign Quebec, the 'soft' industries would be highly vulnerable to changes in Canadian commercial policy. Canadian consumers would probably not bear the costs of protecting the soft industries of a sovereign Quebec; nor could they be expected to bear the cost of adjustment as a sovereign Quebec embarked upon a needed process of restructuring its economy.

The high price that Canadians would have to continue to pay to support Quebec's soft industries would certainly make a customs union with a sovereign Quebec a bad deal. From Quebec's perspective, even a customs union would not be enough to protect its textiles and clothing industry. This would require a continuation of jointly administered import restraints, an arrangement that would be an even worse deal for Canada than a customs union. All the trade and investment rules between an independent Quebec and the rest of Canada would be much stricter than current arrangements.

Another sector that might be adversely affected might be science, research, and development. Quebec might lose important research funding. Scientific collaboration could be more difficult if researchers inside and outside Quebec weren't able to meet through funding agencies. Federal agencies pay for much of the research conducted in Canada. A sovereign Quebec would probably see its portion of research funding go to other provinces without being able to fill the gap. At present, Quebec is overrepresented in research grants attained.[20]

Even Quebec's pride and joy, its vast hydroelectric resource, could prove problematic to a sovereign Quebec. Already, there is reduced demand in New York state for Quebec's electrical power. There are low-cost alternatives as well, and the New York Power Authority objects to Quebec's apparent efforts to sidestep environmental restrictions on its planned 3 billion-watt $12.6 billion Great Whale River Power Plant Project.

In fact, New York's concerns were such that it finally decided in March 1992 to cancel its $17 billion hydroelectricity contract. New York Governor Mario Cuomo asserted that his state no longer needed the 1000 megawatts of power it had planned to buy, and that Hydro's price was too high. Hydro-Québec officials insisted that the project would continue nevertheless. New York cancelled its contract because of its electricity surplus, its low-cost alternative sources of energy, and its environmental concerns. But the cancellation also demonstrates again how vulnerable the Quebec economy is to external shocks. In fact a major deal was cancelled in 1994.

Phase II of the project, which involves the flooding of the thousand-square-mile Great Whale River basin, is on hold. In April 1994 the New York Power Authority announced that it would not be going through with its contract to buy U.S. $5 billion watts of power. The power authority's president, David Freeman, stressed that 'we don't need the power, the price is too high, and there are unresolved environmental questions in Quebec.'[21]

Hydro-Québec's success is integral to a strong Quebec credit rating. It is an obvious sign of the dynamism of the Quebec economy. When it takes a substantial financial hit, as it did with the New York state cancellation, the economic viability of a sovereign Quebec is further called into question.

Hydro-Québec had more U.S. dollar debt than any corporation in the industrialized world, except for a few survivors of the takeover battles of the 1980s. Hydro-Québec plans to double this debt to pay for even larger projects. Also, native land claims remain contentious and the agreement with Newfoundland for power from Churchill Falls would be placed in danger by sovereignty. As expected, American and other potential investors are hesitant to become further involved, given the political and economic uncertainties.[22]

The symbolic importance of hydroelectricity sales to Quebec's future should not be understated. In February 1993 Hydro-Québec chairman Richard Drouin declared on national television that Hydro-Québec was one of the three pillars of an independent Quebec's economy. The others were the government-run pension fund and credit union.

Senior Quebec government officials downplay the importance of the cancelled hydro deals with New York. They stress that Quebec's hydro exports to the United States are worth slightly less than the trade in men's suits and slightly more than fresh meat. They note that between 30 and 40 per cent of all Quebec–U.S. trade consists of intracompany shipments and are less vulnerable to external shocks. This is quite true. But it is also true that to most Quebecers, hydro sales are a vital symbol of the province's self-reliance. The shock of New York's two contract cancellations, notwithstanding the minor financial damage it might have caused, did great harm to the self-confidence of Quebecers.

SOVEREIGNTY'S POTENTIAL IMPACT ON BUSINESS IN QUEBEC

What will happen to small and medium-sized businesses in a sovereign Quebec? Quebec has a high proportion of these businesses concentrated in consumption-oriented services. This means that they are more vulnerable to economic cycles and obsolescence as North America's economy shifts from consumption to production.

For example, if one has a small to medium-sized business in Quebec and is thus importing in limited quantities, then products requiring French manuals, technical data, or repair diagrams will be extremely difficult to get. Translation costs would be prohibitively expensive for most U.S. and Canadian firms. Test equipment, consumer goods, and other industrial supplies will likely be received in English or not at all since the Quebec market represents 1 per cent of gross sales. The vast majority of American firms will decide that shipments identified only in French are not cost-effective.

If goods must be received in French, but suppliers outside Quebec are reluctant to comply, then the business owner or manager will be forced to buy Quebec-only products. What will happen to the sales and buying power of that firm? Will the Quebec small business be competitive with its Canadian competitors, let alone its American rivals who can seek business anywhere virtually without restrictions? If times become more difficult, will the small business person's bank, which is nationally chartered at present, offer similar credit terms? Will new financing be needed from a Quebec- chartered institution?

Uncertainty arising from sovereignty-association or sovereignty could prompt financial institutions to impose a premium of 2 to 3 per cent on the borrowing costs of small businesses. Large enterprises could offer lower prices than smaller companies and be at a fundamental advantage. What would happen to federally chartered banks in Quebec? Would there be a dislocation of the money supply after sovereignty?

In addition, if Quebec ran large budget deficits to finance high interest rates, at least in the seven- to ten-year transition period following sovereignty, would there be any funding available to support product innovation, plant upgrading, research and development, and worker education and retraining? If no funds were available, this would hamper Quebec business in general, but small and medium-sized enterprises would be particularly disadvantaged. As a related concern, would a sovereign Quebec be able to provide pension and health benefits, day care, and higher education support for workers?

A sovereign Quebec might impose foreign currency constraints, which would impair the small business person's ability to purchase foreign products. Could an international product supplier rely on the creditworthiness of the Quebec small business for normal, regular payment terms? Until a level of trust was established, business might be conducted on a 'cash only' basis.

Under sovereignty, anglophone and allophone business leaders would be wary of unwritten government preferences for secretly awarding contracts to francophones. This might not be the choice of government leaders, who might well be sympathetic to the plight of minority-run businesses. However, they must respond to their majority constituency.

A sovereign Quebec might become defensive and close its doors to certain imports, fearing a silent industrial takeover by Canada or the United States. There could be a tug-of-war over markets and technology, a breakdown in franchising agreements, and the diversion of goods from normal distribution channels. Parallel importation could occur. There might then be anarchy in the way manufacturers, distributors, and retailers operate in the new state. There might emerge a 'grey' market whereby a small business, unable to merchandise from its original source and having exhausted all legitimate options, obtains goods from an American or offshore supplier. Stores in Quebec that are loyal to their qualified distributor or manufacturer would be threatened by this grey market. Such a phenomenon could be a major irritant to companies that have been promised guaranteed protection or exclusivity from their suppliers. In a society where uncertainty prevails, as in a newly sovereign Quebec, this grey market could proliferate without restraint.

If a Quebec company is franchised, it can sell outside the province. It can obtain a licence to sell anywhere in Canada and, if its volume is sufficient, it can sell at competitive prices. Would the company be allowed to win such a licence in a sovereign Quebec? If not, how could the business purchase small quantities at reasonable prices?

Of course, a sovereign Quebec could immediately establish a favourable business environment. It could collect just and equitable taxes, relax the language laws pertaining to commercial signs, attract foreign investment, and otherwise reassure the small business person. Certainly, this would be its intention. But in a climate of uncertainty, this would be an exceedingly difficult task.[23]

How might small companies adapt to sovereignty compared to large companies? Probably not very well. Big companies are more likely to have the financial muscle to survive a long difficult adjustment after sovereignty. They can shift assets and jobs to more stable countries unlike small ones. In addition, big companies are more likely to receive government subsidies to protect jobs and cushion the shock. Small business would be faced with a slump in consumer buying, cutbacks in consumer spending, a crunch on parts sold to manufacturers and on corporate expansion and modernization. Unlike big business, the small players would have little recourse. But small business is the real job provider in the economy. Its inability to get meaningful help from an overburdened Quebec or Canada would cause further hardship and economic dislocation.

At this point, several short-term negative implications and very few positive implications of sovereignty for Quebec have been discussed. The negative implications include the uncertainty that might cause investor nervousness; difficulties in accumulating capital; higher taxes, interest rates, and unemployment; reduced access to goods and services; and, in general, a reduced standard of living for the Quebecer. Again, these might be purely short-term phenomena. It is nearly impossible to predict long-term economic growth prospects accurately. This point should be stressed. Investors must play a guessing game. How much should they invest in a nation that may or may not fracture? How seriously might a breakup affect investment returns? How difficult will subsequent Canada-Quebec negotiations be? How long might they drag on? Which industries will be most hurt? What will be the increased risk of lending to national or provincial governments? What risks would now be entailed in lending to big and/or small businesses? These must be confusing and annoying dilemmas to investors. Presumably, they would be tempted to decide that, in the short run, the risks would be such that they would be better off putting their money and resources elsewhere.

There is another concern, however, expressed most often by business leaders in both Quebec and the rest of Canada. This is a frustration with the economic costs of constitutional haggling. Many feel that the economy, not constitutional reform, should be the first priority of the federal government. Some have argued that the federal government used the constitutional issue to deflect attention from the ongoing economic malaise and the lack of fiscal options owing to the state of Canada's public finances. Political uncertainty has also exacerbated the recession by adding a risk premium to Canadian interest rates, increasing the volatility of the Canadian dollar, and reducing the attractiveness of investing in Canada. The unity debate also diverts attention from the perceived 'real' problems to be faced in the transition to free trade and globalization. Regional input with respect to development policy, it is argued, is needed to meet these global economic challenges. For Canada to compete in the increasingly integrated global economy, substantial investments would be required to increase productivity. Also, infrastructure must be upgraded, the environment must be protected, and education and health services have to be improved. Therefore, business leaders contend that access to capital at an affordable cost is essential. This requires a solution to Canada's budget problems. Such a remedy would require discipline and cohesion among all levels of government and among all Canadians. But these vital goals, it is assumed, cannot be adequately addressed until the unity issue is resolved and political uncertainty ended. Following the failure of the Charlottetown Agreement, however, Canada is in limbo. Economic planning is difficult and the economy sputters along without realizing its full potential. Uncertainty causes businesses, governments, and individuals to put off investment decisions. This delay slows any economic recovery.

The unity crisis aggravates other existing problems that must be on the minds of investors. These include Quebec's deteriorating fiscal situation, the lack of demographic growth, and the relatively poor workplace preparation of the next generation of workers. It is difficult to be optimistic about a rapidly improving investment climate.

At least two other fundamental issues are worthy of comment. First, how would debts and assets be divided between a sovereign Quebec and Canada? Second, what sort of currency arrangements, if any, could a sovereign Quebec negotiate with Canada?

7

Quebec Sovereignty and the Debt

The Canadian economy is mired in a recession in 1994. Furthermore, the federal debt increased from 15 per cent of national income in 1981 to 40 per cent in 1992. It was $72 billion in 1980 and rose to $352 billion in 1990. As of 1993 it was about $400 billion. In the past decade, Canada has experienced faster debt accumulation than any other large industrial country except Italy (and Italy has a much higher household savings rate than does Canada). The contrast between the failure of the federal government to control its deficit and the success of the Quebec government in achieving a balanced budget is striking. This clearly adds to the relative discredit in which the central government is held in the province. What this has meant for Canada as a whole, among other things, is declining confidence on the part of international investors and limited financial manoeuvrability. It has meant fewer benefits for the provinces than before at sometimes greater expense.

In February 1990, former finance minister Michael Wilson set forth measures that, it was hoped, would lower the deficit to $28.5 billion in 1991, and to $14 billion by 1994.[1] These measures included the selling of the crown corporation Petro-Canada, plus a two-year freeze on increases in transfer payments to the provinces for health, post-secondary education, and welfare. In addition, outright grants to businesses were largely eliminated, and government business loans were made much more difficult to obtain. It was hoped that the highly unpopular Goods and Services Tax (GST), which went into effect on 1 January 1990, would provide the government with enough revenues to make substantial inroads into the deficit. It has been something less than a great success. In fact, the government of Jean Chrétien has promised to replace it with something else. Of course, the GST alone could not solve the budget deficit dilemma.

Jacques Parizeau and others maintain that Ottawa's lack of control over spending and borrowing and its attendant budget deficits have destabilized the

Canadian economy. This large accumulated debt has contributed to high interest rates and debt-servicing costs. In turn, these have restricted business investment, destabilized provincial finances, and led to unilateral reductions in transfers to the provinces. As noted, the contrast between the federal and Quebec governments in balancing their respective budgets is stark.[2] Also, many nationalists claim, as did the Bélanger-Campeau report, that federalism is no longer profitable for Quebec. They argue that Quebec receives equalization payments, but Ottawa spends less in Quebec than in the other provinces, resulting in a zero balance. 'So why not opt out?'[3]

Parizeau has also intimated that, if Quebec and Canada could not agree on what share of the debt Quebec is responsible for, it might not pay any share at all. He knows that this is an idle threat, however. Any hint of Quebec disowning its previous debt obligations would create a crisis in the foreign investment community, which would then boycott the new government's fiscal policies. Bankers do not like lending money to countries that do not repay their debts. The Quebec government depends heavily on foreign money to finance everything from hydroelectric dams to high schools. As of 31 December 1990, Quebec owed foreign investors $19.4 billion. This is more than a quarter of the government's total debt of $76.1 billion. If Quebec were a sovereign nation, the Quebec bonds held by Canadians would also become foreign debt, raising the dependence on foreign investors considerably, although the provincial finance ministry treats the number held by Canadians outside Quebec as confidential.

According to Grant Reuber of the University of Toronto, Quebec would have a substantial bargaining advantage in resolving the question of how to divide up the national debt. 'Canada's public debt is, and would remain, an obligation of the government of Canada. It could not be imposed on Quebec. Quebec would probably assume some of the debt only in exchange for federal government assets held in Quebec and other considerations. Quebec would set the price, which would be conditioned by the reality that ultimately – as an established sovereign state – Quebec would be free to expropriate the assets on its own terms.' Reuber goes on to argue that if Quebec secedes, Canada might find itself financially constrained, and its ability to assist disadvantaged areas and establish common national standards for social services would be hampered. It should be noted that the Parti Québécois proposes that people and goods would circulate freely between Quebec and Canada, but customs offices would be set up along the border to collect duties on Canadian goods entering Quebec.

Reuber's view is a particularly optimistic one, however. Most studies predict that Quebec will be obligated to service a substantial debt. We shall return to this point, but first it is worth examining what a sovereign Quebec's share of the debt would be. Several studies from outside Quebec suggest that the figure might be between 25.5 per cent and 32 per cent of the total of $450 billion (the biggest per foreign debt of any nation) which corresponds to its share of the population.[5]

As a study by the Business Council on National Issues (BCNI) notes, there are also tens of billions of dollars of other federal liabilities (unfunded public service pension liabilities, loans provided by the Farm Credit Corporation, the Export Development Corporation, guaranteed student loans). The assets and liabilities of the Bank of Canada would also have to be considered.[6] The study suggests that there are at least four criteria for dividing assets and debts: on the basis of population, gross domestic product, federal revenues collected in each province, or the proportion of the federal debt incurred on behalf of each prov-ince over time.[7] All of these criteria have their own set of problems. According to the BCNI, if Quebec resisted paying its mandated fair share, Ottawa could threaten to withhold repayment of its debt to individuals and institutions in Quebec, which could disrupt financial markets and the provincial economy at a time when Quebec would be most in need of economic stability to reassure nervous investment markets.

The Bélanger-Campeau report took a different view. It noted that a sovereign Quebec's deficit would rise to $9.8 billion, but maintained Quebec would not be liable legally to take on its share of the national debt, only its share of interest payments on that debt. Nonetheless, although not legally bound to do so by international law, a sovereign Quebec would assume its share of the national debt, the report went on. The percentage, however, would be based on the province's share of Canada's total assets (18.5 per cent), and not on its share of the population (25.5 per cent). The Bélanger-Campeau report insisted that international law supported the notion that the debt would remain in the hands of the federal government if the political system changed. The federal government would still finance its debt on world markets, but Quebecers, rather than sending their share of the interest on the debt to the federal government, would send it to Quebec.

These opinions are important, because they emphasize that any negotiation of Quebec's sovereignty would be in the framework of international, as well as Canadian, law. Furthermore, they leave the impression that international precedent leans towards favouring the 'successor state' or Quebec, rather than the 'predecessor state' or Canada. Note the unresolved discrepancy. Would a sovereign Quebec be responsible for 25.5 per cent or 18.5 per cent of the debt?

In addition, could there be mutually acceptable agreements about ownership of federal assets in Quebec and Quebec's assets in the rest of Canada? International agreements and understandings, such as the Defense Production Agreement or jurisdiction over the St Lawrence Seaway, would have to be reconciled. This begs the question of how the rest of Canada would respond to sovereignty. Would the rest of Canada trade with Quebec to the same degree as at present? What would become of the common external tariff? Why should Quebec's tariff structure be practiced by Ontario? Why should Canada protect Quebec's place in the World Trade Agreement (WTA)? Could Quebec protect itself adequately in the WTA or the North American Free Trade Agreement? Quebec sovereigntists stress that all existing agreements would be retained by Quebec, but is it really so simple?

Jacques Parizeau maintains that all outstanding debts can be split in an equitable manner. Where the debt is for public works, it would be split according to assets. Major physical assets that are not so easily divided, like rail lines, would require minor adjustments to devise fairly. Parizeau notes that a bigger but solvable problem may be how to divide unfunded pension liability for public servants.[8] He insists that there will be a net outpayment from Quebec to Canada. Furthermore, almost all of the splitting of debts and assets would be just 'accounting.' Only a small number of issues would require negotiation or arbitration.

This sounds very promising. However, what if the division of debt and assets is an acrimonious affair? In fact, dividing assets might be particularly difficult. Whereas the debt is a concept that is hard for most people to understand, assets are tangible things that people can see and comprehend. We know what natural resources, bridges, and highways look like. These negotiations might be both difficult and costly in terms of administrative expenditures.

In one study, it was demonstrated that division of the federal debt could be especially difficult as the divided debt would carry increased risk premiums. Agreeing on a formula to divide the debt, and designing the institutions necessary to administer the division, could be particularly difficult. There might also be a great migration of labour and capital from vulnerable regions to more secure ones.[9] Perhaps as many as one million people would leave the Atlantic provinces, Manitoba, Saskatchewan, and Quebec and look for new economic opportunities in Ontario, Alberta, and British Columbia. In any case, the division of the debt would likely be a contentious zero-sum game in which, if one party gained by obtaining a reduced share of the debt, the other would necessarily lose by having to accept a relatively larger share.

In addition, there is no precedent in international law for the distribution of debts and assets in the Canadian situation. Quebec and Canada officials would have to determine the principles to be followed.

There are other potential difficulties. The Bélanger-Campeau Commission secretariat stated that a sovereign Quebec could survive comfortably if it kept economic links with the rest of Canada. In fact, the report maintained that Quebec might be better off than the rest of Canada. It would have a deficit comparable to several west European countries. The debt would account for 56 per cent of Quebec's gross domestic product, compared with 65.6 per cent in the rest of Canada. Australia's debt as a per centage of GDP was 55.6 per cent, Denmark's was 55.3 per cent and the United States' was 54.5 per cent.

There were problems with this analysis, however. Its findings were based on 1991 figures as of the end of March, and it did not consider the economic instability that might hit a sovereign Quebec. Also, the respected Quebec economist Marcel Côté put the deficit of a sovereign Quebec closer to $12 billion, and possibly as high as $15 billion. This deficit would have to be paid in increased taxes, lower services, or both. Côté pointed out that international investors who buy Canadian and Quebec government bonds would be looking for signs that a sovereign Quebec was assuming its fair share of the Canadian debt. They would not be interested in investing in a debt-ridden economy. It could take years before Quebec could develop a bond market to finance its debt. In addition, Quebec's finances would probably be worse after sovereignty. The deficit and debt would probably rise. Whereas Canada could finance its debt by raising interest rates to attract capital, a sovereign Quebec without its own currency or monetary policy would not be able to do this.

If Quebec's share of the Canadian debt comes to about $100 billion, the first budget of a sovereign Quebec would be in the vicinity of $140 billion, since the existing provincial debt is $40 billion. Côté believes that a Quebec premier would have to delay indefinitely a declaration of sovereignty until financing was found for the deficit. Imposing higher taxes or spending cuts would be politically suicidal. An independent Quebec would have a heavy fiscal load and few new government programs. According to Côté, the economic costs of sovereignty would be substantial.[10]

Quebec's provincial debt is one of the highest in Canada – an independent Quebec would be a heavily indebted new country. Also, an independent Quebec would forego equalization payments that currently account for roughly 12 per cent of provincial revenues. Quebec would also forego transfer payments that have historically benefited it.

The servicing of Quebec's debt, plus its share of Canada's debt, would therefore have to be financed by a smaller revenue base than at present, even after Quebec took full control of taxes from Ottawa. The smaller revenue base, in turn, would probably mean higher taxes or reduced government services. Quebec could borrow more money, but a heavily indebted new country might have to pay a premium rate in international markets which, again, would put fiscal pressure on the government. As Jeffrey Simpson notes, it is a fascinating paradox that if Canada's debt were lower, Ottawa could deliver more generous programs in Quebec. However, since the debt is so high, the problems Quebec would have without Canada would be that much greater.[11] Since Canada's debt payments would be diminished, 'governments would have to pay higher interest rates to persuade investors to buy their bonds.'[12]

Nevertheless, to keep its credit rating and credibility in international markets intact, Quebec cannot afford to default on this obligation (contrary to Jacques Parizeau's assertions). Yet the inevitable bickering over how much of Canada's debt Quebec should actually pay might generate a perception of internal instability that could drive off foreign investment. In April 1990, for example, as the Meech Lake Accord foundered, the Deutsche Bank of West Germany advised investors to cut down on their Canadian bond holdings; similarly, investors from other countries sold more than $1 billion in Canadian government bonds. Whether risk-averse foreign investors will find that the attractions of an independent Quebec's markets outweigh the minuses of perceived instability – because of arguments over the national debt or because of the overall increased indebtedness of a sovereign Quebec – is an open question.

To be more specific the Deutsche Bank reported that in 1987, after the Meech Lake Accord was signed, Quebec paid a premium of 40 basis points on its five-year bonds over a comparable bond issued by the federal government. After Meech's failure in June 1990, the risk premium was 58 points and by March 1991, it had widened to 89 points. The comparable spread between five-year Ontario bonds and Canada bonds was 62 points, more than a quarter point less.[13]

Interest rate levels are determined by a number of factors of which politics is just one, but it is an important factor. The Deutsche Bank also predicted that the Quebec deficit would rise in 1991–2 while the federal deficit would stabilize during this period. It also predicted that Quebec's financial requirements would rise while the federal government's requirements would decline.

Economist Paul Boothe has noted that a transition could be made from a national debt in the name of all Canadians to a system in which the debt is shared by a sovereign Quebec and possibly other small regions.[14] However, such a transition would likely be a difficult one. One possibility is that Canada could recall its debt and then reissue all but Quebec's share of the bonds and treasury bills. Quebec would have to float new issues to make up the difference. But, it would be difficult to decide who should get the new Canada bonds and who should get the Quebec bonds. In addition, bondholders might cash in their bonds in favour of other securities. Also, there would be a question of whether Quebecers could go to the financial markets for such a large amount all at once without scaring off investors.

Alternatively, Quebec might replace federal debt as it matures with Quebec bonds until it had assumed its share of the debt. Here again such an action might frighten investors. Finally, Quebec might reach some other agreement with Ottawa to pay its share of the interest and principal. What remains most unclear is what would happen if investors demanded too high a price to buy Quebec bonds and treasury bills, or what would be the investor response if the Quebec economy declined after independence.[15]

Despite its substantial debt, Canada has maintained an excellent credit rating (although it has experienced downgrades in 1993, as previously noted). This is because of its vast resource base and its status as a country of refuge. A small sovereign Quebec would not be as attractive in this regard. Nor would Quebec have a financial market capable of meeting its needs at first, thus forcing it to pursue external markets, as noted. Given its debt and lack of historical financial management success, Quebec will have trouble attracting external help.

The Bélanger-Campeau Commission report revealed that many Quebecers believe that the province can secede from Canada and then easily negotiate the maintenance of close financial and economic ties. This assumption may be unwarranted, for all sorts of complications might ensue. There is no legal or constitutional basis for secession of a province from the Canadian federation.

The Bélanger-Campeau Commission secretariat argued that a sovereign Quebec's share of the debt should be the same as its share of federal assets, such as airports, post offices, and government offices. But federal assets are a poor measure of the future flow of earnings in Quebec and in the rest of Canada. Federal subsidies have nurtured Canadians' health, education, and welfare.

The federal government has supported key Quebec industries – sometimes at the expense of other provinces. While those investments do not show up in balance sheets of federal government assets, they are a prime determinant of future income. If one could quantify the value of these federal government subsidies, then Quebec's real share of the federal debt would be much higher than the figure suggested by the Bélanger-Campeau analysis. This might well force higher taxes and other financial costs in a sovereign Quebec.

Ultimately, Quebec could not renounce payment of its share of the national debt, and it probably could not borrow large sums from wary investors. If it could take on its share of the debt, interest charges would quintuple the annual deficit.[16] It would be difficult to find Canadian investors willing to take on such a risk given more attractive investments elsewhere, and especially in the United States.

TABLE 10

Estimates of Quebec's budget deficit in Year 1 of independence (hypothetical estimates using fiscal year 1990/91 as the base year)

Bélanger-Campeau	$10 billion
Fortin	$13 billion
McCallum	$15 billion
Economic Council of Canada	$15 billion
Côté	$16 billion
Grady	$22 billion

SOURCES: Four of the estimates (all but 'Economic Council' and 'Côté') were taken directly from Pierre Fortin, 'L'impact du passage à la souveraineté sur le déficit budgétaire du Québec' (paper presented at a conference sponsored by *Les Affaires*, Montreal, 23 March 1992). Fortin made certain adjustments to the original estimates in order to make them comparable.

The 'Economic Council' estimate is from Economic Council of Canada, *A Joint Venture: The Economics of Constitutional Options*, Twenty-Eight Annual Review (Ottawa: Supply and Services Canada 1991), 81. The figure of $15 billion is based on the council's estimate of the impact of sovereignty on the Quebec budget, in combination with Fortin's estimate of the consolidated deficit under federalism ($9.8 billion).

The 'Côté' estimate is from Marcel Côté, 'Souveraineté: le coûts de transition' (notes for the conference, 'Project '90,' Université du Québec á Montréal, March 1992, Mimeographed). Other original sources are as follows: Secrétariat de la Commission sur l'avenir politique et constitutionnel du Québec [Bélanger-Campeau Commission], Analyse pro forma des finances publiques dans l'hypothése de la souveraineté du Québec,' in Bélanger-Campeau Commission, *Éléments d' analyse économique pertinents à la révision du statut politique et constitutionnel du Québec*, The Canada Round 5 (Toronto: C.D. Howe Institute 1991); John McCallum, Remarks to Commission sur le processus de détermination de l'avenir politique et constitutionnel du Québec, Assemblée nationale, Quebec, 4 December 1991, table 1; and Patrick Grady, *The Economic Consequences of Quebec Sovereignty* (Vancouver: Fraser Institute 1991).[18]

Reprinted from John McCallum, *Canada's Choice: Crisis of Capital or Renewed Federalism* (Toronto: C.D. Howe Institute 25 June 1992).

One 1991 study published by the C.D. Howe Institute is especially pessimistic about a sovereign Quebec's prospects. In *Parting as Friends: The Economic Consequences for Quebec*, McGill University professors John McCallum and Chris Green suggest that Quebec would face an annual budget deficit of $15 billion during the first five years of independence, a debt that would double by the fifth year.[17] This massive debt would make borrowing on international money markets very difficult. Spending cuts of 10 to 15 per cent would have to be imposed. The public sector would be reduced by 5 per cent, and taxes would have to be raised by 15 per cent. If correct, this analysis suggests an economic disaster. McCallum has summarized the results of several studies predicting Quebec's budget deficit in the first year of independence. His table is reprinted here (see table 10).

Ghislain Dufour, head of the powerful Quebec employers' group, the Conseil du patronat, revealed that a survey of its members found that 65 per cent believed that the province would suffer economically for five years after it became sovereign. Foreign investment would diminish.[19] Independence would not be attained quickly nor easily. Quebec sovereigntists will have to devote far more attention to the economic costs of creating a new nation. The romance of a sovereign Quebec is enticing, but the accountants' dull balance sheets make clear that the romance may be fleeting and that the real world economic challenges will be taxing and difficult.

8

Quebec Sovereignty and Currency Concerns

One of the most politically sensitive aspects of the Quebec sovereignty debate involves currency issues. In particular, there is an ongoing discussion about whether an independent Quebec should initiate its own currency, or adopt the Canadian or even the American currency. Most pro-sovereignty politicians and political analysts have shied away from this contentious issue. If Quebec adopts the Canadian dollar, would they have a say over Canadian monetary policy? Would the rest of Canada agree? Would Quebec's role be only consultative or would it have a veto role? Former prime minister Brian Mulroney, for one, maintained that a sovereign Quebec would not be permitted to use the Canadian dollar, although no one really knows how he could have prevented this from happening if Quebec political leaders were insistent.

There are those who argue that it would be to a sovereign Quebec's advantage to have its own currency. Many sovereigntist leaders, although not Jacques Parizeau, have asserted that a distinctive currency further legitimizes political sovereignty. There would also be seigniorage to be earned for Quebec.

In fact, if a sovereign Quebec did decide to create its own currency, it would have a number of options. It could peg its new currency to the Canadian dollar or the U.S. one, perhaps at a level that favours Quebec exports to the rest of Canada. The Quebec Chamber of Commerce makes the point that other small countries have their own currency, so this option is not unheard of. Nevertheless, it is not clear that foreign and Canadian investors would display the required confidence in this Quebec dollar or Frontenac, or whatever it might be called. No country created since the Second World War has a currency that trades freely on international markets, with the exception of Israel – a special case. It is not clear that Quebecers would be content to see their private savings converted to a new Quebec currency rather than holding onto their Canadian dollars. Indeed it is likely that Quebecers would want to soften the economic impact of independence with a shared currency.

Creating a new currency creates risks because new governments are often tempted to revalue their money, enabling them to repay their debts with cheaper currency. Investors prefer currencies that have a track record of maintaining their value. Also, a Quebec currency might be less stable than Canada's because Quebec's economy is smaller and less diversified. No matter how prosperous and well-managed a Quebec dollar might be, the Quebec economy would be vulnerable to booms and busts to a greater degree than would Canada's economy.

Professor Thomas Courchene of Queen's University believes that Confederation has failed economically.[1] It would be in Quebec's interest, he says, to adopt its own currency instead of using the Canadian or American dollar. It should not use a currency controlled by the rest of Canada, nor should the other provinces want Quebec to retain the Canadian dollar since its economic policies would necessarily affect the value of the currency. This is not to say that Quebec should separate, Courchene insists, because the costs of independence would be prohibitive.

If Quebec creates its own currency, it would have to be able to vary it against its Canadian counterpart. If not, it would simply be a nuisance and the equivalent of Canadian money, according to an important study authored by David Laidler.[2] Laidler concludes that Quebec has a strong economic interest in remaining part of the Canadian monetary system, even if it moves to greater political independence. The maintenance of a monetary union would promote the continued existence of a common market for goods, services, capital, and labour. According to Laidler, these ties would require political supervision and probably a decentralized federation.

A number of writers agree that there are two attractions of maintaining the Canadian dollar as a common currency. First, it would facilitate trade flows between Quebec and the rest of Canada, and, second, the Canadian dollar is recognized internationally as a legitimate, convertible currency.

David Laidler argues that, although a Quebec currency might be viable, Quebec's best option is to retain economic ties with Canada. Foreign leaders would support such a decision, since most would be indifferent to Canada's constitutional problems so long as their loans were repaid. Furthermore, any decision by Quebec to introduce its own money would be costly since it would be more than just a national symbol and could not simply be launched by government decree. People would have to be persuaded to use it and to have confidence in its value and stability. Quebec authorities would have to promise full convertibility, but this would limit Quebec's use of such devices as dual exchange rates. In addition, wages, salaries, prices, and contracts would have to be converted from the Canadian dollar into the new Quebec currency, with painful adjustments for all.

In any case, a Quebec currency would have problems because Canada's debts outweigh its assets, and many of the debts are internationally owned. As a result, neither Canada nor Quebec could tinker with the currency without probable negative consequences.[3] Trade with the rest of Canada would become more cumbersome, international capital markets would demand a premium on funds invested, and Quebec would have to battle inflation to establish the new currency's credibility.

Quebec's former premier Robert Bourassa has noted that Quebec could not adequately protect its economic interests if it were to create its own currency.[4] On the other hand, a common currency would require the establishment of a common market with no trade barriers to ensure the free flow of goods, services, capital, and labour. If Quebec were to accept a common currency, it would have to harmonize its fiscal policy with Canada (on taxes and government spending). Bourassa has also asserted that economic integration leads to a common parliament elected through universal suffrage, since you cannot have taxation without representation. This is a debatable point of course. By contrast, Parti Québécois leader Jacques Parizeau insists that a political union would be unnecessary. He points to the Ontario NDP government's budget as distinct from federal government fiscal policy. This is an example of states sharing a currency but not pursuing common fiscal policies. However, Parizeau is quick to maintain that a sovereign Quebec would welcome a common monetary policy and close consultation or complete consultation on fiscal policy.

This is his 'carrot' to federalists. His 'stick' is that Canada might have to pay Quebec's share of the national debt if it refused to negotiate a common currency after sovereignty. Indeed, the PQ leader has even hinted that a sovereign Quebec could destroy the Bank of Canada by using Quebec's existing holdings of Canadian dollars as a fiscal weapon. This is just an idle threat, of course, but it is clear that, if a sovereign Quebec does choose to retain the Canadian dollar, Parizeau seems resigned to having virtually no say on monetary policy and muses that Quebec has no influence on Canadian monetary policy anyway.

The federal government would not give Quebec a say in monetary policy, in part because of federalist anger at the new nation, but mostly because western Canada and the Maritime provinces, which have demanded changes in monetary policy, do not have substantial representation either. Instead, the federal government insulates the dollar from political pressures by concentrating power over monetary policy in the hands of the governor of the Bank of Canada. To jeopardize this arrangement by splitting authority over the central bank would risk unleashing inflationary forces that could destroy the dollar's value.

Ironically, while many sovereigntists suggest that a sovereign Quebec use the Canadian dollar, this would leave the Bank of Canada in control of Quebec's interest rates.[5] For years, both the Quebec government and prominent businessmen have excoriated the Bank of Canada for its conservative monetary policies. This policy was said to be designed for the needs of Ontario, keeping interest rates too high for Quebec's less robust economy and the dollar too expensive for the good of Quebec's exporters. If Quebec were to keep the Canadian dollar, it would be as if it were admitting that, despite all this hostile talk, the central bank's despised anti-inflationary policy is exactly what Quebec needs to attract investment and keep voters' savings secure.

If it maintains the Canadian dollar after sovereignty, Quebec would be the only industrialized country in the world to have its monetary policy controlled by another country. There are, however, some Third World countries in this situation. The U.S. dollar circulates as the local currency in Panama, for instance. This has caused some problems for Panamanian exports. Since Panama cannot devalue its currency each time one of its trading partners does, Panamanian exports become more expensive in the other country, hurting export earnings.

Parizeau's willingness to let Canada make monetary policy is not a universally held position within the Parti Québécois. PQ Vice-President Bernard Landry has suggested that an independent Quebec be allowed to name the Bank of Canada governor 'once in five short mandates or twice in four longer mandates.'[6] He has also called for Quebec representation on the bank's board and staff. Landry argues for some Quebec power to direct the bank to narrow the gap between Canadian and U.S. interest rates. If these recommendations were not followed, Landry maintained, Quebec would institute its own currency as other small nations do, without the fear of a credibility crisis driving down the value of a Quebec currency. A weak currency would make it easier for Quebecers to sell their goods externally, thereby boosting the currency, he says. It would be difficult to convince the federal government or the rest of Canada of the merits of this argument. But many experts agree that the debate over Quebec's future, while wrenching and negative, could offer a positive opportunity to revamp Canada's central bank. One popular idea is to provide a full-time source of regional input to the bank, either by beefing up the board of directors or by locating some senior deputy bank governors in different parts of Canada.[7] The Bank of Canada would resist these changes, however. In fact, bank officials insist that regional views are already addressed in federal monetary policy making.

Paradoxically the Parti Québécois has blamed the 'Made in Ontario' monetary policy of the Bank of Canada for economic strife and higher unemployment in Quebec than in Ontario. But by using the Canadian dollar it would be supporting that monetary policy. In addition, an independent Quebec would have less influence, and not more, on the Bank of Canada's decisions. Some economists think that the mere act of splitting the country would oblige the Bank of Canada to tighten monetary policy for a few years so that investors would not pull out capital assets.

Parizeau wants a sovereign Quebec to retain the Canadian dollar, even if it would have no influence on monetary policy. He notes Quebec has no influence on Canadian monetary policy at present anyway. Even so, a single currency would be controlled by a single central bank. But one must then question how a central bank can have two political masters, even if one of the two is ostensibly benign. Former Quebec premier Bourassa criticized the Bank of Canada for its tight monetary policy. There would be tremendous pressure on the political leaders of a sovereign Quebec to risk higher inflation by using monetary policy to expand the Quebec economy more rapidly.

But a sovereign Quebec could make the Canadian dollar legal tender, with or without the permission of the federal government. This is probably a realistic option. In this computerized age, money crosses borders easily, and the Bank of Canada could not stop Quebec from using Canadian dollars unless it restricted the dollars that people could take out of Canada – an unlikely prospect.

This is not to say that the rest of Canada will be happy about the situation. Economic analyst Frank Dabbs has noted: 'Once Quebec secedes, the national bond and the parliamentary dominance that has served Quebec's interests in Confederation will be gone. What remains of Canada may not be in the generous mood Quebec expects.'[8] The situation will be watched closely by investors, for the Canadian currency, as a reserve currency, would be greatly affected by Quebec's fiscal and trade actions. It may also be that other Canadian banks would place constraints on Quebec's freedom of action. What if a Quebec currency was excluded from the overnight cheque-clearing system used by Canadian banks? U.S. investment analyst Robert Blohm asserts that Canadian banks would not want to cover for an overnight payment failure by Quebec financial institutions.[9]

Nevertheless, there may be advantages for Canada in sharing its currency. It is profitable to provide another country's money. The Bank of Canada earns about $2.6 billion a year by printing bank notes for about two cents and selling them for about face value. Quebec accounts for about $600 million of that profit. Also, by issuing money, the Canadian government can borrow from Quebec without having to pay nominal interest on the loan, as long as Quebecers want to keep this currency. Parti Québécois leaders add that 'a common currency will simplify producer and merchant calculations, facilitate competition between local enterprises in each sector, and maintain the integration of markets.'[10] Clearly, Quebec sovereigntists want to use the Canadian dollar to facilitate their new economy's international acceptance. Moreover, Quebec companies would avoid the transaction costs of doing business with the rest of Canada if the same currency were used. This is to the advantage of Canada as well. Many of the business contacts, labour agreements, and other economic ties linking Canadian firms with Quebec would still exist after sovereignty, and a common currency would make it much easier to preserve these mutually profitable relationships. Thus, Canadian interests might be best served if Quebec retained the Canadian dollar.

What would happen to the value of the Canadian dollar with Quebec's independence? Jacques Parizeau predicts little change. Robert Bourassa disagrees. Others suggest that by using the Canadian dollar, a sovereign Quebec would live with Canada's inflation rate, and thus nothing would change. On the other hand, if outside investors sell Canadian dollars following sovereignty, the Canadian currency's foreign-exchange value would fall. In this regard, although sympathetic to the sovereignty movement, economist Pierre Fortin has acknowledged that it is a 'paradox' for sovereigntist business leaders to reject federalism because of high interest rates.

Some critics have pointed out that, if it agrees to use the Canadian currency, Quebec might also have to accept surveillance and constraints on its fiscal policy while having only a non-veto minority voice in monetary policy outcomes such as interest rates and the exchange rate of the dollar. As noted, one frequently cited model for Quebec is the European Economic Community which is trying to integrate its twelve member countries into economic and monetary union in an effort to boost Europe's international competitiveness, increase economic integration, and promote political union. To this end, the European nations are trying to coordinate budgets and economic policies, establish a European system of central banks, or Eurofed, to manage monetary policy, and create one single currency. These innovations demand that each country surrender sovereignty in the economic sphere and possibly the political sense, a decision that Great Britain, for one, has been reluctant to make. It is hard to predict if Quebec could subject its budget and debt policies to outside surveillance and discipline. Furthermore, Canada might balk at including Quebec in a common currency without some say over Quebec's economic policies. A Quebec running high budget deficits or accumulating a large public debt could jeopardize the Bank of Canada's policies and force Canadians to pay higher interest rates and face tight money.

It is ironic that Quebec sovereigntists cite Europe's move toward greater financial and economic integration as a reassuring model to follow. What they obscure is that the European countries are moving in exactly the opposite direction of what the sovereigntists want Quebec to do. The Europeans are moving from sovereignty towards confederation. They plan to establish institutions that would curb the independence of member states even more than they are curbed now. By contrast, Quebec's leaders promote a move from confederation towards sovereignty. They seek greater freedom of action for Quebec, not less.

Another problem could be competing policies. One observer cites the possibility of Canada supporting high wage settlements and rising prices, while Quebec chooses controls on prices and wages.[11] The two are obviously incompatible, and trade barriers might be necessary to prevent an unacceptable flight of money.

Ultimately, an arrangement whereby the two nations are pursuing their own fiscal priorities and macroeconomic policies may prove impractical. In addition, a deal whereby Quebec has no say over monetary policy might prove unworkable in the long run, for its political sovereignty could well be compromised.

In one notable poll, the public in Quebec and the rest of Canada agreed that if Quebec should become sovereign, it should be permitted to retain the currency of Canada.[12] In Quebec, 80 per cent of respondents agree, and 59 per cent in the rest of Canada support a shared currency. Obviously, most Canadians would favour economic stability, not recriminations, in a post-sovereignty environment. Should a sovereign Quebec not be allowed to use the Canadian dollar, however, it has been suggested that it might create its own currency and peg it to the American dollar. In this way, it might benefit from the advantages of a less inflationary economy and lower interest rates. Yet it could retain its sovereignty by having its own money, or so the argument goes. By linking its currency to the U.S. dollar, the Quebec currency would gain international confidence. Here again, the United States might object to such an argument, or the loss of monetary policy authority might prove untenable to Quebec leaders. Also, a Quebec currency pegged to the U.S. dollar might make it difficult for the remaining provinces to do business with Quebec and vice-versa, while north-south trade and capital flows would be intensified. The economic position of the rest of Canada, and the viability of its currency, might be compromised. In addition, a crisis of confidence in the Quebec currency could spark a massive outflow of funds into American securities and real estate. The idea of pegging a Quebec currency to the American dollar appears to be a non-starter. Of course, the Canadian dollar is rarely if ever allowed to exceed or fall below the value of the U.S. dollar by more than about 35 per cent.

It is clear that all of the currency options available to Quebec – creating its own currency and pegging it to the Canadian or U.S. dollar, letting its own currency float freely on international markets, using the Canadian currency, or even using the U.S. dollar – are highly problematic. None of the rosy economic scenarios of the sovereigntists appear likely.[13] Indeed, the economic arguments for Quebec's sovereignty are not persuasive, at least in the short run.

THE ECONOMIC RISKS AND CHALLENGES OF SOVEREIGNTY

In the transition period following sovereignty, Quebec stands to face severe economic challenges. These challenges would include questions concerning:

- the effects of uncertainty on every aspect of economic life in the new nation;
- the ability of Quebec to gain access to resources from the rest of Canada;
- the degree to which Quebec could trade and invest with the rest of Canada;
- angry reactions to Quebec's sovereignty within Quebec and in the rest of Canada;
- the end of transfer payments from the federal government;
- the emigration of many of Quebec's 'best and brightest' to Canada and the United States;
- difficulties in negotiating territorial and jurisdictional issues with Canada;
- a reduced standard of living in Quebec, at least in the short run;
- the mechanics of negotiating economic issues with Canada in the absence of the federal arbiter;
- potential risks to services such as portable health care guarantees;
- the diminution of Quebec's importance on the world stage, in international organizations;
- the expenses of a Quebec military, diplomatic corps, public service;
- the nervousness of international investors in the unstable investment climate during the transition period following sovereignty;
- the concern of much of Quebec's business elite about the implications of sovereignty;
- new economic institutions Quebec would have to create to stabilize its economy;
- how trade issues, including the North American Free Trade Agreement, would be negotiated;
- how north-south trade issues would be handled, as opposed to east-west ones;
- how Quebec's small and medium-sized businesses would compete given the new restrictions that they might face;
- how capital investment might be attracted to Quebec;

- how higher taxes, higher interest rates, and higher unemployment would be faced;
- how the national debt and national assets would be assessed and divided. Can Quebec and Canada meet their debt obligations satisfactorily without each other?
- whether Quebec should institute its own currency, with all the attendant risks of uncertainty, or share the Canadian currency, but have no say over monetary policy.

Perhaps this listing paints too harsh a picture. It is possible that the transition period following sovereignty might be smooth and economically stable. Many sovereigntists make just this point. It should also be noted, however, that many of these sovereigntists dismiss the studies predicting economic reversal as biased or irrelevant. They are politicians after all, with a political goal to pursue. But it is not clear that they have carefully examined the results of these studies, nor have they addressed directly some of the concerns listed at the end of this chapter.

Sovereignty is not just a romantic goal promoting political and social change. It may also have severe economic consequences that must be evaluated and prepared for. Beyond this, the uncertainty of sovereignty, and the questions that accompany this uncertainty, give one pause about the sovereignty goal itself. Is sovereignty worth the economic pain that might ensue? It is a question that Quebecers will have to answer for themselves. But it is absolutely vital that they have as much information as possible so that they can make an informed choice.

9

The U.S. View of Post-Sovereignty Quebec–U.S. Relations

The constitutional crisis in Canada has not gone unnoticed by the U.S. government, because the United States has substantial economic and political interests in the future stability of Quebec and Canada. American political leaders have been explicit in their support for an intact Canada, and they worry about the uncertainty that sovereignty could promote. Indeed, the State Department, the National Security Council, and the Central Intelligence Agency (CIA)[1] have filed reports on Canada's linguistic divisions since 1961, and even before.[2] Every U.S. president, without exception, has favoured a strong, united Canada. An independent Quebec would probably be a good, stable ally, but a united Canada is a known commodity that is clearly perceived to be in the U.S. national interest. The United States would not take any action to encourage Quebec's sovereignty. At the same time, American officials have made clear that the United States will not interfere in Canada's internal affairs.

Non-interference implies that the United States favours a strong and united Canada, but it is not expected to promote it overtly. U.S. armed forces would not invade Quebec, nor would it impose economic sanctions on the province. The United States would watch the situation closely and do nothing, at least until sovereignty was attained by Quebec. Furthermore, American officials would not hesitate from working amicably with a sovereign Quebec, should it emerge.

In addition, the United States would be expected to provide whatever non-military support Canada asked for, as long as it was clear that Canadian officials had done the asking and the United States was not intruding where it was not wanted. As part of this policy, the United States has always notified Canadian diplomats of requests by Canadian provincial representatives to discuss policy questions with U.S. diplomats, so that the Canadian government can supervise such contacts.

The United States would not interfere for several reasons. First, it would be inappropriate and wrong for it to interfere in the internal affairs of any democratic nation, and particularly its closest ally. In addition, no matter what action it might take, that action would be regarded, at the very least, as an irritant by Quebec and Canadian officials. The United States has no interest in becoming an issue itself. In fact, the U.S. position has been widely respected by both Canadian federalists and Quebec sovereigntists thus far, specifically because the U.S. government has said so little about the issue. It should also be noted that there does not yet exist a long-term U.S. policy regarding a sovereign Quebec, nor is there likely to be one until the event occurs, if indeed it does. American officials will respond only when a crisis emerges. There are no long-term scenarios for U.S. action in the event of Quebec's sovereignty.

An important point to keep in mind, however, is that there is not yet a widespread perception in Washington that U.S. interests would be so adversely affected by Quebec's sovereignty as to warrant subtle (or not-so-subtle) intervention. Nor is this likely to change. But if it does, if the threat of sovereignty were somehow to have devastating economic implications or strategic costs for the United States, then American officials would undoubtedly rethink their position. Again, the chances of this are remote, but they cannot be ruled out completely.

But there is something more. Some American officials believe that the sovereignty issue is 'unresolvable' and will be 'a permanent and salient feature of Canadian culture and politics.'[3] Although American officials are generally pleased that the U.S. priorities in the binational relationship – most notably, trade, environmental concerns, security arrangements, drug interdiction, the Fulbright educational exchange, and political concerns – are being addressed effectively, they remain concerned the sovereignty issue will not go away and must be an ongoing consideration.

Many American politicians and public servants follow major events in Canada and in Quebec closely. In fact, more government officials in Washington devote attention to Canada than to any other single country, including the former Soviet Union. The State Department has formed a monthly luncheon group to discuss U.S.–Canada (and particularly Quebec) issues. Until 1993, there was a deputy assistant secretary of state focused just on Canada, the only single country to have such a monitor. Because of budget cutbacks, that position no longer exists. But the office of Canada and the Canada desk remain prominent within the Department of State. There is also an office of Canada in the Commerce Department. Powerful American political leaders like Senators George Mitchell and Edward Kennedy, New York Governor Mario Cuomo, and former presidential adviser John Sununu are much more knowledgeable about Canada than were their predecessors. In fact, Senator Daniel Patrick Moynihan is on record in July 1990 as stating that, if Quebec were to become independent, it would remain a part of the free trade agreement. Minnesota Congressman James Oberstar declared in March 1994 that the United States would quickly recognize an independent Quebec if a sovereignty referendum passed. It is worth noting that in June 1990 the *New York Times* reported that classified State Department and CIA studies still point to the security, trade, and environmental disruptions that Quebec's independence would bring. There is a recognition in the reports that there is no threat to U.S. interests, however.

This being said, declassified U.S. government documents reveal that the U.S. government has harboured serious doubts about Canada's viability without Quebec. Because of its concerns about Canada's constitutional strife, in 1977 the State Department evaluated the likely scenarios in Quebec, including sovereignty, sovereignty-association, and maintenance of the status quo. The status quo was seen as preferable to any other option, but a settlement on the basis of a special status for Quebec would be better than Canada's dissolution.

Jean-François Lisée's *In the Eye of the Eagle* brilliantly discusses the extent to which U.S. government authorities have watched Canada throughout its history.[4] One ongoing theme of Lisée's book is that an independent Quebec would be a nuisance for the United States, but the latter is nothing if not pragmatic and would work with whatever nations emerged north of the border. Lisée shows how the U.S. State Department has been well aware of the implications of the devolution of powers to the provinces, a special status for Quebec, and the angry reactions that could emerge in the rest of Canada. The author also stresses, however, that there is no evidence of U.S. involvement in Canadian internal affairs.

The U.S. State Department does anticipate some problems if Canada grows more decentralized. According to high-level sources, it might be harder for the United States to negotiate with a peripheralized Canada promoting conflicting policies. In addition, there is the possibility that a Canadian prime minister could use the United States as a 'whipping boy' in an effort to build national unity. In the period following sovereignty, should it occur, U.S. interest will be focused more on Canada than on the new Quebec nation. Canada is more important in the long run. Mexico will become more important to the United States than would Quebec. Indeed, Quebec would not be a major player in world affairs. However, it was emphasized repeatedly by those interviewed for this volume that the United States would not intervene, although it favours a strong united Canada, and that it would work with a sovereign Quebec if it emerges.

It should also be stressed that U.S. officials are not convinced that Quebec will become independent. In a July 1990 speech, then U.S. ambassador Edward Ney predicted that Canada would survive: 'The failure we have just witnessed (of Meech Lake) was not that of a nation, but only of a constitutional proposal.'[5] Former president George Bush had made it clear that he had no interest in meddling in Canada's domestic politics. 'This is not a point at which the U.S. ought to involve itself in the internal affairs of Canada.'[6] Bush had also been quoted as stating that the United States is 'very, very happy with one unified Canada.'[7] President Clinton's national security adviser, Anthony Lake, has said that he was 'optimistic' that Quebec would not become sovereign.

During the last few decades, an ongoing concern in Quebec was whether the United States might try to prevent Quebec from attaining political independence. Sovereignty proponents pointed to the examples of Chile in 1973 or Greece in the late 1960s for evidence of U.S. involvement in the internal affairs of sovereign nations. Jean-François Lisée makes clear, however, that the United States has no such ambitions in Quebec. He reports that the United States might not demonstrate any support for Quebec independence – a surprise to René Lévesque and other separatist leaders who guessed that the United States would equate their movement with the positive experience of the U.S. revolutionary war – but the United States would not hinder the movement either.

Some American observers assert that Quebec's sovereignty movement is a threat to the United States because Quebecers now regard themselves as a 'nation' or a 'people' rather than just a constituent unit of Canada. Although this is not a widely held view in the United States, there is some fear that Spanish-speakers concentrated in the southwest and far west might demand similar nationhood. Certainly this is a position articulated and promoted by U.S. English, a well-heeled interest group which has helped to pass English-only official language legislation in eighteen U.S. states. They have had no success on the national level, however.[8]

U.S. policy is to not officially recognize any sub-units of nations.[9] Rather, it respects the territorial integrity of all countries (or of all allies). As a result, the United States does not officially support secessionist movements in India's Punjab, nor would it play an overt role in Canada's internal challenge. Canada is not regarded as a special case, at least in official terms.

In practice and as noted above, the United States has long maintained that an independent Quebec would be a viable country and a good neighbour. It acknowledges that Quebec would likely support all of Canada's existing defence and economic commitments and remain a staunch supporter of American policies in a broad sense. The most pertinent reason for U.S. opposition to Quebec's sovereignty, then, has less to do with Quebec per se and more to do with the fractionalization of Canada that could result. Other provinces might pursue independence, or at least greater autonomy, and this would result in confusion about policies and difficult international negotiations. Should there be only a restructured, more decentralized federation including Quebec, the United States might still have to deal with one or more strong provinces able to block treaties between Canada and the United States – a power that is specifically discussed in the Canadian constitution. It is also possible that Canadian 'navel-gazing' over its internal problems might distract its attention from important bilateral issues. Trade, energy, environment, fishing, and other issues may be put on the back-burner until Canada overcomes its constitutional problems.

The sovereignty of Quebec would have dramatic implications for Quebec–Canada–U.S. relations, according to the American Law Institute's restatement of the Foreign Relations Law of the United States, 14 May 1986, section 210(3).

When part of a state becomes a new state, the new state does not succeed to the international agreements to which the predecessor state was party, unless, expressly or by implication, it accepts such arguments and the other party or parties thereto agree or acquiesce.[10]

Of course, it is in Quebec's interest to maintain close and amicable relations with the United States, since such a relationship would contribute to economic and political stability. Since most francophone Quebecers are favourably disposed to the United States, this is a likely scenario.

At this time, U.S. officials have reserved judgment on how to respond to the consequences of a sovereign Quebec. It is not clear if they would pursue a free trade agreement with Quebec with the same criteria that exist between Canada and the United States. Nor has the United States decided how it would respond to any boundary disputes between Quebec and Canada or between Canada, Quebec, and the United States. As with so much else in American political life, American policies towards Canada and Quebec will depend, at least in part, on how effective Canada, Quebec, and the other provinces are as lobbyists in Washington. In this regard, the lobbying techniques employed by Canada's native people in Washington might be instructive. The Cree of Northern Quebec are engaged in a boundary dispute with the Quebec government and fear the implications of an officially French language law on their predominantly English-speaking population. The Cree also worry about access to mineral rights and claims they hold over the land situated near the James Bay hydroelectric project. Their grievances must be taken seriously, and the United Nations has demonstrated some support for their plight. What is particularly interesting for our purposes, however, is that they have brilliantly lobbied the U.S. Congress, U.S. executive branch agencies, the media, and the public. By contrast, the Mohawks, whose grievances might be as legitimate as the Cree, have little money or know-how about the ways of Washington. They have relied on legal proceedings or on the efforts of the Canadian Embassy to make their case. In Washington, almost no one knows who they are, and their successes have been few.

As of 1994, the government of Quebec had not been as successful as it might have been in Washington. Although Quebec maintains government offices in several American cities, it has had trouble getting a hearing from the players that matter on political issues. Of course, the Canadian Embassy acts as a check on some of the activities of the Quebec government in the United States. Nevertheless, Quebec officials have made serious mistakes. For example, officials in the United States of provincially owned Hydro-Québec do not seem to receive the support that they should from Quebec government officials, particularly if a hydroelectricity sale encounters problems. There was at one time an obvious rivalry between officials of the Quebec government and officials of Hydro-Québec posted in the United States and it may still exist. Although hydroelectricity is only Quebec's eighth most important export, following paper products, aluminium, cars, airplane motors and parts, electronic parts and semi-conductors, and various wood products, electricity has become the tangible personification of Quebec's economic self-sufficiency. Its inability to conclude a massive sale with New York state in 1992 and then again in 1994 were both a symbolic blow to Quebec's pride and a modest economic hardship. In the recent past, rather than reassuring American officials about the future of Quebec–U.S. relations, Quebec representatives often unnerved, or at least concerned, the Americans. Nevertheless, since 1992 the delegate general, Reed Scowen, has been a calming influence. With new personalities in place, the problems of the past may no longer be so acute.[11]

ANNEXATION BY THE UNITED STATES

A number of senior Canadian officials have speculated that Quebec's sovereignty would lead to U.S. annexation of all or part of Canada. Obviously, this is an extremely controversial position. Former Canadian ambassador to the United States Allan Gottlieb has warned that the decentralization of Canada would lead inevitably to U.S. annexation because a decentralized Canada would not have the leverage it needs to trade with the United States and other parts of the world. Liberal Prime Minister Jean Chrétien maintained when he was in opposition that Quebec's separation would be an invitation for the rest of Canada to join the United States. In other words, Chrétien believes that, if Quebec were to separate, Canada would disintegrate and ultimately subsume itself into another nation.

If annexation were to occur, Quebec would be faced with a dilemma: Stay out of the new continental union and risk economic oblivion, or join and face cultural oblivion.[12] If the rest of Canada joined the United States, Quebec's importance would sharply diminish.

A few American newspaper columnists, most notably Patrick Buchanan, have speculated about annexing all or part of Canada. Buchanan has gone so far as to talk to Parti Québécois leaders about the prospect. This latter-day example of Manifest Destiny is attractive to many Americans because of the goodwill they feel towards Canada and the vast storehouse of natural resources in Canada that would be most welcome additions to U.S. industrial strength. Some provinces, especially British Columbia, Alberta, and Ontario, might be particularly attractive to U.S. annexationists. (Atlantic Canada might not be so welcome.) Presumably, the United States would then enjoy an economic boom and be better able to compete with its economic rivals. It is unlikely that Canadians would go along with this idea, of course. Indeed, there is no strong effort in Canada to promote annexation of one or more provinces by the United States. This does not indicate an anti-American bias in Canada, but a realization that Canada is a different country with its own system of laws, cultural attitudes, and history. This attitude has been held since the United Empire Loyalists fled the United States and its repugnant (to them) system of republican government. Free market or laissez-faire policies did not frighten those new Canadians, nor did the British crown and the parliamentary system. The separation of powers was anathema to them, however.

To this day, most Canadians would reject the division-of-powers model which has been so successful, but so specific, in the United States. This has been demonstrated in a Gallup Canada poll which revealed that only 13 per cent of Canadian adults favoured joining the United States. In British Columbia, 86 per cent said that they did not want their province to become a state, a clear rebuff to those Americans who would dearly love to add prosperous provinces like British Columbia or Alberta to their nation.[13] An Angus Reid poll published in February 1991 also showed little support for annexation. In that survey only 4 per cent of Canadians were interested in economic union with the United States, including less than 10 per cent of Canadians in western Canada. A subsequent poll published in January 1993 revealed that only 20 per cent of Canadians favoured annexation.[14] One survey after another demonstrates limited support for integration into the United States. On the other hand, according to one poll, as many as 37 per cent of Canadians believe that Canada will become a part of the United States within the next 50 years.[15] They see this as inevitable, even if the vast majority of Canadians do not now favour this option. However, this may have been a reflection of anti-Mulroney feeling.

A decision not to join the United States does not necessarily imply that most Canadians' first allegiance is to the federal government. Until the late 1980s, a number of surveys had indicated that their first tie is to their province, not Ottawa.[16] Exceptions usually included residents of southern Ontario and English-speaking Quebec, although even in Ontario there have been substantial declines in the numbers who identify themselves as Canadian in the last five years.[17] This strong provincial allegiance gave the Canadian provinces more discretionary authority than any other federal constituent units in the world, with the possible exceptions of the Swiss cantons. To be fair, the Spicer Commission called the findings of these surveys into question, and by 1993 and 1994 surveys began to reveal that Canadians outside Quebec were now first Canadians and only secondly provincial residents.[18] Quebecers still considered themselves Quebecers first, however.

Over the last few years, the American press has been fairly sympathetic to the Quebec independence movement. The *Washington Post, New York Times, Wall Street Journal, Business Week,* and *Time,* among other publications, have published editorials supporting the will of the Quebec electorate and acknowledging that the United States can live with an independent Quebec, if necessary. However, there is no evidence beyond the musings of a few newspaper columnists that the United States would necessarily welcome the addition of new U.S. states at this time. Indeed, the addition of new states could upset the Republican-Democratic state balance, or could significantly alter the politics of race or ethnicity. Could provinces run by the New Democratic Party easily meld into the U.S. system? The political structure of the new states would have to change to accommodate the U.S. system of separation of powers. It may be that the United States is fixed at fifty states with no particular interest in adding more, particularly if these additions could themselves threaten American national harmony.

There is another related point. Puerto Rico, Guam, and the District of Columbia all have statehood movements. Their accession to statehood would likely precede any former Canadian provinces. As a result, the former provinces might be in the awkward position of being U.S. protectorates, territories, commonwealths, or some equivalent, but not immediately states, resulting in less effective representation in the Congress and a reduced say in national public policy making. Even if a province were to become a state, its influence would be diminished within a larger federation. A new state would only have two senators among many. Given the different U.S. federal-constituent relationship, a new state would have to give up many of the constitutional powers that it had as a Canadian province. Canadian provinces have more of a constitutional jurisdiction than virtually any other federation. Presumably much of this would be lost in the more centralized U.S. federation.

Misleading and silly commentaries on Canada's problems have been published in the U.S. press. These stories misinform the reader, but their circulation is widespread and therefore cannot be ignored. One of the more ridiculous articles appeared in *U.S.A. Today* and was authored by founder Al Neuharth. He compared the Quebec situation to the 'rebelmania' (his quotes) in eastern Europe, asserted that a divided Canada could not compete effectively, and suggested that both official language groups 'respect each other's motherland slogan or anthem of "Vive la France" and "God Save the Queen."'[19] This ridiculous diatribe is worth noting only because millions of Americans read such nonsense. Similarly, prior to the 26 October 1992 referendum, the *Baltimore Sun* commented: 'If Canadians don't adopt some constitution soon, no one outside of Canada will understand or sympathize.' Of course, Canada would have had a constitution, no matter the referendum result.

Of particular interest is the extent to which Canadians care about what the American press are writing about them. The Canadian press write stories about what the American newspapers are printing, and they put these American views on the front page. As is usually the case, Canadians fail to realize (a) that the attention span of the American press towards almost anything involving Canada is notoriously limited, and (b) that Canada is but one of many nations with which the United States has important interests (the opposite is not the case of course). Unless there is a direct threat to the U.S. national interest, an unlikely prospect at best, the United States will respond pragmatically to whatever nation or nations emerge north of the border. To reiterate, however, there is virtually no chance that the United States would interfere in Canada's internal affairs. Former U.S. ambassador Ney has asserted: 'There's no takeover mentality. No one should believe there are bogeymen south of the border just waiting to scoop up this or that.'[20]

The Quebec press frequently complain that their American counterparts are too sympathetic to the anglophone minority. The French-language service of the Canadian Press News Service has bemoaned the fact that the American press present the English-speaking community of Quebec as a victim, deprived of its rights to freedom of expression by being forbidden commercial signs in English. Quebecers are extremely sensitive to the image of the province presented in the United States. Almost every unflattering article about Quebec in the U.S. press causes a flap in political and journalistic circles in Quebec.[21]

Only a small minority of the American public has devoted any but the most limited attention to Canada's constitutional plight. There is little empirical evidence of how the American public may regard Canadian political issues since it is assumed they know little about them. One recent exception, however, is a May 1992 poll which revealed that 35 per cent of the sample agreed that 'the French-speaking population in Canada has a unique culture which makes it a distinct society in North America.' In addition, 47 per cent indicated that they would be unmoved by Quebec's leaving Canada to become an independent country. Forty-two per cent said they would be more saddened than pleased about such an eventuality, and 5 per cent answered they would be happy about the dissolution of Canada. Perhaps most telling was the finding that 53 per cent of Americans perceived the relationship between Canada's two European founding peoples as generally harmonious and only 47 per cent were aware of the possibility of Quebec leaving the Canadian federation.[22]

In addition, 76 per cent of the respondents thought that if a majority of Quebecers voted for sovereignty, the U.S. government should not intervene in any way. Fourteen per cent wanted the American government to try to keep Quebec within Canada, and 4 per cent wanted the United States to promote Quebec's sovereignty.

In another survey of western U.S. élite perceptions of the Canadian constitutional crisis, the findings revealed that 45 per cent of the sample believed that Quebec had no right to separate from Canada.[23] Thirty per cent felt it did. On the normative question of whether Quebec *should* be a separate country, only 4 per cent agreed, and 77 per cent disagreed. Most of the sample believed that the United States should not help or hinder the process if Quebec were to separate. But 56 per cent did agree that Quebec–U.S. relations would worsen post-sovereignty. Fifty-three per cent also believed that economic ties would be weakened. It should be stressed, however, that these surveys represent the views of an élite western sample. Most Americans know little about the situation. Their views, of course, are likely to be shaped by these élites.

QUEBEC SOVEREIGNTY, THE CANADA–U.S. FTA AND NAFTA

In large part, Quebec's future prosperity is dependent on its trade with the United States. Quebec's sales to the United States amount to over $20 billion a year. Quebec's total gross domestic product is $150 billion. Each Quebec worker produces, on average, $6000 worth of goods and services for the American market each year. Over 75 per cent of Quebec's exports go to the United States, and exports to New York state alone are greater than those to France, England, Belgium, Holland, and Italy combined.

U.S. government officials are intensely aware of the possible implications of Quebec's sovereignty for the Canada–U.S. Free Trade Agreement (FTA). In fact, as Sheldon Gordon of the *New York Times* asserts, 'any fragmentation of Canada would, at the very least, complicate the U.S. security and commercial links with its nearest ally and most important trade partner.'[24] There are 170 bilateral treaties between Canada and the United States. Existing environmental protection agreements, law enforcement regulations and cooperation, and transportation and communications ties may all have to be reversed to accommodate the new situation. In fact, it is not outside the realm of possibility that the United States, faced with difficult issues such as how to incorporate Quebec into NORAD and how to retain friendly political relations with Canada as a whole (including access to its natural resources), would choose not to include Quebec in the free trade agreement. Even if it did, the tax write-offs and capitalization policies that have been used to assist the francophone business community may well be seen by the U.S. government as unfair subsidies. In fact, given the difficulties Canada has already experienced with the United States over pork and other commodities, such quarrels seem inevitable.[25] How an independent Quebec would figure in North American Free Trade Agreement is unclear.

On the other hand, the American business community might support the entry of a sovereign Quebec into the NAFTA. In 1990 leading business barometer, *Business Week*, called for:

A framework that would allow Quebec to seek its own course, accommodate the rest of Canada, and foster the latest initiative for freer trade between the U.S. and Mexico. Right now, the flow of trade and investment across the Canadian and Mexican borders is exploding, but the creation of a North American community is taking place piecemeal. President Bush seems to be taking the first steps, in recognizing the need for a broad free-trade zone, eventually encompassing the whole Western Hemisphere. The specter of balkanization must not haunt the Americas.[26]

U.S. trade with Quebec is substantial. It accounts for one-half of all current U.S.–Mexico trade. It compares to the volume of U.S. trade with France or Italy. It is twice the trade that exists between the U.S. and Brazil and is nine times greater than that between the United States and Chile, the likely next partner to NAFTA.

If Quebec becomes independent, it will want to remain a partner in the existing free trade agreement between Canada and the United States. It remains to be seen, however, how effective a divided or balkanized Canada can be as a trading partner compared to a united Canada. It is in the U.S. interest to have a strong and united Canada in order to address together the increased competition that the North American trading partners confront worldwide.

However, the Canada–U.S. FTA has weakened the economic incentives for the provinces to remain in Canada. With the far broader U.S. market open to the provinces, they no longer need a guaranteed position in the much smaller Canadian market. The free trade agreement gave many Quebec businesses the confidence that they could make it alone. For many of the Quebec corporate élite, the fear of independence has eroded.

Nevertheless, if the economic downturn continues, if Quebec hydroelectricity or paper sales decline, if the manufacturing sector diminishes, or if existing economic safety nets prove unreliable, then confidence in the prospect of an independent Quebec will likely decline. Of course, the United States would almost certainly pursue a free trade agreement with Quebec. However, U.S.– Quebec negotiations might reflect the changed economic conditions at the time, placing the United States in a position of great strength. Quebec would need a free trade agreement far more than the United States. All of the existing provisions of the Canada–U.S. deal might not apply in a subsequent Quebec–U.S. deal, but Quebec would have to accept the provisions set by the United States.

Parti Québécois leader Jacques Parizeau has asserted that a sovereign Quebec would be prepared to retain all of the economic arrangements with Canada and the United States that now exist. Parizeau believes that a free flow of goods, services, capital, and perhaps labour is likely to be maintained between a sovereign Quebec and Canada. In fact, he asserts that the free trade agreement would require only minor modifications, such as representation for Quebec on affected commissions and tribunals. Furthermore, Parizeau has predicted that with sovereignty, Quebec businesses would be prepared to deal with their customers in their own language, including English, since the French language would no longer be threatened in Quebec. Language laws could be relaxed, and trade in turn would be enhanced.[27] Parizeau has since backtracked on this position and is now uncertain about the extent to which language laws would be relaxed after sovereignty is achieved. This is important, however. At present, less than one-half of 1 per cent of all American goods are sold to Quebec. The United States supplies bilingual labelling on their exported goods to satisfy Canada's national requirements. However, the costs of shipping products unilingually labelled in French would be prohibitive for such a small market.

There is an irony here that is worth noting briefly. Most nationalist Quebecers who favour a free trade agreement with the United States see no threat to their distinctive language and culture. Quebec is arguably the most pro–free trade province. Quebecers support the deal for its perceived economic advantages and because of the international legitimacy that would be accorded a sovereign Quebec that is part of a trade deal.

However, U.S. culture and its English language are not a threat because Quebec is French-speaking which provides a linguistic shelter. By contrast, English-speaking Ontario is a perceived threat. It may be true that the U.S. language and culture will not threaten the French language, but the issue should not be dismissed out of hand. In fact, one could argue that some provisions of the French-language charter could be ruled unfair trading practices.

Another reason why Quebec might be a stronger supporter of freer trade than Ontario is that a higher proportion of Ontario-based companies are branch plants of U.S. parent corporations. Ontario firms can more easily leave the province under NAFTA and this situation poses risks to Ontario of downward wage pressure, job loss, and investment diversion. By contrast, Quebec companies are more likely to be Quebec- or Canadian-owned.

Pierre Fortin of the Université du Québec à Montréal agrees that it would serve the United States' best commercial and strategic interests to retain the free trade agreement with a sovereign Quebec. He asserts that U.S.–Quebec trade is comparable in magnitude to U.S. trade with Japan, but without the hidden non-tariff barriers that exist in the latter case. Fortin also has made the point that Quebec is more receptive than is the Canadian federal government to U.S. direct investment.[28]

It might be the case that the United States would welcome a sovereign Quebec into NAFTA under existing conditions. The United States values Quebec as an economic ally. It puts a high priority on preserving economic stability no matter what political changes occur in Canada. It is certainly a convenience to have the same tariff rules apply throughout North America. To renegotiate the FTA with a sovereign Quebec under different terms than with Canada could be difficult. For example, the existing transportation agreements were negotiated carefully, and accommodation was not easily reached. Renegotiating this aspect might be long and costly.

Nevertheless, if Quebec were to enter into free trade negotiations with the United States, it might face serious obstacles. First, an angry and vengeful rest of Canada might hinder the talks. Also, the U.S. negotiators are expert at their task and could be expected to take whatever advantage becomes available. They might be sympathetic to Quebec's plight, but this would not affect their policy-making strategies. Since Quebec would want a deal more than the United States, and since Quebec is a tiny trading partner, it would be vulnerable. In addition, former Canadian free trade negotiator Simon Reisman has suggested that negotiating with Quebec might not be the United States' first priority; concluding a deal with Chile and Brazil might come first.[29]

Professor Thomas Courchene of Queen's University adds that Quebec would lose the free ride it gets as a province in FTA negotiations with the United States. As a province, it works within the larger, more powerful Canada to promote its interests. Without Canada, it might face increased U.S. pressure over the environmental impact of the massive James Bay Phase II power project, subsidized electricity exports to the United States, and the way Quebec regulates financial institutions.[30]

Real-world problems that might emerge include how the trading partners might deal with countervailing duties. How many panels would have to be set up? The existing structure provides for only three. This issue is probably a manageable one, but it is a nuisance nevertheless.

There could be another problem. The North American Free Trade Agreement, unlike the free trade agreement, has docking procedures. The founding members to the agreement can reject a new member. Accession to NAFTA is dependent on economic performance, compatibility, and economic principles. Jacques Parizeau maintains that Quebec has nothing to fear since Quebec's economy is completely integrated with its North American partners.[31] But Parizeau wants Chile to be the first new partner, ahead of Quebec, because the docking criterion is new and he does not want Quebec to be the test case of the three conditions. He also fears that a vengeful Canada could stall Quebec's entry into North American Free Trade Agreement. This may be a legitimate fear.[32]

FTA negotiations between the United States, Quebec, and Canada might be difficult. The United States would likely demand that Quebec change certain of its policies. The Congress is in an angry mood, and individual members of Congress with grievances against Quebec could raise these issues when the subject of a new trade deal is discussed. An FTA with Quebec would require legislation in the U.S. Congress since it would not be covered by the current fast-track authorization.

A sovereign Quebec would support a comprehensive free trade agreement with Canada, the United States, and Mexico. But Quebec's absence from the Canadian federation could leave a Canada divided by anti–free trade interests in Ontario, where the New Democratic Party government is on record as opposing NAFTA, and a pro–free trade Alberta and likely British Columbia. (notwithstanding its NDP government). There is no guarantee that a future Canadian government post-sovereignty would agree to participate in NAFTA. This would badly aggravate existing regional tensions in Canada. It could also force tariff barriers to rise between Canada and Quebec.

Even if Canada remains part of a free trade agreement, both it and Quebec will be smaller economic players. Small governments are more efficient, but they tend to be underfinanced. They are more responsive to majority will, but less responsive to minorities. Small governments are generally less effective in promoting their interests within the world community, unless they are sophisticated and urbanized countries like the Netherlands. A smaller Quebec would have less leverage with the United States in any free trade deal than it would if it had remained a part of Canada.

There is another potential problem. Washington would not be likely to pursue free trade negotiations with Quebec if Ottawa frowned upon it. The United States would not want to jeopardize the more vital U.S.–Canada relationship. In fact, Bloc Québécois leader Lucien Bouchard has speculated that an independent Quebec might have to rely on a friendly U.S. government to keep other provinces from trying to punish it by cutting trade links. He has stated that 'the Americans would not let any Canadian province close its borders.'[33] With all due respect to Mr Bouchard, this is preposterous. On the other hand, if a sovereign Quebec could build friendly ties with Canada, then the United States would probably look upon a Canada–Quebec–U.S. deal more favourably. The United States recognizes that U.S.–Quebec trade tensions would be experienced only at the margin. Furthermore, a U.S.–Canada–Quebec–Mexico trade coalition might offer expanded trade options. This is an optimistic view, of course.

In fact, it is not clear that the rest of Canada would 'play along,' at least in the short run. The accession clause in the North American Free Trade Agreement makes clear that the United States, Mexico, and Canada all have a veto on other countries that wish to join. Also, the NAFTA accession clause makes it clear that the admission of other countries would be only on terms and conditions required by the United States, Mexico, and Canada, and any other countries who join the agreement in the interim. As noted earlier, this puts Quebec's array of subsidized industries at risk. In short, Quebec would have to clear the same hurdles as Chile or any new entrant into the NAFTA.

In addition, trade deals impose costs on the weaker partner, as Canada has discovered with the United States. In fact, if Quebec becomes sovereign, its population of 6.8 million would have less clout than it had as a province in a country with 26.8 million people. In addition, Quebec has a distinctive system of cooperation in provincial investment between government, business, and financial institution. It is a system of industrial organization that would be antithetical to the United States and would thus face enormous pressures to change. More specifically, Quebec's programs of subsidizing certain industries, which were acceptable to the United States so long as Quebec was a province, might not be tolerated if Quebec becomes an independent nation-state pursuing a free trade agreement. Quebec protects various industries, such as wine, liquor, dairy products, film, and the United States might demand an end to these subsidies. Frequent U.S. trade complaints could stymie free trade negotiations. Quebec's government-controlled agencies like Hydro-Québec or the Caisse de dépôt et placement du Québec, or financial institutions like the Mouvement Desjardins, which exert enormous control on the provincial economy, would face U.S. pressure. In fact, a week before the Charlottetown referendum the U.S. International Trade Commission's annual report on U.S. trade agreements referred to Quebec's subsidies as potentially problematic. The ITC subsequently declared that a sovereign Quebec would need to gain the Congress' approval before joining the FTA or NAFTA. If the United States believes that there is too much government influence in the Quebec economy, then it might argue that Quebec companies are receiving an unfair advantage in terms of competitiveness and trade. This might lead to a plethora of U.S. countervail cases. The existing FTA gained some protection for subsidized companies by offering concessions in other areas.

As former U.S. deputy chief negotiator of the FTA William Merkin has noted: 'There wasn't as much attention paid to any one particular province as there would be if Quebec came to the U.S. as its own country ... issues Quebec didn't have to address in the basic agreement would suddenly come to the front ...'[33]

One result might be that Quebec's financial institutions might be made subject to takeover by U.S. financial firms; or the Caisse de dépôt et placement du Québec might be prevented from subsidizing Quebec business; or Quebec might decide that the economic costs of an FTA outweigh the potential benefits; or Hydro-Québec might be prohibited from offering extremely attractive prices to attract investment. (It has recently been found to have secret contacts with thirteen multinational corporations to provide them with power at rates far below the production costs. Indeed, it is not clear that Hydro-Québec's proposed Great Whale Project would go ahead if the company were not selling its power at subsidized rates.) The United States might target issues related to Quebec's procurement procedures, or its financial services industry, or its industrial subsidies or import quotas. The United States might demand that Quebec treat imported goods as favourably as its own and dismantle existing barriers against the goods and services from the rest of Canada.

As of the present, the U.S. government has not decided what it would do with regard to a free trade agreement with a potentially sovereign Quebec. Nor have U.S. officials decided if they will announce to the press that they have made no decisions regarding future Quebec–U.S. relations, thereby contradicting the Parizeau position that the United States will trade with a sovereign Quebec, if it comes to that. What is clear is that there is great uncertainty in this aspect of future economic relations after sovereignty, as in most other aspects of the political and economic relations between the United States, Canada, and a sovereign Quebec.[34]

There is another point which cannot bode well for sovereigntists in Quebec. Since 1991, the U.S. trade representative branch of the Department of Commerce has become much more aggressive in pursuing perceived violations of U.S. trade law and GATT regulations. In particular, it has begun to go after subunits of other governments that are perceived to be in violation of GATT rulings. In 1992, the U.S. trade representative retaliated against the province of Ontario for its apparent failure to comply with GATT rules concerning beer prices. From a U.S. government perspective, the Canadian federal government was perceived as unable to rectify the situation and the U.S. government had to act in the national interest. Similarly, U.S. government officials are concerned that some provinces will not enforce GATT rules concerning standards on, for example, pharmaceutical-testing labs. The Canadian government appears unwilling to act and U.S. officials signal that they might be forced to. The U.S. trade representative has always been within its rights to penalize a subunit of government in violation of GATT rules. Now, however, they face strong domestic pressures to act upon their grievances.

Another related case concerned Quebec's subsidization of magnesium products. In interviews, U.S. officials revealed that they might not support a sovereign Quebec's accession to NAFTA if such subsidies continue. Quebec officials respond that they are already dismantling many of their subsidies, no matter the political future. There is truth to this, but U.S. officials are wary of the slow pace of this process. Of course, magnesium is not the only industry at issue. Hydroelectricity, agriculture, and government procurement procedures are also of concern to U.S. officials. Taken together, Quebec's efforts to subsidize certain industries resemble, for several U.S. government officials interviewed, a managed economy not unlike Japan's MITI. This may or may not be an impediment to Quebec's accession to NAFTA. It is an issue that should be taken very seriously by sovereigntists.

U.S. government officials stress that they do not know what the implications of sovereignty will be for the United States. The Quebec–U.S. relationship is intertwined and the uncoupling of the Canada–Quebec tie would have unforseen consequences for the U.S. There is enormous relief, however, that both Canada and Quebec are friendly to the U.S. and not disposed to harm its interests postsovereignty.

U.S. officials, like their counterparts in other parts of the world, express real concern that sovereignty is even a possibility in such a democratic and prosperous nation. One lamented that if Canada can fragment, what hope does a struggling, fledgling, ethnically divided nation like Russia have? What prospects does any divided society have? Nevertheless, although government officials are very concerned about the potential for sovereignty, they assiduously avoid the 'what if' game. They are 'firefighters' who deal with crises only when they present themselves. They cannot afford to devise long-term scenarios which will inevitably be wrong.

During the George Bush presidency, Canada had a fairly high profile within the U.S. government bureaucracy. George Bush and Brian Mulroney had a warm personal relationship, and along with the shared interests of the two nations, the personal relationship helped smooth potential problems and promoted government-to-government cooperation. It would not be an exaggeration to suggest that the administration was predisposed to be positive towards Canada. Within the bureaucracy, the State Department might have been most pro-Canada. The U.S. trade representative and Department of Commerce were most likely, within the bureaucracy, to challenge Canadian interests. The National Security Council (NSC), reporting directly to the president, occupied the middle ground but had the ear of the president. The influence of the NSC might have been most obvious when it advised President Bush to allow a memorandum of understanding with Canada on the contentious softwood lumber issue. The trade representative did not support this action but was overruled. How various constituencies within the Washington bureaucracy will perceive Canada–U.S. relations during the Clinton presidency remains to be seen.

10

Where Is the Peaceable Kingdom Headed?

Canada's constitutional problems remain unresolved. At present, it appears that Quebec will attain a greater degree of autonomy and possibly full independence. Quebec's sovereignty, if it occurs, might well have some short-term negative economic consequences, but both Quebec and Canada would remain politically democratic, culturally vital, and economically prosperous, and both would retain two of the highest living standards in the world.

Both nations would go to great lengths to ensure that they can provide an attractive environment for trade and investment. Both nations would continue to respect all of their international obligations. Both would remain among the most progressive and dynamic societies in the world. In addition, Canada might serve as a model to other nations struggling to accommodate diverse groups while ensuring a satisfactory level of national unity. Some observers suggest that a Canadian 'superstructure' or sovereignty-association might provide an example to fractured federations such as the former Soviet Union and Yugoslavia.[1] Indeed, some have suggested that the 'Commonwealth of Independent States,' which emerged from the old Soviet Union, might be a step towards sovereignty-association. Here again, however, the comparison cannot be carried too far. Those nations face conditions that are unique to their situations, and no complete application of a Canadian-style system would be appropriate. Tinkering with the constitution might provide positive results, but this is as far as it could go.

Of course, the leaders of the Parti Québécois have been portraying Canada in the worst possible light. They have decided that Canadian federalism is a brutal centralizing force and that its economic and social policies have been uniformly bad. The federal bilingualism policy is called a miserable failure. The future looks even worse than the past, given the federal government's seemingly unsolveable financial problems.

The trouble is, of course, that these accusations by Quebec are not quite true. Canadian federalism is not brutally centralizing. In fact, along with Switzerland, Canada is among the most decentralized federations in the world today. It is so decentralized today it can elect an avowed separatist/sovereigntist as the leader of the official opposition in parliament! Federal economic policies have not been perfect, but on balance they have promoted prosperity in Canada and in Quebec. Indeed, if federal economic policies were such a disaster, Quebec's business class would not have grown so self-confident. Also, Canada's financial problems are not insoluble. Canada's social policies such as medicare, unemployment insurance, old age pensions, and equalization payments have been quite successful. Federal bilingualism policy has enjoyed some success within the federal public sector and has helped preserve the cultural identity of Canada's francophone communities outside Quebec.

It is also hard to imagine a centralized Canada, given the difficulties that Canadian officials have had in building a sense of national unity throughout the country. Canadians look to their provinces to redress their grievances. The Canada–U.S. Free Trade Agreement and increased Canadian trade links with Mexico and Latin America have increased the ties between Canada and its southern neighbours.[2] Toronto's access to Lake Ontario has promoted its links to Chicago, Cleveland, Pittsburgh, Detroit, and other American Great Lakes cities. Many British Columbians have long thought of themselves as having closer economic ties to Washington state, Oregon, and California then they do to central Canada. The erosion of national institutions such as the Canadian Broadcasting Corporation, the National Film Board, and Via Rail (the national passenger railroad system) because of budget cutbacks have made the job of creating national unity symbols much more difficult.

If this decentralization is so pervasive, then what is motivating Quebec to seek greater autonomy? On one level, one can point to the familiar concerns about protecting the distinctive French language and culture. This concern is still valid although less so after the successful implementation of French language laws. Just as important, however, is that French-speaking Quebecers find it demeaning that people outside of Quebec have a 'say' in what goes on in Quebec. Language is less an issue than a symbol for these people, who are most prominent in the élite class. For them, the real issue is how to maintain a French-speaking nation free of perceived interference from the federal government.

But there are other factors as well. Quebec is facing a shrinking labour pool and tax base. Quebec's population growth is one of the lowest in Canada. Many of its best, brightest, and most productive young people have left. Also distressing is that the high school dropout rate in the province is an extraordinarily high 39 per cent. Industrial investors will be suspicious of such an ill-trained workforce. Quebec students' math skills are among the lowest in the nation. With the limited earning potential that this lack of education implies, Quebec's workforce of tomorrow will have difficulty paying for the social benefits and pensions to which Quebecers are accustomed. There are other social problems of rising numbers of babies born out of wedlock, of persistent unemployment, of a workforce consisting of only 2.9 million people, of low numbers of new immigrants, of an aging workforce, and so on. The immediate question is how would sovereignty be helpful in ameliorating these pervasive problems, if at all? There is no obvious answer to this query.

That is not to say that constitutional changes are not required. Canada is a large nation with diverse cultural, economic, and social needs varying from region to region. The federal government should devise policies that treat everyone equitably. It should recognize that some measure of decentralization is necessary. Similarly, constitutional changes that require the unanimous approval of parliament and all the provinces are doomed to failure. Meech Lake and the Charlottetown Agreement proved that.

There is reason to hope that Quebec's demands might be accommodated in large part. Most Canadians recognize that Canada's constitutional structure is threatened. A majority of Canadians may be willing to consider various constitutional options and alternatives when the country emerges from recession and when new politics are in place. All three federal parties agree that Quebec's distinctiveness must be recognized. The federal position is faced with serious obstacles, however. A large number of Quebecers still support some degree of sovereignty. Regional animosities are extensive. High taxes and a weak economy are creating bitterness, and most political leaders are not inspiring trust.

To meet Quebec's demands, the Charlottetown accord had to guarantee powers that go beyond those provided for in the Meech Lake Accord. These included an official recognition of Quebec's distinctiveness, a federal withdrawal from certain provincial spending areas, and a further devolution of powers over education, culture, and immigration. Other provinces had been offered similar powers. And yet this was not enough for Quebec voters.

One other interesting development is the July 1991 decision by Merrill Lynch to advise its clients to invest in Quebec and Hydro-Québec bonds. Reasons cited included the reduced chances of Quebec's sovereignty and Ontario's record deficit. Merrill Lynch predicted that trading relationships would return to their pre-Meech Lake position. This decision, although demonstrating confidence in the Quebec economy, must be worrisome to sovereigntists. They have insisted that outside investors are losing faith in a Quebec within a debt-ridden Canada but would eventually increase their holdings in a sovereign Quebec. This Merrill Lynch decision belies the sovereignty stance. More recently, in

1994 the Bank of Montreal's investment unit sent written assurances that if Quebec's political situation becomes so volatile that its office can no longer function in Montreal, then customers' accounts will be moved to Toronto.

It should also be noted that Quebecers are now less bitter about Meech's failure. Their priorities are economic, not constitutional. Also, they were not alone in rejecting Charlottetown. The relationship between English-speaking and French-speaking Canadians is not particularly hostile, although there are exceptions to this. Relationships between the two linguistic groups are less divisive than in Belgium, for example.[3] However, federalists are quick to point out that if Quebec's anger or sense of rejection is ebbing, that is not to say that the crisis is over. In fact, complacency in the rest of Canada could also push Quebec to sovereignty.[4] Prime Minister Jean Chrétien has pledged not to reopen the 'Constitutional File,' by which he means the Quebec sovereignty issue. He understands that support for sovereignty in Quebec increases when Quebecers feel humiliated by the rest of Canada, as many of them did following the failure of the Meech Lake Accord. So Prime Minister Chrétien will avoid confrontations with Quebec. He will also strive not to be seen as favouring Quebec. Federal money will be dispensed neutrally so as not to infuriate the rest of Canada. Trying to be seen as favouring all of Canada, and no one distinct society, is the prime minister's necessary but difficult task.

Polls reveal that Canadians are in a cynical mood. The success of the Reform party is one example of this. In addition, the recession has hit harder in Canada than it has in the United States. Interest rates are higher, unemployment is more pervasive, and government spending is down. Throughout the country, economic concerns dwarf the public's attention to the constitutional challenge that Quebec is making.

This is simultaneously instructive and disquieting. The focus on the nation's economic problems in the rest of Canada, rather than Quebec's challenge, offers only modest hope that constitutional change can occur in the next few years. Aggravating this situation is the fact that Quebec will not negotiate with the other provinces, but only with Ottawa. Finally, it is not clear that the rest of Canada particularly cares about what happens to Quebec, so long as its self-determination effort does not affect Canada adversely in economic terms. In short, the rest of Canada may not be prepared to respond appropriately to Quebec's challenge. Jacques Parizeau confidently suggests that his timetable is clear. A 1994 Quebec provincial election will return the PQ to power. In 1995, the sovereignty referendum will pass and the victory will be complete.

Notwithstanding Mr Parizeau's confident tone, Quebec may or may not go it alone. Most 1992 surveys revealed that a majority of Quebecers favoured sovereignty-association. It is one thing to express such a view in a survey however, and another to vote for sovereignty in a referendum. A few weeks prior to the 1980 referendum, a substantial majority expressed support for sovereignty. What changed then, and what might still be valid, is that a referendum campaign galvanizes forces for and against sovereignty. The media focuses on the issue. Information is readily available. The relative benefits and costs of sovereignty are debated. Voters in 1980 were better informed and more aware of the consequences of the final vote. Finally, survey results may represent an expression of anger and bitterness without cost. Voting for sovereignty demands clear-headed action. Also, it may not be enough to get a simple majority to create a sovereign Quebec. Analysts differ as to whether 75 per cent, or 65 per cent, or 50 per cent plus 1 votes are necessary.

There is bitterness in many Canadian circles about the free trade agreement, the Goods and Services Tax, the recession, regional political alienation, and, of course, Quebec's challenge. The post-Meech Lake, post-Charlottetown, post–1993 federal election cynicism seems quite pervasive, according to prominent pollsters like Conservative Allan Gregg, Liberal Angus Reid, and others. The economic, political, and/or constitutional problems that will have to be faced include:

- How will federal and provincial powers be reallocated? Quebec's assumption of much of the power over immigration is just the first step.
- How will English and French language interests be reconciled?
- Can the fusion of powers in Canada's government be reduced so that backbench MPs are able to vote their conscience once in a while?
- How will the Canadian party system be altered now that the Reform party and the Bloc Québécois have emerged as players on the parliamentary scene?
- How are foreign investors likely to react given Canada's constitutional uncertainty?
- In this regard, how will the NAFTA be affected, if at all, by a sovereign Quebec?
- If Canada somehow muddles through intact, how will it accommodate its competing interests?
- What will be the impact of the recession on Quebec's sovereignty aspirations?
- If Quebec goes it alone, how will the rest of Canada react?
- Similarly, if Quebec goes it alone economically, can it pay its debts, protect its assets, institute a legitimate, convertible, stable currency or share Canada's currency, continue making transfer payments, retain its current borders, and retain the allegiance of its diplomats, soldiers, and other public servants?

- How will the Quebec business class respond to Quebec's constitutional challenge?
- To what extent can the European Union be regarded as a model for Canada's future, with or without Quebec?
- How will the United States respond to a sovereign Quebec?

This last question is truly a wild card. An American military invasion or economic sanctions are unlikely, as noted. But U.S. vital interests will inevitably be affected by changes in Canada. American officials do not have long-term plans or scenarios about Canada's constitutional plight. Instead, they put out the fires when they occur. Should Quebec attain sovereignty, only then will the U.S. government decide what are its best interests at that time. U.S. actions cannot be reliably predicted, and this is disconcerting. If the United States cannot decide how to respond until the event occurs, then there are limits to how the Quebec and Canadian governments can plan to react to the American response. Quebec and Canadian officials would, no doubt, immediately move to reassure the U.S. government and international investors that all is well. But would this be enough? Would not the dramatic events and period of uncertainty necessarily frighten external observers?

So where do we stand? Francophone Quebecers are concerned about the future of their language and culture. Political sovereignty may be a vehicle to protect their distinctive character. There would be important costs, but they are probably manageable. A sovereign Quebec might suffer political uncertainty for a time, and it might have less international influence than if it were a part of Canada, but they would be acceptable costs.

The economic arguments for sovereignty are not persuasive, however. In fact, these costs are probably unacceptable, especially in a time of recession. It is reasonable to believe that many of the most talented Quebecers would leave and not be replaced. International investors would initially be worried and frightened, and many would put their holdings elsewhere. Relations with Canada would be acrimonious until the bitterness subsides and working arrangements are made. Division of the debt, sharing a currency, and mutually holding assets would all force difficult, angry negotiations.

Perhaps Canadian officials will agree to sovereignty-association rather than just sovereignty for Quebec. If so, relations would be easier. In fact, in the long run this is a strong possibility. But in the short run, both Canada and Quebec would suffer severe economic dislocation. Again, it should be stressed that Quebec's economy, and its polity, would be viable post-sovereignty. This was never the issue. The point is that neither Quebec nor Canada can be as strong apart as they can be together. The quality of life would diminish in both nations after sovereignty.

Of course, there are serious inequities in Canada's political and economic system. The Charlottetown Agreement was a substantial effort to redress these problems. But it was not enough. In addition, political institutions in Canada like the Senate and House of Commons may or may not be reformed. But it seems a near-certainty that all of the provinces will gain more powers from the federal government. The result could be a more representative and open political system as part of one of the most decentralized federal systems in the world today.

Where are we, then? First, it should be understood that nationalism is an ongoing feature of Quebec political life. It may be less obvious at times, particularly during an economic recession, but it is always present. Second, sovereignty will always have an appeal for many francophone Quebecers. Support for sovereignty is highly volatile, however. In times of economic plenty, it is a particularly romantic, attractive ideal. It is interpreted in various ways by Quebecers, but all sovereigntists agree that at the least it must include Quebec's ability to be an effective nation able to govern its own political affairs.

What distinguishes the current sovereignty movement from previous ones is the modicum of support from Quebec's business class. This most conservative class of Quebec workers is, at least, not virulently opposed to sovereignty. They might not support it wholeheartedly, but most do not vigorously fight it. This is a great change from previous years when the Quebec business class led the anti-sovereignty movement.

Where does this leave Quebec and Canada? In the next few years, when economic conditions improve, Quebec may well decide that the benefits of federalism, in terms of shared political and national institutions, are outweighed by the costs of giving up a portion of its sovereignty. If Quebec can have a sovereignty-association relationship with Canada, a reasonable possibility in the long run, then a politically independent Quebec will become a real possibility – perhaps a probability. This will not happen immediately. It may take seven to ten years, but it is a distinct possibility.

Should Quebec not become sovereign, it will be because it has gained enough concessions from Canada to enable it to play a profound role in deciding its own future. Quebec and the other major provinces will have assumed jurisdiction over many formerly federal responsibilities. Canada will become, even more than it is now, a confederation with the preponderant powers held by the provinces.

This may be a good thing in the long run. It is certainly a trend in several other nations, although few if any of these are modern, democratic, industrialized states. Canadian nationalists will be devastated. But most Canadians and Quebecers will continue to lead peaceful, relatively prosperous lives. There would be a period of great sadness and bitterness in Canada after sovereignty, but it would end as most Canadians and Quebecers proceeded to get on with things.

Some scholars have suggested that, post-sovereignty, the rest of Canada might decentralize or fragment, join the United States, or remain united. In the short run, the latter is likely. In the long run, the situation cannot be accurately predicted with any confidence.

Could Canada's plight have been avoided? A simple answer might be that if Canada had had a revolution, a civil war, or a single national language imposed, it might not face a threat of dissolution. But no Canadian would think the costs of those events acceptable.

We are left to conclude that Quebec's emergence as a modern, self-confident, economically viable nation, seeking much greater powers to pursue its own political destiny, was a natural progression. In the long run, there may be no democratic means to counter the sovereignty movement or accommodate Quebec's interests successfully. As painful as this may be for Canadian federalists, both inside and outside Quebec, sovereignty may be inevitable, and all will have to accept the new reality. We shall find out soon enough.

Bill 101: Charter of the French Language*

Bill 101 passed Quebec's National Assembly on August 26, 1977, shortly after the Parti Québécois came to power in the province. Prescriptive down to the tiniest detail, the legislation was aimed at preserving a language and culture perceived to be threatened. While many would agree that Bill 101 has reversed the erosion of French and elevated the economic status of Quebec's francophones, it has done so by sharply restricting the rights of anglophones and other linguistic minorities. Although some provisions have been invalidated by Canada's Supreme Court, the law remains largely intact. In the abridged text that follows, a number of technical, administrative, and repetitive sections have been omitted.

Preamble

Whereas the French language, the distinctive language of a people that is in the majority French-speaking, is the instrument by which that people has articulated its identity;

Whereas the Assemblée Nationale du Québec recognizes that Québecers wish to see the quality and influence of the French language assured, and is resolved therefore to make of French the language of Gouvernement and the Law, as well as the normal and everyday language of work, instruction, communication, commerce and business;

Whereas the Assemblée Nationale du Québec intends in this pursuit to deal fairly and openly with the ethnic minorities, whose valuable contribution to the development of Québec it readily acknowledges;

Whereas the Assemblée Nationale du Québec recognizes the right of the Amerinds and the Inuit of Québec, the first inhabitants of this land, to preserve and develop their original language and culture;

* As printed in James Crawford, ed., *International Perspectives on Language Politics* (Chicago: University of Chicago Press 1992), 435–45.

Whereas these observations and intentions are in keeping with a new perception of the worth of national cultures in all parts of the earth, and of the obligation of every people to contribute in its special way to the international community;

Therefore, Her Majesty, with the advice and consent of the Assemblée Nationale du Québec, enacts as follows:

Title I. Status of the French Language

Chapter I. The Official Language of Québec

1. French is the official language of Québec.

Chapter II. Fundamental Language Rights

2. Every person has a right to have the civil administration, the health services and social services, the public utility firms, the professional corporations, the associations of employees and all business firms doing business in Québec communicate with him in French.
3. In deliberative assembly, every person has a right to speak in French.
4. Workers have a right to carry on their activities in French.
5. Consumers of goods and services have a right to be informed and served in French.
6. Every person eligible for instruction in Québec has a right to receive that instruction in French.
7. French is the language of the legislature and the courts in Québec.
8. Legislative bills shall be drafted in the official language. They shall also be tabled in the Assemblée Nationale, passed and assented to in that language.
9. Only the French text of the statutes and regulations is official.
10. An English version of every legislative bill, statute and regulation shall be printed and published by the civil administration.
11. Artificial persons addressing themselves to the courts and to bodies discharging judicial or quasi-judicial functions shall do so in the official language, and shall use the official language in pleading before them unless all parties to the action agree to their pleading in English.
12. Procedural documents issued by bodies discharging judicial or quasi-judicial functions or drawn up and sent by the advocates practising before them shall be drawn up in the official language. Such documents may, however, be drawn up in another language if the natural person for whose intention they are used expressly consents thereto.
13. The judgments rendered in Québec by the courts and by bodies discharging judicial or quasi-judicial functions must be drawn up in French or be accompanied

with a duly authenticated French version. Only the French version of the judgment is official.

Chapter IV. The Language of the Civil Administration

14. The Government, the government departments, the other agencies of the civil administration and the services thereof shall be designated by their French names alone.
15. The civil administration shall draw up and publish its texts and documents in the official language. This section does not apply to regulations with persons outside Québec, to publicity and communiqués carried by news media that publish in a language other than French or to correspondence between the civil administration and natural persons when the latter address it in a language other than French ...
18. French is the language of written internal communications in the Government, the government departments, and the other agencies of the civil administration.
19. The notices of meeting, agendas and minutes of all deliberative assemblies in the civil administration shall be drawn up in the official language.
20. In order to be appointed, transferred or promoted to an office in the civil administration, a knowledge of the official language appropriate to the office applied for is required ...
22. The civil administration shall use only French in signs and posters, except where reasons of public health or safety require use of another language as well ...
29. Only the official language shall be used on traffic signs. The French inscription may be complemented or replaced by symbols or pictographs.

Chapter V. The Language of the Semipublic Agencies

30. The public utility firms, the professional corporations and the members of the professional corporations must arrange to make up their services in the official language. They must draw up their notices, communications and printed matter intended for the public, including public transportation tickets, in the official language ...
34. The professional corporations shall be designated by their French names alone.
35. The professional corporations shall not issue permits in Québec except to persons whose knowledge of the official language is appropriate to the practice of their profession ...

Chapter VI. The Language of Labour Relations

41. Every employer shall draw up his written communications to his staff in the official language. He shall draw up and publish his offers of employment or promotion in French.

42. Where the offer of employment regards employment in the civil administration, a semipublic agency or a firm required ... to have a francization certificate, establish a francization committee or apply a francization programme, as the case may be, the employer publishing this offer of employment in a daily newspaper published in a language other than French must publish it simultaneously in a daily newspaper published in French, with at least equivalent display.

43. collective agreements and the schedules to them must be drafted in the official language ...

45. An employer is prohibited from dismissing, laying off, demoting or transferring a member of his staff for the sole reason that he is exclusively French-speaking or that he has insufficient knowledge of a particular language other than French.

46. An employer is prohibited from making the obtaining of employment or office dependent upon the knowledge of a language other than the official language, unless the nature of the duties requires the knowledge of that other language. The burden of proof that the knowledge of the other language is necessary is on the employer, at the demand of the person or the association of employees concerned, or as the case may be, the Office de la langue française ...

49. Every association of employees shall use the official language in written communications with its members. It may use the language of an individual member in its correspondence with him ...

Chapter VII. The Language of Commerce and Business

51. Every inscription on a product, on its container or on its wrapping, or on a leaflet, brochure or card supplied with it, including the directions for use and the warranty certificates, must be drafted in French. This rule applies also to menus and wine lists. The French inscription may be accompanied with a translation or translations, but no inscription in another language may be given greater prominence than that in French ...

53. Catalogues, brochures, folders and similar publications must be drawn up in French.

54. Except as provided by regulation of the Office de la langue française, it is forbidden to offer toys or games to the public which require the use of a non-French vocabulary for their operation, unless a French version of the toy or game is available on no less favourable terms on the Québec market.

55. Contracts pre-determined by one party, contracts containing printed standard clauses, and the related documents, must be drawn up in French. They may be drawn up in another language as well at the express wish of the parties ...

57. Application forms for employment, order forms, invoices, receipts and quittances shall be drawn up in French.

58. Except as may be provided under this act or the regulations of the Office de la

langue française, signs and posters and commercial advertising shall be solely in the official language.

59. Section 58 does not apply to advertising carried in news media that publish in a language other than French, or to messages or a religious, political, ideological or humanitarian nature, if not for a profit motive.

60. Firms employing not over four persons including the employer may erect signs and posters in both French and another language in their establishments. However, the inscriptions in French must be given at least as prominent display as those in the other language ...

63. Firm names must be in French ...

67. Family names, place names, expressions formed by the artificial combination of letters, syllables or figures, and expressions taken from other languages may appear in firm names to specify them, in accordance with other acts and with the regulations of Office do la langue française ...

71. A non-profit organization devoted exclusively to the cultural development or to the defense of the peculiar interests of a particular ethnic group may adopt a firm name in the language of the group, provided that it adds a French version.

Chapter VIII. The Language of Instruction

72. Instruction in the kindergarten classes and in the elementary and secondary schools shall be in French, except where this chapter allows otherwise ...

73. In derogation of section 72, the following children, at the request of their father and mother, may receive their instruction in English:

(a) a child whose father or mother received his or her elementary instruction in English, in Québec;

(b) a child whose father or mother domiciled in Québec on 26 August 1977, received his or her elementary instruction in English outside Québec;

(c) a child who, in his last year of school in Québec before 26 August 1977, was lawfully receiving his instruction in English, in a public kindergarten class or in an elementary or secondary school;

(d) the younger brothers and sisters of a child described in paragraph (c) ...

79. A school body not already giving instruction in English in its schools is not required to introduce it and shall not introduce it without express and prior authorization of the Ministère de l'education ...

Chapter IX. Miscellaneous

89. Where this act does not require the use of the official language exclusively, the official language and another language may be used together.

90. Subject to section 10, anything that, by prescription of an act of Québec or an act

of the British Parliament having application to Québec in a field or provincial jurisdiction, or a regulation or an order, must be published in French and English may be published in French alone. Similarly, anything that, by prescription of an act, a regulation or an order, must be published in a French newspaper and in an English newspaper, may be published in a French newspaper alone ...

Title II. The Office de la Langue Française and Francization

Chapter II. The Office de la Langue Française

100. An Office de la langue française is established to define and conduct Québec policy on linguistics research and terminology and to see that the French language becomes, as soon as possible, the language of communication, work, commerce and business in the civil administration and business firms.
101. The Office is composed of five members, including a president, appointed by the Gouvernement for not more than five years ...
113. The Office shall:
   (a) standardize and publicize the terms and expressions approved by it;
   (b) establish the research programmes necessary for the application of this act;
   (c) draft the regulations within its competence that are necessary for the application of this act and submit them for consideration to the Conseil de la langue française in accordance with section 188;
   (d) define, by regulation, the procedure for the issue, suspension or cancellation of the francization certificate;
   (e) assist in defining and preparing the francization programmes provided for by this act and oversee the application thereof;
   (f) recognize, on the one hand, the municipal bodies, school bodies, health services and social services that provide services to persons who, in the majority, speak a language other than French, and, on the other hand, the departments that have charge of organizing and giving instruction in a language other than French in the school bodies.
114. The Office may:
   (a) adopt regulations within its competence under this act, which shall be submitted for examination to the Conseil de la langue française;
   (b) establish terminology committees and determine their composition and their terms and conditions of operation and, as may be required, delegate such committees to the departments and agencies of the civil administration;
   (c) adopt internal management by-laws subject to approval by the Gouvernement;
   (d) establish by by-law the services and committees necessary for the attainment of its purposes;
   (e) subject to the Act respecting the Ministère des affaires intergouvernementales,

make agreements with any other agency or any government to facilitate the application of this act;

(f) require every teaching institution at the college or university level to file a report on the language used in its manuals and state its observations in that respect in its annual report;

(g) assist the agencies of the civil administration, the semipublic agencies, business firms, the different associations, and individuals, in refining and enriching spoken and written French in Québec ...

Chapter III. The Commission de Toponymie

122. A Commission de toponymie is established at the Office de la langue française ...

125. The Commission shall:
   (a) establish the standards and rules of spelling to be followed in place names;
   (b) catalogue and preserve place names;
   (c) establish and standardize geographical terminology, in cooperation with the Office;
   (d) officialize place names;
   (e) publicize the official geographical nomenclature of Québec;
   (f) advise the Gouvernement on any question submitted by it to the Commission relating to toponymy ...

128. Upon the publication in the *Gazette officielle du Québec* of the names chosen or approved by the Commission, the use of such names becomes obligatory in texts and documents of the civil administration and the semipublic agencies, in traffic signs, in public signs and posters and in teaching manuals and educational and research works published in Québec and approved by the Ministère de l'education ...

Chapter V. Francization of Business Firms

136. Business firms employing fifty or more employees must, from the date determined under section 152, which shall not be later than 31 December 1983, hold a francization certificate issued by the Office.

137. From 3 January 1979, any firm required to hold a francization certificate is guilty of an offence if it does not hold one.

138. A francization certificate attests that the business firm is applying a francization programme approved by the Office, or that French already enjoys the status in the firm that such programmes are designed to ensure ...

141. The francization programme is intended to generalize the use of French at all levels of the business firm. This implies:
   (a) the knowledge of the official language on the part of management, the members of the professional corporations and the other members of the staff;

(b) an increase at all levels of the business firm, including the board of directors, in the number of persons having a good knowledge of the French language so as to generalize its use;

(c) the use of French as the language of work and as the language of internal communication;

(d) the use of French in the working documents of the business firm, especially in manuals and catalogues;

(e) the use of French in communications with clients, suppliers and the public;

(f) the use of French terminology;

(g) the use of French advertising;

(h) appropriate policies for hiring, promotion and transfer.

142. Francization programmes must take account of the situation of persons who are near retirement or of persons who have long records or service with the business firm.

143. Francization programmes must take account of the situation relations of business firms with the exterior and of the particular case of head offices established in Québec by business firms whose activities extend outside of Québec ...

151. The Office may, with the approval of the Minister [responsible for application of this act] and on condition of a notice in the *Gazette officielle du Québec*, require a business firm employing less than fifty persons to analyze its language situation and implement a francization programme ...

152. The Office may, by regulation, establish classes of business firms according to the nature of their activities and the number of persons they employ. For each class so established, it may fix the date on which francization certificates become exigible, se the terms on which certificates are issued and prescribe the obligations of the firms holding certificates ...

Title III. The Commission de Surveillance and Inquiries

158. A Commission de surveillance is established to deal with questions relating to failures to comply with this act ...

168. The investigation commissioners and the staff of the Commission de surveillance cannot be prosecuted for acts done in good faith in the performance of their duties.

169. The investigation commissioners shall make the inquiries provided for by this act.

170. The inspectors shall assist the investigation commissioners in the performance of their duties, verify and establish facts that may constitute offences against this act and submit reports and recommendations to the investigation commissioners on the facts established.

171. The investigation commissioners shall make an inquiry whenever they have reason to believe that this act has not been observed.
172. Business firms to which the Office has issued or is about to issue a francization certificate are subject to an inquiry where so requested by the Office.
173. Any person or group of persons may petition for an inquiry.
174. Petitions for inquiry must be in writing and be accompanied with indications of the grounds on which they are based and identification of the petitioners. The identity of a petitioner may be disclosed only with his express authorization ...
182. When, after an inquiry, an investigating commissioner considers that this act or the regulations hereunder have been contravened, he may put the alleged offender in default to conform within a given delay. If the investigation commissioner considers that the offence has continued beyond such delay, he shall forward the record to the Attorney-General for his consideration and, if necessary, institution by him of appropriate penal proceedings ...

Title IV. Conseil de la Langue Française

188. The Conseil shall:
   (a) advise the Minister on the questions he submits to it relating to the situation of the French language in Québec and the interpretation or application of this act;
   (b) keep a watch on language developments in Québec with respect to the status and quality of the French language and communicate its findings and conclusions to the Minister;
   (c) apprise the Minister of the questions pertaining to language that in its opinion require attention or action by the Gouvernement;
   (d) advise the Minister on the regulations prepared by the Office.
189. The Conseil may:
   (a) receive and hear observations of and suggestions from individuals or groups on questions relating to the status and quality of the French language;
   (b) with the approval of the Minister, undertake the study of any question pertaining to language and carry out or have others carry out any appropriate research;
   (c) receive the observations of any agency of the civil administration or business firm on the difficulties encountered in the application of this act and report it to the Minister;
   (d) inform the public on questions regarding the French language in Québec ...

Title V. Offences and Penalties

205. Every person who contravenes a provision of this act other than section 136 or of

a regulation made under this act by the Gouvernement or by the Office de la langue française is guilty of an offence and liable, in addition to costs:

(a) for each offence, to a fine of $25 to $500 in the case of a natural person, and of $50 to $1,000 in the case of an artificial person;

(b) for any subsequent offence within two years of a first offence, to a fine of $50 to $1,000 in the case of a natural person, and of $500 to $5,000 in the case of an artificial person.

206. A business firm guilty of an offence contemplated in section 136 is liable, in addition to costs, to a fine of $100 to $2,000 for each day during which it carries on a business without a certificate ...

208. Any court of civil jurisdiction, on a motion by the Attorney-General, may order the removal or destruction at the expense of the defendant, within eight days of the judgment, of any poster, sign, advertisement, bill-board or illuminated sign not in conformity with this act ...

Title VI. Transitional and Miscellaneous Provisions

211. Every person who has complied with the requirements of section 35 of the Official Language Act (1974, chapter 6) in respect of bilingual public signs shall have until 1 September 1981 to make the required changes, in particular to change his bill-boards and illuminated signs, in order to comply with this act.

212. The Gouvernement shall entrust a minister with the application of this act. Such minister shall exercise in regard to the staff of the Office de la langue française, that of the Commission de surveillance and that of the Conseil de la langue française the powers of a department head.

Canadian Charter of Rights and Freedoms*

Canada's 1982 Constitution, which Quebec refused to sign, included a Charter of Rights and Freedoms that made official bilinguilism binding on all provinces. According to an earlier precedent set by the Supreme Court of Canada, provincial legislatures could go beyond, but not diminish the language rights guaranteed under the constitution. The 1982 Charter established two important principles: a fundamental equality between English and French and a goal of advancing the 'equality of status or use' of both languages. Also, it included a section providing for linguistic minority rights in education.*

Official Languages of Canada

16. (1) English and French are the official languages of Canada and have equality of status and equal rights and privileges as to their use in all institutions of the Parliament and government of Canada ...

(3) Nothing in this Charter limits the authority of Parliament or a legislature to advance the equality of status or use of English and French.

17. (1) Everyone has the right to use English or French in any debates and other proceedings of Parliament ...

18. (1) The statutes, records and journals of Parliament shall be printed and published in English and French and both language versions are equally authoritative ...

19. (1) Either English or French may be used by any person in, or in any pleading in or process issuing from, any court established by Parliament ...

* James Crawford, ed., *International Perspectives on Language Politics* (Chicago: University of Chicago Press 1992), 433. For further legal analysis, see André Tremblay, 'The Language Rights,' in *The Canadian Charter of Rights and Freedoms: Commentary*, ed. Walter S. Tarnopolsky and Gérald-A. Beaudoin (Toronto: Carswell Co. 1982).

20. (1) Any member of the public in Canada has the right to communicate with, and to receive available services from, any head or central office of an institution of the Parliament or government of Canada in English or French, and has the same right with respect to any other office of any such institution where

(a) there is a significant demand for communications with and services from that office in such language; or

(b) due to the nature of the office, it is reasonable that communications with and services from that office be available in both English and French ...

21. Nothing in sections 16 to 20 abrogates or derogates from any right, privilege or obligation with respect to the English and French languages, or either of them, that exists or is continued by virtue of any other provision of the Constitution of Canada.

22. Nothing in sections 16 to 20 abrogates or derogates from any legal or customary right or privilege acquired or enjoyed either before or after the coming into force of this Charter with respect to any language that is not English or French.

Minority Language Educational Rights

23. (1) Citizens of Canada

(a) whose first language learned and still understood is that of the English or French linguistic minority population of the province in which they reside, or

(b) who have received their primary school instruction in Canada in English or French and reside in a province where the language in which they received that instruction is the language of the English or French linguistic minority population of the province, have the right to have their children receive primary and secondary school instruction in that language in that province.

(2) Citizens of Canada of whom any child has received or is receiving primary or secondary school instruction in English or French in Canada, have the right to have all their children receive primary and secondary school instruction in the same language.

(3) The right of citizens of Canada under subsections (1) and (2) to have their children receive primary and secondary school instruction in the language of the English or French linguistic minority population of a province

(a) applies wherever in the province the number of children of citizens who have such a right is sufficient to warrant the provision to them out of public funds of minority language instruction; and

(b) includes, where the number of those children so warrants, the right to have them receive that instruction in minority language educational facilities provided out of public funds.

Enforcement

24. (1) Anyone whose rights or freedoms, as guaranteed by this Charter, have been infringed or denied may apply to a court of competent jurisdiction to obtain such remedy as the court considers appropriate and just in the circumstances.

(2) Where, in proceedings under subsection (1), a court concludes that evidence was obtained in a manner that infringed or denied any rights or freedoms guaranteed by this Charter, the evidence shall be excluded if it is established that, having regard to all the circumstances, the admission of it in the proceedings would bring the administration of justice into disrepute.

General

25. The guarantee in this Charter of certain rights and freedoms shall not be construed so as to abrogate or derogate from any aboriginal, treaty or other rights or freedoms that pertain to the aboriginal peoples of Canada including

(a) any rights or freedoms that have been recognized by the Royal Proclamation of October 7, 1763; and

(b) and rights or freedoms that may be acquired by the aboriginal peoples or Canada by way of land claims settlement ...

Future Institutional Structures as Discussed by Ronald L. Watts*

One may identify in broad terms a continuum of alternative structural models. These fall into three broad categories. The first are various *federal forms*. Common to them all is the distinguishing mark of federations as political systems in which sovereignty is constitutionally divided between central and provincial governments. The second are various *confederal forms* where the definitive characteristic is that sovereignty ultimately resides with the constituent political units but a superstructure is established to deal with common policies subject to the assent of the constituent units. The third is the *separation* of the current federation into two or more independent successor states.

A fundamental choice to be made is which of these basic forms of political organization is to provide the future framework for political institutions within the geographic space that is now Canada. The strategies of political negotiators will vary according to whether they are seeking some form of revised federalism, some form of confederalism, or complete economic and political independence.

Of the nine options listed below, the first five represent different forms of federalism, options six to eight different forms of confederalism, and the last complete separation into two or more independent states.

1. *Status quo federalism.* The Canadian federal structure devised in 1867 has for nearly a century and a quarter proved remarkably effective and flexible through many changing conditions. Nevertheless, the post-Meech Lake conditions and the strategic factors outlined previously suggest that the existing federal structure is unlikely to be tenable

---

* Reprinted with permission from Ronald L. Watts, 'Canada's Constitutional Options,' in *Options for a New Canada*, ed. Ronald L. Watts and Douglas M. Brown (Toronto: University of Toronto Press 1991), 24–7.

for more than an interim period of a few years. At the very least it is no longer acceptable to a majority in Quebec. Furthermore, it is the source of much dissatisfaction not only in western Canada but also in the Atlantic provinces and the Territories, and among the aboriginal peoples.

2. *A rebalanced federation.* The distribution of jurisdiction and the structure of central institutions might be modernized to make the Canadian federal system more effective in contemporary conditions. Central powers might be increased in some areas and decreased in others. For example, federal jurisdiction might be enhanced to ensure the freer movement of people, goods and services. The European Community is often cited, even in Quebec, as a superior example to Canada in this respect. Indeed, the Allaire report of the Quebec Liberal Party advocates 'a stronger economic union' although it specifies few specific federal instruments to achieve this. At the same time jurisdiction over some other areas where centralization is not a prerequisite for effectiveness might be devolved to the provinces. This would go a significant distance towards meeting the concerns of Quebec and of some other provinces while also improving efficiency. Central institutions and structures (e.g., the Senate) might also be modernized.

3. *A more decentralized federation.* This solution would involve a devolution of some programs and responsibilities (e.g., industrial development, training and communications) and of some taxing powers (in place of shared-cost programs). This alternative would accord with the apparent centrifugal trends in Quebec and in Canadian opinion elsewhere. Dissatisfaction within the business community with the current inefficiency of the deficit-ridden federal government and with the excessive overlaps in the operations of the federal and provincial governments provides a strong impetus for greater decentralization. It is unlikely, however, to be supported by centralists outside Quebec or by those in the Atlantic provinces and Manitoba concerned that a weaker central government would be unable to undertake effective redistribution of resources through regional development and equalization programs. Nevertheless, the western premiers at their post-Meech Lake meeting in July 1990 did appear to give some support to this alternative. If there were sufficient devolution, such a model might be acceptable to Quebec. The Allaire report of the Quebec Liberal Party has advanced an extreme example of this variant of federalism. A critical issue in designing a more decentralized federation would be identifying the degree of central jurisdiction still required to maintain an effective federal system including an effective economic union. (This proposal would probably not be acceptable to western Canada).

4. *A more radically asymmetrical federation.* The 1867 constitution included some elements of asymmetry. A more radical asymmetry would enable concerns of centralists outside Quebec to be reconciled with the desires in Quebec for greater devolution.

Efforts to increase moderately the degree of asymmetry within the Canadian federation as proposed in the Meech Lake Accord failed, however, to receive the support required for ratification. Nevertheless, faced with the realization of a potential breakup of the federation as the only alternative, a more radically asymmetrical federation might be accepted. The clearest example of such an arrangement is the Malaysian federation where there is a marked greater autonomy for the two Borneo states. The experience of that federation indicates both that such an arrangement is feasible but that there may be limits to how far such arrangements can go (e.g., in Malaysia the conditions which led to Singapore's departure). A more asymmetrical federal structure in Canada might take the form of 'opt-out federalism,' (through a more extensive variant of section 7 of the Meech Lake Accord allowing provinces to opt-out of certain federal programs). Or it might take the form of 'opt-in federalism,' starting with greater devolution but providing arrangements for individual provinces to delegate powers back to the federal government. The Allaire report of the Quebec Liberal Party has proposed leaving room for such a possibility. This could be done by a more extensive variant of section 94 of the *Constitution Act, 1867.* An alternative device enabling *de facto* asymmetry would be to specify areas of concurrent jurisdiction with provincial paramountcy as has already been done under section 94A of the *Constitution Act, 1867* relating to jurisdiction over pensions. In any alternative involving substantial asymmetry there would be serious questions about the appropriate role to be played by the representatives of those constituent units having greater jurisdictional autonomy when federal policy in those areas is being deliberated within the central institutions. (This proposal would probably not be acceptable to western Canada).

5. *A binational federation.* This would be a federation in which the two constituent units would be Quebec and the rest-of-Canada, the latter taking either a unitary form or more likely existing as a federation within a federation. There have been examples elsewhere of a federation within a federation. Experience elsewhere suggests, however, that bipolar political unions have been notoriously unstable. Furthermore, the population ratio of 3:1 between the two units would raise major problems in arriving at agreement on appropriate representation with the central institutions. Any Quebec proposal of parity with the other nine provinces in a binational federation is likely to be strongly resisted by the rest-of-Canada. (This proposal would probably be unacceptable to the rest of Canada).

6. *A confederalism of regions.* In this model there would be a loose confederation of four or five regional units with the prairies and the Atlantic provinces (or at least the Maritimes) each constituting a single unit. The grouping of the smaller provinces into larger units would enable the new units to match the capacity of Ontario, Quebec and

British Columbia to exercise extended powers. A very real difficulty with this solution is that it would require the willingness of the smaller provinces to coalesce. In this option the central superstructure would have responsibility for coordinating policy relating to economic, monetary and a number of other agreed policy areas. It would be necessary to assess at what point devolution hinders effective economic and monetary union to the detriment of all the constituent units. It would be ironic, just at a time when Europe is evolving from confederalism, because of its inadequacies, towards its own unique form of federalism, for Canada to go in the opposite direction. (This proposal would be very difficult to implement).

7. *Sovereignty-association confederalism.* This solution, advocated by the Parti Québécois and others in Quebec, would take the form of a loose economic confederation in a binational form. It would combine Quebec as one unit and a federation of the other nine provinces as the other unit. The bipolar superstructure would be responsible mainly for the common market and a common currency, and for common armed forces and a few other programs. Such proposals have often suggested that the two components should have parity within the central superstructure (e.g., Parti Québécois proposals in 1979-80). It will probably be difficult, however, to convince the majority in the rest-of-Canada, representing 75 percent of the total population in the confederal superstructure. A further possible problem is that the operation of such a superstructure with only two constituent units is almost certain to produce repeated deadlocks, thus hampering international competitiveness.

8. *A common market.* This might consist of five to ten constituent units with only the minimal central structures and powers necessary for a common market and possibly a monetary union. While avoiding the problems of a bipolar superstructure, such an arrangement is unlikely, even with the increasingly centrifugal attitudes throughout Canada, to meet the desires among most Canadians outside Quebec for effective coordinated national action in a range of policy areas. (This proposal would probably be unacceptable to the rest of Canada).

9. *Two or more economically and politically independent successor-states.* Quebec's complete economic and political separation may be seen by some as a cleaner and neater solution than many of the complex alternatives listed above. It does raise questions, however, of the need to deal with such issues as the allocation of assets and liabilities, the adjustment of boundaries (by referendum?) to meet the wishes of minorities otherwise left on each side, and of transportation arrangements between Ontario and the Atlantic provinces. For a Canada-without-Quebec it raises not only the spectre of 'Pakistanization' but also the prospect of the permanent dominance of Ontario. How

radically would the structure of the rest-of-Canada have to be revised? Would the rest-of-Canada remain as one or become a number of economically and politically independent successor-states? (This is the only option that does not require agreement. It would be a choice by default).

Roadmap Summary Statements

For over 20 years there have emerged a variety of federally and provincially sponsored constitutional reform suggestions. Many of the most prominent have been summarized by the Canada West Foundation and are reprinted by permission.*

GENERAL PRINCIPLES

Canada Clause – since 1979 many have advocated the inclusion of a 'simple and eloquent' statement of the Canadian identity and values – a 'Canada Clause' that would formally acknowledge the distinctiveness of all Canadians, including Quebeckers, aboriginals, and other cultural groups, and thereby foster the development of a strong sense of Canadian identity. Opposition to a Canada clause is based upon the concern that a general statement of Canada's distinctiveness would undetermine and derogate from the acknowledgement of the distinctiveness of Quebeckers and/or aboriginals.

Quebec as a Distinct Society – it is unanimously conceded that because of its language and its different legal system Quebec constitutes a distinct society. Proponents argue that constitutional acknowledgement of this distinctiveness is both symbolically and practically important. Opponents are concerned that a 'distinct society' clause would give the Government of Quebec special powers, would undermine the application of the Charter, and would be a stepping-stone to complete Quebec independence.

Aboriginal Rights – the 1982 Constitution Act recognizes 'existing aboriginal rights.' Those seeking to extend aboriginal rights argue that aboriginal self-government and a

---

* Source: 'Alternatives '91: A Roadmap for Constitutional Change' (Calgary: Canada West Foundation November 1991).

means of settling land claims should also be placed in the constitution. Opposition to aboriginal self-government and entrenched land claims centres upon the need for a precise definition of these terms.

Amending Formula – under the 1982 Constitution Act, most amendments to Canada's constitution can be accomplished with the approval of Parliament and the legislatures of seven provinces with 50% of the population, although some matters such as the role of the Governor General or the amending formula itself require the support of Parliament and all provincial legislatures. The Quebec Government never agreed to this formula and argues that it must have a veto to protect the distinctiveness of Quebec society. Others argue that no province should have a veto because it would hamper the ability of Canadians to change their constitution in the future.

CHARTER OF RIGHTS AND FREEDOMS

Bilingualism – for many, bilingualism is so central a component of the Canadian identity that its constitutional status must be extended, for others, its impact has been so divisive that official bilingualism should be curtailed, or even abandoned in favour of assigning jurisdiction over languages to the provinces.

Multiculturalism – many of the constitutional reports see the preservation and enhancement of Canada's multicultural heritage as a major element of Canadian existence; others see governmental programs of this sort as unnecessary, and each citizen's cultural heritage as his or her own private concern.

Other rights – building upon the widespread popularity of the Charter, some reports want to extend it to include economic rights (mobility of labour, capital, goods, services) and others speak of a 'social charter' that would underpin the rights of Canadians to food, shelter, medical care, and employment. Opponents fear a further erosion of the powers of elected governments in favour of appointed judges.

REGIONAL REPRESENTATION

Senate Reform – rejecting the present Senate as ineffective, many proposals have advocated either an elected Senate to better represent the regions within the national Parliament, or a provincially appointed Senate to facilitate intergovernmental cooperation. Opponents worry that the powers of the national government would be hamstrung by a powerful reformed Senate.

Formalizing First Ministers Conferences – several proposals have suggested a more formal existence and powers for First Ministers Conferences as a means of regional representation and inter-governmental coordination; opponents worry about tying the hands of the national government, or about stressing executive-dominated procedures that preclude a meaningful role for Parliament or the provincial legislatures.

Parliamentary Reform – several proposals suggest a stronger role for individual MPs, and a reduced capacity for strong party discipline through reforms to the committee system, or through more free votes, or through fixed election dates to defuse confidence issues. Opponents fear that such measures would prevent a national government from formulating or pursuing a coherent and effective national policy.

Electoral Reform – some proposals, expressing concern about the way that the vagaries of the single-member district deny major national parties representation in entire regions, have suggested the selection of an additional bloc of MPs to provide an element of proportional representation; opponents worry that tinkering with the electoral system will fragment Commons representation and hamper the emergence of stable majority governments.

JURISDICTIONAL RESPONSIBILITIES

Division of Powers – many proposals have argued the need for a transfer of powers and responsibilities from Ottawa to the provinces, either on a broad range of issues or more narrowly focussed on (for example) natural resources; opponents worry that too massive a transfer of power would rob the federal government of any real capacity for action, and preserve the name of the nation while destroying its substance.

Federal Spending Powers – most proposals would limit, or require provincial ratification of, federal spending in areas of provincial jurisdiction; opponents defend a need for a national role and for national standards.

Immigration – several proposals have accepted the need for Quebec (and sometimes for other provinces) to exercise their shared powers in immigration in order to respond to their specific needs; opponents see federal leadership as critical and a strong provincial role as an abdication of a national responsibility.

Environment – some proposals see the environment as a problem on which only national regulation and national standards can be effective; others fear that because of the close connection between environmental issues and wide variations in local environmental conditions, a strong federal role would undermine provincial control over natural resources.

Economic Union – many proposals have advocated that the federal government retain the necessary authority to manage the economic union. Most reports propose measures to create genuine free trade within Canada across provincial boundaries, overcoming the numerous barriers to interprovincial trade that now exist. Opponents fear that this will work in favour of the large and economically strong provinces to the expense of local small business.

Supreme Court Nominations – many have supported a provincial role in the appointment of judges to the Supreme Court, the final referee of federal provincial disputes; opponents feel that Supreme Court appointments should be a question of professional merit, not regional representation, and worry that too overtly political a ratification process would lower the quality of the Court and undermine its effectiveness.

DIRECT DEMOCRACY

Constituent Assembly – some proposals have suggested a body of citizens specially elected for the drafting of a new constitution; opponents worry that this process would take too long, that its proposals would be unrealistic and impractical, and that it would get in the way of the give and take between governments that will be necessary to achieve a constitutional agreement.

Referenda – some proposals do not want constitutional changes to take effect unless they have been directly approved by the vote of the citizens; opponents fear that this risks derailing detailed negotiations and agreements, and playing into the hands of those who would misrepresent and distort the proposed changes.

Initiatives and Recall – some proposals want more direct citizen involvement in the democratic process by initiating legislative and/or constitutional proposals through public petition, or by being able to call elected representatives to account between general elections; opponents are concerned that such measures could (especially in a parliamentary system) unduly handicap a government and make the legislative process even more difficult and unwieldy.

GENERAL PRINCIPLES

Proposed Changes Reports & Proposals	Canada Clause	Quebec Distinct Society	Aboriginal Rights	Amending Formula
1. Pepin-Robarts Task Force 1979	Includes multi-culturalism and aboriginal rights.	Recognizes the distinctive nature of *all* provinces.	Advocates greater native representation.	Vetoes for Ont., Que., 2 Atlantic prov.'s and 2 western provinces.
2. Strengthening Canada: Government of Alberta 1985				
3. Constitution Act 1982			Recognizes existence of aboriginal rights.	Parliament and 7 provinces totaling 50% of population.
4. Macdonald Royal Commission 1985		Recognizes the duality of Canada.	Settle land claims.	Parliament and 7 provinces totalling 50% of population.
5. Meech Lake Accord 1987		Distinct Society clause placed in body of the constitution.		Federal government and all provinces given veto.
6. Manitoba Task Force October 1991	Recognize national identity, equality of provinces, multicultural heritage, etc.	Replace the word distinct with 'unique.'	Recognize inherent self-gov't, but requires practical definition.	Consider use of constituent assembly and referenda.
7. Reform Party: Principles and Policies 1991	Advocates equality of the provinces.	Advocates equality of the provinces.	Supports aboriginal self-government.	Parliament plus a referendum with a majority in 7 provinces.
8. The Liberal Party of Quebec (Allaire Report 1991)		Distinct Society basic rationale for reform.	Recognizes distinctiveness of First Nations.	Quebec veto.

GENERAL PRINCIPLES (continued)

9. Belanger-Campeau Commission 1991		Distinct society basic rationale for reform.		
10. Report of the Group of 22, 1991			Recognize aboriginal right to self-government.	
11. Beaudoin Edwards Report 1991			Right of assent to amendments which affect them.	Vetoes for Ont, Que, 2 Altantic provinces and 2 western provinces.
12. Northumberland Group 1991			Supports constitutional justice for the First Nations.	
13. A British Columbia Perspective 1991		Rejects further special status, Constitution adequately protects Quebec rights.	Calls for negotiations at the band level.	Parliament and 7 provinces totalling 50% of population.
14. The Spicer Commission 1991	'Simple and eloquent' clause enshrining Canada's identity and values	'Simple and eloquent' clause enshrining Canada's identity and values.	Prompt and fair settlement of land-claims; establishment of self-government.	
15. Government of Canada, September 1991	Affirms Canadian identity, equalities, fairness, democratic principles, etc.	Defined by language, culture, civil law.	Right to self-government recognized.	7 Provinces + 50% and/or unanimous provincial approval.

1

CHARTER OF RIGHTS AND FREEDOMS

Proposed Changes

Reports & Proposals	Bilingualism	Multi-Culturalism	Other Rights
1. Pepin-Robarts Task Force 1979	Federal government bilingual, provinces set own policy.	Provincial responsiblity, with Canada-wide programs.	
2. Strengthening Canada: Government of Alberta 1985	Double majority rule in Senate on language and culture issues.		
3. Constitution Act 1982	Guarantees minority language rights and affirmative action programs.	Provides for preservation and enhancement of multicultural heritage.	Fundamental freedoms, legal, democratic, mobility, and equality rights enshrined.
4. Macdonald Royal Commission 1985	All provinces officially bilingual; double majority rule in Senate	Favours continuation of multiculturalism.	
5. Meech Lake Accord 1987			
6. Manitoba Task Force October 1991	English and French official languages at federal level.	Multiculturalism is a fundamental characteristic of Canada.	Review issues relating to the 'notwithstanding' clause.
7. Reform Party: Principles and Policies 1991	Market oriented territorial bilingualism.	Individuals responsible for maintenance of own heritage.	Property rights entrenched in Constitution.
8. The Liberal Party of Quebec (Allaire Report 1991)	Quebec will safeguard rights of anglophones.		
9. Belanger-Campeau Commission 1991			

CHARTER OF RIGHTS AND FREEDOMS (continued)

10. Report of the Group 22, 1991	No change to legal and Constitutional provisions re: language.		
11. Beaudoin Edwards Report 1991			
12. Northumberland Group 1991	Extended affirmative action on language.		
13. A British Columbia Perspective 1991	Adequately protected.		
14. The Spicer Commission 1991	Review application of official language policy to clarify costs & benefits	Axe all programs except immigrant orientation and reduction of racism.	
15. Government of Canada, September 1991	Guarantees two official languages and affirmative actions programs.	Provides for preservation and enhancement of multiculturalism.	Property rights constitutionalized.

REGIONAL REPRESENTATION

Proposed Changes Reports & Proposals	Senate Reform	Formalizing First Ministers Conferences	Parliamentary Reform	Electoral Reform
1. Pepin-Robarts Task Force 1979	Abolish the Senate.	Advocates a Council of the Federation.	Modify and strengthen committee system.	Add 60 members to the House of Commons by proportional representation using province-wide ridings.
2. Strengthening Canada: Government of Alberta 1985	Triple E – Elected, Equal provincial representation, Effective powers.	First Ministers' Conferences constitutionalized.	Senate structured on a regional, not party basis.	
3. Constitution Act 1982		Constitutional conferences among First Ministers and aboriginals.		
4. Macdonald Royal Commission 1985	Elected the same time as MP's by proportional representation & regional equality.	Formalize all federal–provincial ministerial conferences.		Proportional representation in Senate; add members to the House of Commons, proportional representation by province.
5. Meech Lake Accord 1987	Provincial nominations, federal appointments; further negotiations.	Formalize annual meetings.		
6. Manitoba Task Force October 1991	Elected, equal or equitable; review or delay legislation only.			

REGIONAL REPRESENTATION (continued)

7. Reform Party: Principles and Policies 1991	Triple E – Elected, Equal provincial representation, Effective powers.	Opposes formal First Ministers' Conferences.	Free votes, independent committees.	Fixed elections; four year terms.
8. The Liberal Party of Quebec (Allaire Report 1991)	Abolish; Quebec to ratify federal laws affecting Quebec.	Quebec to deal directly with Ottawa.		
9. Belanger-Campeau Commission 1991				
10. Report of the Group of 22, 1991	Elected or appointed from provinces; feds over-see national standards.			
11. Beaudoin Edwards Report 1991				
12. Northumber-land Group 1991	Welcome 'review' of Senate role.			
13. A British Columbia Perspective 1991	Elected Senate weighted by provincial population.	Advocates the creation of the Council of the Federation.	Free votes in Parliament.	
14. The Spicer Commission 1991	Fundamentally reformed or abolished.		Less party discipline, more free votes.	
15. Government of Canada, September 1991	Elected, more equitable, with limited powers.	Advocates the creation of the Council of the Federation.	More free votes; fewer votes of confidence.	Proportional representation in Senate; Aboriginal representation.

JURISDICTIONAL RESPONSIBILITIES

Proposed changes Reports & Proposals	Division of Powers	Federal Spending Powers	Immigration	Environment
1. Pepin-Robarts Task Force 1979	Abolish reservation and disallowance; clarify and adjust.	Ratified by Council of Federation; provinces opt out with compensation.		
2. Strengthening Canada: Government of Alberta 1985	Abolish reseveration disallowance; provinces to ratify emergency powers.			
3. Constitution Act 1982	Clarify provincial powers over natural resources.			
4. Macdonald Royal Commission 1985	Abolish reservation and disallowance; clarify and adjust.	Non-formal restraints; shared cost program last resort.		
5. Meech Lake Accord 1987		Limits federal spending powers in areas of prov. responsibility.	Share responsibilty; Quebec gains 25% of immigrants.	
6. Manitoba Task Force October 1991	Increased federal involvement in national policy making.	Strenghten equalization; entrench federal funding on health, etc.		
7. Reform Party: Principles and Policies 1991	Re-examine; clarify and re-establish with bias towards decentralization.	Balance budget; programs subject to regional fairness tests.	Based upon economic need.	Federal leadership; harmonization to avoid duplication.

JURISDICTIONAL RESPONSIBILITIES (continued)

8. The Liberal Party of Quebec (Allaire Report 1991)	Repatriation of nearly all powers to Quebec.	Eliminate direct federal spending in Quebec.	Share authority.	
9. Belanger-Campeau Commission 1991	Argues for greater decentralization.			
10. Report of the Group of 22, 1991	Expand provincial powers, preserve federal role, abolish reservation and disallowance.	Federal and provincial govt.'s restricted to spending on own jurisdiction.		Provincial responsibility; fed's control int'l air and water regulations.
11. Beaudoin Edwards Report 1991	Entrench delegatory powers in Constitution.			
12. Northumberland Group 1991	Supports federal govt's authority to establish national standards; opposes decentralization.	Supports federal govt's authority to establish national standards; opposes decentralization.		
13. A British Columbia Perspective 1991	Concurrency with provincial paramountcy; some decentralization.	To be decided by the Council of the Federation.	Increased provincial powers.	Increased provincial powers.
14. The Spicer Commission 1991	Effectiveness increased when programs close to people.			
15. Government of Canada, September 1991	Expand provincial powers; federal government to regulate the economic union.	Provincial government cooperation required.	Shared responsibility with all provinces.	Preservation of the environment constitutionalized.

DIRECT DEMOCRACY

Proposed changes Reports & Proposals	Economic Union	Supreme Court Nominations	Constituent Assembly	Referenda	Initiatives and Recall
1. Pepin-Robarts Task Force 1979	Remove barriers to inter-provincial trade.	Nomination in consulta-tion with provincial Attorney General's ratified by Council of Federation.	Not necessary 'at this time.' (1979)	Constitu-tional change ratified by majority in four regions.	
2. Strength-ening Canada: Government of Alberta 1985		Nominations ratified by First Ministers.			
3. Constitu-tion Act 1982					
4. Macdonald Royal Com-mission 1985	Free move-ment of produce, goods, and services.	Opposes provincial rep. except for Quebec; elected Senate should ratify.			
5. Meech Lake Accord 1987		Prov nomination of judges; Quebec nominates 3 civil law judges.			
6. Manitoba Task Force October 1991	Work towards the elimination of inter-provincial barriers.	Federal-provincial consultative process advocated.	Use of const. assembly should be considered.	Use of referenda should be considered.	

DIRECT DEMOCRACY (continued)

7. Reform Party: Principles and Policies 1991	Remove barriers to inter-provincial trade.	Senate ratification and regional representation.	Constituent assembly necessary.	Ratify constitutional change.	Advocates initiatives and recall.
8. The Liberal Party of Quebec (Allaire Report 1991)	Remove barriers to inter-provincial trade.	New community tribunal in Que. to replace Canadian Supreme Court.		Referendum on Quebec sovereignty.	
9. Belanger-Campeau Commission 1991			Necessary for use in Quebec upon separation.	Referendum on Quebec sovereignty. (1992)	
10. Report of the Group of 22, 1991	Remove barriers to inter-provincial trade.				
11. Beaudoin Edwards Report 1991		Entrench three judges from Quebec.	Rejected; favours representative committee of Parliament.	Optional, non-binding constitutional referendums at P.M.'s discretion.	
12. Northumberland Group 1991					
13. A British Columbia Perspective 1991		Nominations ratified by Council of the Federation.	Too difficult to create; federal-provincial negotiations adequate.	Encourages use of referenda process.	
14. The Spicer Commission 1991			Encourages possible usage.	Encourages further exploration.	

DIRECT DEMOCRACY (continued)

15. Government of Canada, September 1991	Free movement of capital, goods, services, and labour constitutionalized	Provinces and Territories to submit lists of nominees.

APPENDIX E

A Roadmap for National Unity*

GENERAL PRINCIPLES

Quebec as a Distinct Society – The linguistic and cultural uniqueness of Quebec is an obvious historical and sociological fact. Proponents of a 'distinct society' clause argue that constitutional recognition of this distinctiveness is both symbolically and practically important. Symbolically, it gives the people of Quebec a needed reassurance about their place within Canada. Practically, it gives the Quebec legislature either greater powers or greater freedom in the exercise of existing powers to protect and promote that uniqueness. Opponents worry that such recognition would: 1) be an implicit rejection of the formal equality of all provinces; 2) give the legislature of that province alone significant and possibly expanding powers; 3) undermine the even application of the Charter of Rights and Freedoms to Canadians in all parts of the country; and, 4) be simply a waystation on the road to complete Quebec independence.

The 'distinct society' argument has become linked to the idea of a 'Canada Clause' – a statement of a broader range of the values which are central elements to Canada's identity which would serve to provide the larger context within which the uniqueness of Quebec's 'distinct society' is a single (albeit a very important) element. Critics see this as an implicit derogation from the acknowledgement of the distinctiveness of Quebec. There is also a concern that it should be an eloquent, even a poetic statement, rather than a shopping list.

Aboriginal Self-Government – An earlier concern for native rights led to the 1982 inclusion of Section 35 ('existing aboriginal rights') in the Constitution. More recent demands have centred around the recognition of self-government, preferably seen as an

---

* Reprinted with permission from 'Alternatives '92: A Roadmap for National Unity' (Calgary: Canada West Foundation March 1992).

inherent right rather than one which is to be granted by government. Supporters see the principle as an affirmation and practical realization of Aboriginal rights, as well as a way of escaping the enervating paternalism of the reserve system. Critics worry about the potentially open-ended implications of such an undefined concept, and about the extent to which Aboriginal self-government might take individuals and territory outside the Charter or even outside Canada.

Senate Reform – The purposes of Senate reform are twofold: 1) to provide the citizens of Canada's outlying provinces with more meaningful representation in Ottawa; 2) to provide the people's elected representatives with a means to check the near absolute power of the Prime Minister's Office. There are three key dimensions to reform: the selection of Senators, the number of Senators per province, and the specific powers and responsibilities of a reformed Senate. The general consensus of recent proposals regarding *selection* is that Senators should be directly elected, although questions remain about the appropriate electoral system (proportional representation or plurality vote) and about the timing (whether or not they should be simultaneous with federal or provincial general elections). The second dimension relates to *representation* within the Senate. This poses a Catch-22. There is a general recognition of a need for greater representation for Atlantic and Western provinces, but a desire to keep Quebec's and Ontario's representation at existing levels. The third issue relates to the *responsibilities* of a reformed Senate: whether it should have an absolute veto or be subject to possible override by the Commons on all legislation or on special categories of legislation.

Critics of Senate reform worry about the possibility of deadlock and ungovernability, or the frustration of the wishes of a democratic majority. Supporters of Senate reform see it as giving the citizens of the smaller provinces some assurance that they will not be neglected in favour of, or sacrificed to, the interests of the central provinces.

Division of Powers – Criticism of the Constitution over the last two decades has frequently suggested that some federal powers could be exercised more usefully and in a more focused way by provincial governments. A variety of schemes (such as Quebec's Allaire Report) for such devolution have emerged. On the other hand, the Meech Lake Accord was attacked for 'giving away the store' and enfeebling federal capacity; accordingly, the 1991 federal proposals suggested both a modest devolution to the provinces and a new federal legislative power in support of the economic union.

Recent discussions have suggested asymmetry as a solution – that is, a situation in which the legislature of Quebec would exercise powers not necessarily exercised by any or all of the other legislatures. This could be achieved through legislative delegation, through formal special status, or through provisions for legislative concurrency available to all provinces but taken up more readily and extensively by Quebec. Supporters of the idea see it as a flexible way of squaring Quebec's demands for more powers with

English-Canadian support for a strong national government. Critics worry about the status of Quebec MPs should the asymmetry surpass modest proportions, and about the capacity of the federal government should several of the larger and wealthier provinces follow Quebec's lead and take up more extensive powers.

Amending Formula – Under the *1982 Constitution Act*, most amendments to Canada's Constitution require the approval of Parliament and the legislatures of seven provinces with 50% of the population. A limited category of matters such as the role of the Governor General and the amending formula itself require the support of Parliament and all provincial legislatures. The Quebec government has never agreed to this formula, arguing that it must have a veto to protect the distinctiveness of Quebec society. Some recent proposals have tried to incorporate this demand in the general form of a 'regional veto' system requiring the agreement of Ontario, Quebec, the Atlantic region, and the West.

Some critics argue that no province should have a veto because it would hamper the ability of Canadians to change their Constitution in the future. Others complain that giving a veto to some but not all provinces creates 'first' and 'second' class provinces. A further concern is that reopening the question of the amending formula necessarily triggers the unanimity requirement, rather than the general amending formula, for the package of constitutional changes now under consideration.

Economic Union – It is a frequently mentioned anomaly that since the Canada–US Free Trade Agreement, many goods can cross the border between Canada and the United States more easily than they can cross the borders between the various provinces. Our present Constitution prohibits customs barriers to inter-provincial trade, but not the variety of non-customs barriers that have emerged in this century. Many proposals have contemplated a provision in the Constitution ensuring the free movement of people, goods, services and capital within the Canadian federation. Federal proposals originally suggested a federal legislative authority in support of such free movement and in the promotion of fiscal and economic harmonization, but this aspect of the question has received little support.

Supporters of the constitutionalization of a Canadian economic union suggest it as creating the larger domestic market that will make Canadian economic activities more effective and more competitive internationally. Opponents feel that this will work in favour of the large and economically strong provinces at the expense of local, small businesses, and that it will disproportionately benefit those provinces already active in interprovincial trade at the cost of those provinces whose production is more directed to local and international markets.

Social Charter – Some recent proposals have raised concerns about the possible erosion of Canada's national social programs, such as Medicare and the Canada Assistance

Plan – either as a consequence of the devolution of greater powers and responsibilities to the provincial governments, or because of the dwindling fiscal capacity of the national government, or as part of a levelling effect of the demands of an increasingly competitive international environment. To forestall these worries, they have suggested entrenching a Social Charter or covenant to affirm these rights and to protect citizens from their abridgment. On more general terms, the approval of a Social Charter for the European Community suggests that the formal affirmation of such rights is an appropriate move in its own right. Opponents worry about the future cost implications of such entrenched guarantees, especially if they are subject to interpretation and enforcement by judges whose expertise and priorities do not include the assessment of fiscal capacity or expenditure consequences.

Constitutional Process – There have been recurrent demands for an extensive and formal public involvement in the ongoing process of constitutional change, both for the immediate package and for any future change that might be contemplated. This sometimes takes the form of proposals for a constituent assembly, either as a preferred option at the present time or as a 'fall back' position should the present initiatives fail. Alternatively, some support national or provincial constitutional referendums as a way of both creating and registering public approval of the constitutional package. Opponents of the ideas worry about the impact of such measures on the constricted time frame of constitutional change, about the difficulty of making the inevitable and necessary trade-offs in the glare of a public campaign rather than in the give-and-take of executive meetings, and about the increased risk of failure.

Text of the Charlottetown Agreement

I. UNITY & DIVERSITY

A. People and communities

1. Canada Clause

A new clause should be included as Section 2 of the Constitution Act, 1867, that would express fundamental Canadian values. The Canada Clause would guide the courts in their future interpretation of the entire Constitution, including the Canadian Charter of Rights and Freedoms.

The Constitution Act, 1867, is amended by adding thereto, immediately after Section 1 thereof, the following section:

'2.(1) The Constitution of Canada, including the Canadian Charter of Rights and Freedoms, shall be interpreted in a manner consistent with the following fundamental characteristics:

(a) Canada is a democracy committed to a parliamentary and federal system of government and to the rule of law;

(b) the Aboriginal peoples of Canada, being the first peoples to govern this land, have the right to promote their languages, cultures and traditions and to ensure the integrity of their societies, and their governments constitute one of three orders of government in Canada;

(c) Quebec constitutes within Canada a distinct society, which includes a French-speaking majority, a unique culture and a civil law tradition;

(d) Canadians and their governments are committed to the vitality and development of official-language minority communities throughout Canada;

(e) Canadians are committed to racial and ethnic equality in a society that includes citizens from many lands who have contributed, and continue to contribute, to the building of a strong Canada that reflects its cultural and racial diversity;

(f) Canadians are committed to a respect for individual and collective human rights and freedoms of all people;

(g) Canadians are committed to the equality of female and male persons; and

(h) Canadians confirm the principle of equality of the provinces at the same time as recognizing their diverse characteristics.

(2) The role of the legislature and Government of Quebec to preserve and promote the distinct society of Quebec is affirmed.

(3) Nothing in this section derogates from the powers, rights or privileges of the Parliament or the Government of Canada, or of the legislatures or governments of the provinces, or of the legislative bodies or governments of the Aboriginal peoples of Canada, including any powers, rights or privileges relating to language and, for greater certainty, nothing in this section derogates from the aboriginal and treaty rights of the Aboriginal peoples of Canada.'

2. Aboriginal Peoples and the Canadian Charter of Rights and Freedoms

The Charter provision dealing with Aboriginal people (Section 25, the non-derogation clause) should be strengthened to ensure that nothing in the Charter abrogates or derogates from Aboriginal, treaty or other rights of Aboriginal peoples, and in particular any rights or freedoms relating to the exercise or protection of their languages, cultures or traditions.

3. Linguistic Communities in New Brunswick

A separate constitutional amendment requiring only the consent of Parliament and the legislature of New Brunswick should be added to the Canadian Charter of Rights and Freedoms. The amendment would entrench the equality of status of the English and French linguistic communities in New Brunswick, including the right to distinct educational institutions and such distinct cultural institutions as are necessary for the preservation and promotion of these communities. The amendment would also affirm the role of the legislature and government of New Brunswick to preserve and promote this equality of status.

B. Canada's Social and Economic Union

4. The Social and Economic Union

A new provision should be added to the Constitution describing the commitment of the governments, Parliament and the legislatures within the federation to the principle of the preservation and development of Canada's social and economic union. The new provision, entitled The Social and Economic Union, should be drafted to set out a series of policy objectives underlying the social and the economic union, respectively. The provision should not be justiciable.

The policy objectives set out in the provision on the social union should include, but not be limited to:

• Providing throughout Canada a health-care system that is comprehensive, universal, portable, publicly administered and accessible;
• Providing adequate social services and benefits to ensure that all individuals resident in Canada have reasonable access to housing, food and other basic necessities;
• Providing high-quality primary and secondary education to all individuals resident in Canada and ensuring reasonable access to postsecondary education;
• Protecting the rights of workers to organize and bargain collectively; and,
• Protecting, preserving and sustaining the integrity of the environment for present and future generations.

The policy objectives set out in the provision on the economic union should include, but not be limited to:

• Working together to strengthen the Canadian economic union;
• The free movement of persons, goods, services and capital;
• The goal of full employment;
• Ensuring that all Canadians have a reasonable standard of living; and,
• Ensuring sustainable and equitable development.

A mechanism of monitoring the Social and Economic Union should be determined by a First Ministers' Conference.

A new provision should be drafted to clarify the possible relationship between the new section and the existing Canadian Charter of Rights and Freedoms.

A clause should be added to the Constitution stating that the Social and Economic Union does not abrogate or derogate from the Canadian Charter of Rights and Freedoms.

5. Economic Disparities, Equalization and Regional Development

Section 36 of the Constitution Act, 1982, currently commits Parliament and the Government of Canada and the governments and legislatures of the provinces to promote equal opportunities and economic development throughout the country and to provide essential public services of reasonable quality to all Canadians. Subsection 36(2) currently commits the federal government to the principle of equalization payments. This section should be amended to read as follows:

Parliament and the Government of Canada are committed to making equalization payments so that provincial governments have sufficient revenues to provide reasonably comparable levels of public services at reasonably comparable levels of taxation.

Subsection 36(1) should be expanded to include the territories.

Subsection 36(1) should be amended to add a commitment to ensure the provision of reasonably comparable economic infrastructures of a national nature in each province and territory.

The Constitution should commit the federal government to meaningful consultation with the provinces before introducing legislation relating to equalization payments.

A new Subsection 36(3) should be added to entrench the commitment of governments to the promotion of regional economic development to reduce economic disparities.

Regional development is also discussed in item 36 of this document.

6. The Common Market

Section 121 of the Constitution Act, 1867, would remain unchanged.

Detailed principles and commitments related to the Canadian Common Market are included in the political accord of August 27, 1992. First Ministers will decide on the best approach to implement these principles and commitments at a future First Ministers' Conference on the economy. First Ministers would have the authority to create an independent dispute resolution agency and decide on its role, mandate and composition.

II. INSTITUTIONS

A. The Senate

7. An Elected Senate

The Constitution should be amended to provide that Senators are elected, either at large by the population of the provinces and territories of Canada or directly by the members of their provincial or territorial legislative assemblies.

Federal legislation should govern Senate elections, subject to the constitutional provision above and constitutional provisions requiring that elections take place at the same time as elections to the House of Commons and provisions respecting eligibility and mandate of Senators. Federal legislation would be sufficiently flexible to allow provinces and territories to provide for gender equality in the composition of the Senate.

Matters should be expedited in order that Senate elections be held as soon as possible, and, if feasible, at the same time as the next federal general election for the House of Commons.

8. An Equal Senate

The Senate should initially total 62 Senators and should be composed of six Senators from each province and one Senator from each territory.

9. Aboriginal Peoples' Representation in the Senate

Aboriginal Peoples' Representation in the Senate should be guaranteed in the Constitution. Aboriginal Senate seats should be additional to provincial and territorial seats, rather than drawn form any province or territory's allocation Senate seats.

Aboriginal Senators should have the same role and powers as other Senators, plus a possible double majority power in relation to certain matters materially affecting Aboriginal people. These issues and other details relating to Aboriginal representation in the Senate (numbers, distribution, method selection) will be discussed further by governments and the representatives of the Aboriginal peoples in the early autumn of 1992(*).

10. Relationship to the House of Commons

The Senate should not be a confidence chamber. In other words, the defeat of government-sponsored legislation by the Senate would not require the government's resignation.

11. Categories of Legislation

There should be four categories of legislation:
1) Revenue and expenditure bills ('Supply bills');
2) Legislation materially affecting French language or French culture;
3) Bills involving fundamental tax policy changes directly related to natural resources;
4) Ordinary legislation (any bill not falling into one of the first three categories).

Initial classification of bills should be by the originator of the bill. With the exception of legislation affecting French language or French culture (see item 14), appeals should be determined by the Speaker of the House of Commons, following consultation with the Speaker of the Senate.

12. Approval of Legislation

The Constitution should oblige the Senate to dispose of any bills approved by the House of Commons, within 30 sitting days of the House of Commons, with the exception of revenue and expenditure bills.

Revenue and expenditure bills would be subject to a 30-calendar-day suspensive veto. If a bill is defeated or amended by the Senate within this period, it could be repassed by a majority vote in the House of Commons on a resolution.

Bills that materially affect French language or French culture would require approval by a majority of Senators voting and by a majority of the Francophone Senators voting. The House of Commons would not be able to override the defeat of a Bill in this category by the Senate.

Bills that involve fundamental tax policy changes directly related to natural resources would be defeated if a majority of Senators voting cast their votes against the bill. The House of Commons would not be able to override the Senate's veto. The precise definition of this category of legislation remains to be determined.

Defeat or amendment of ordinary legislation by the Senate would trigger a joint sitting process with the House of Commons. A simple majority vote at the joint sitting would determine the outcome of the bill.

The Senate should have the powers set out in this Consensus Report. There would be no change to the Senate's current role in approving constitutional amendments. Subject to the consensus, Senate powers and procedures should be parallel to those in the House of Commons.

The Senate should continue to have the capacity to initiate bills, except for money bills.

If any bill initiated and passed by the Senate is amended or rejected by the House of Commons, a joint sitting process should be triggered automatically.

The House of Commons should be obliged to dispose of legislation approved by the Senate within a reasonable time limit.

13. Revenue and Expenditure Bills

In order to preserve Canada's parliamentary traditions, the Senate should not be able to block the routine flow of legislation relating to taxation, borrowing and appropriation.

Revenue and expenditure bills ('supply bills') should be defined as only those matters involving borrowing, the raising of revenue and appropriation as well as matters subordinate to these issues. This definition should exclude fundamental policy changes to the tax system (such as the Goods and Services Tax and the National Energy Program).

14. Double Majority

The originator of a bill should be responsible for designating whether it materially affects French language or French culture. Each designation should be subject to appeal to the Speaker of the Senate under rules to be established by the Senate. These rules should be subject to appeal to the Speaker of the Senate under rules to be established by the Senate. These rules should be designed to provide adequate protection to Francophones.

On entering the Senate, Senators should be required to declare whether they are Francophones for the purpose of the double majority voting rule. Any process for challenging these declarations should be left to the rules of the Senate.

15. Ratification of Appointments

The Constitution should specify that the Senate ratify the appointment of the Governor of the Bank of Canada.

The Constitution should also be amended to provide the Senate with a new power to ratify other key appointments made by the federal government.

The Senate should be obliged to deal with any proposed appointments within 30 sitting days of the House Commons.

The appointments that would be subject to Senate ratification, including the heads of the national cultural institutions and the heads of federal regulatory boards and agencies, should be set out in the specific federal legislation rather than the Constitution. The federal government's commitment to table such legislation should be recorded in a political accord.(*)

An appointment submitted for ratification would be rejected if a majority of Senators voting cast their votes against it.

16. Eligibility of Cabinet

Senators should not be eligible for Cabinet posts.

B. The Supreme Court

17. Entrenchment in the Constitution

The Supreme Court should be entrenched in the Constitution as the general court of appeal for Canada.

18. Composition

The Constitution should entrench the current provision of the Supreme Court Act, which specifies that the Supreme Court is to be composed of nine members, of whom three must have been admitted to the civil law bar of Quebec.

19. Nominations and Appointments

The Constitution should require the federal government to name judges from lists submitted by the governments of the provinces and territories. A provision should be made in the Constitution for the appointment of interim judges if a list is not submitted on a timely basis or not candidate is acceptable.

20. Aboriginal Peoples' Role

The structure of the Supreme Court should not be modified in this round of constitutional discussions. The role of Aboriginal peoples in relation to the Supreme Court should be recorded in a political accord and should be on the agenda of a future First Ministers' Conference on Aboriginal issues(*).

Provincial and territorial governments should develop a reasonable process for consulting representatives of the Aboriginal peoples of Canada in the preparation of lists of candidates fill vacancies on the Supreme Court(*).

Aboriginal groups should retain the right to make representations to the federal government respecting candidates to fill vacancies on the Supreme Court(*).

The federal government should examine, in consultation with Aboriginal groups, the proposal that an Aboriginal Council of Elders be entitled to make submissions to the Supreme Court when the court considers Aboriginal issues(*).

C. House of Commons

21. Composition of the House of Commons

The composition of the House of Commons should be adjusted to better reflect the principle of representation by population. The adjustment should include an initial increase in the size of the House of Commons to 337 seats, to be made at the time Senate reform comes into effect. Ontario and Quebec would each be assigned 18 additional seats, British Columbia four additional seats, and Alberta two additional seats, with boundaries to be developed using the 1991 census. An additional special Canada-wide redistribution of seats should be conducted following the 1996 census, aimed at ensuring that, in the first subsequent general election, no province will have fewer than 95 per cent of the House of Commons seats it would receive under strict representation-by-population. As a result of this special adjustment, no province or territory will lose seats, nor will a province or territory which has achieved full representation-by-population have a smaller share of House of Commons seats than its share of the total population in the 1996 census.

The redistribution based on the 1996 census and all future redistributions should be governed by the following constitutional provisions:

(a) A guarantee that Quebec would be assigned no fewer than 25 per cent of the seats in the House of Commons;

(b) The Section 41(b) of the Constitution Act, 1982, the 'fixed floor,' would be retained;

(c) Section 51(a) of the Constitution Act, 1867, the 'rising floor,' would be repealed;

(d) A new provision that would ensure that no province could have fewer Commons seats than another province with a smaller population;

(e) The current provision that allocates two seats to the Northwest Territories and one seat to Yukon.

A permanent formula should be developed and Section 51 of the Constitution Act, 1867, should be adjusted to accommodate demographic change, taking into consideration the principles suggested by the Royal Commission on Electoral Reform and Party Financing.

22. Aboriginal Peoples' Representation

The issue of Aboriginal representation in the House of Commons should be pursued by Parliament, in consultation with representatives of the Aboriginal peoples of Canada, after it has received the final report of the House of Commons Committee studying the recommendations of the Royal Commission on Electoral Reform and Party Financing(*).

D. First Ministers' Conferences

23. Entrenchment

A provision should be added to the Constitution requiring the Prime Minister to convene a First Ministers' Conference at least once a year. The agendas for these conferences should not be specified in the Constitution.

The leaders of the territorial governments should be invited to participate in any First Ministers' Conference convened pursuant to this constitutional provision. Representatives of the Aboriginal peoples of Canada should be invited to participate in discussions on any item on the agenda of a First Ministers' Conference that directly affects the Aboriginal peoples. This should be embodied in a political accord(*).

The role and responsibilities of First Ministers with respect to the federal spending power is outlined at item 25 of this document.

E. The Bank of Canada

24. The Bank of Canada

The Bank of Canada was discussed and the consensus was that this issue should not be pursued in this round, except for the consensus that the Senate should have a role in ratifying the appointment of its Governor.

III. ROLES AND RESPONSIBILITIES

25. Federal Spending Power

A provision should be added to the Constitution stipulating that the Government of Canada must provide reasonable compensation to the government of a province that chooses not to participate in a new Canada-wide shared-cost program that is established by the federal government in an area of exclusive provincial jurisdiction, if that province carries on a program or initiative that is compatible with the national objectives.

A framework should be developed to guide the use of the federal spending power in all areas of exclusive provincial jurisdiction. Once developed, the framework could become a multilateral agreement that would receive constitutional protection using the mechanism described in Item 26 of this report. The framework should ensure that when the federal spending power is used in areas of exclusive provincial jurisdiction, it should:

(a) contribute to the pursuit of national objectives;

(b) reduce overlap and duplication;

(c) not distort and should respect provincial priorities; and

(d) ensure equality of treatment of the provinces, while recognizing their different needs and circumstances.

The Constitution should commit First Ministers to establishing such a framework at a future conference of First Ministers. Once it is established, First Ministers would assume a role in annually reviewing progress in meeting the objectives set out in the framework.

A provision should be added (as Section 106 (a) (3)) that would ensure that nothing in the section that limits the federal spending power affects the commitments of Parliament and the Government of Canada that are set out in Section 36 of the Constitution Act, 1982.

26. Protection of Intergovernmental Agreements

The Constitution should be amended to provide a mechanism to ensure that designated agreements between governments are protected from unilateral change. This would occur when Parliament and the legislature(s) enact laws approving the agreement.

Each application of the mechanism should cease to have effect after a maximum of five years but could be renewed by a vote of Parliament and the legislature(s) readopting similar legislation. Governments of Aboriginal peoples should have access to this mechanism. The provision should be available to protect both bilateral and multilateral agreements among federal, provincial and territorial governments, and the governments of Aboriginal peoples. A government negotiating an agreement should be accorded equality of treatment in relation to any government which has already concluded an agreement, taking into account different needs and circumstances.

It is the intention of governments to apply this mechanism to future agreements related to the Canada Assistance Plan(*).

27. Immigration

A new provision should be added to the Constitution committing the Government of Canada to negotiate agreements with the provinces relating to immigration.

The Constitution should oblige the federal government to negotiate and conclude within a reasonable time an immigration agreement at the request of any province. A government negotiating an agreement should be accorded equality of treatment in relation to any government which has already concluded an agreement, taking into account different needs and circumstances.

28. Labour Market Development and Training

Exclusive federal jurisdiction for unemployment insurance, as set out in Section 91 (2) (a) of the Constitution Act, 1867, should not be altered. The federal government should retain exclusive jurisdiction for income support and its related services delivered through the Unemployment Insurance system. Federal spending on job-creation programs should be protected through a constitutional provision or a political accord(*).

Labour market development and training should be identified in Section 92 of the Constitution as a matter of exclusive provincial jurisdiction. Provincial legislatures should have the authority to constrain federal spending that is directly related to labour market development and training. This should be accomplished through justiciable intergovernmental agreements designed to meet the circumstances of each province.

At the request of a province, the federal government would be obligated to withdraw from any or all training activities and from any or all labour market development activities, except Unemployment Insurance. The federal government should be required to negotiate and conclude agreements to provide reasonable compensation to provinces requesting that the federal government withdraw.

The Government of Canada and the government of the province that requested the federal government to withdraw should conclude agreements within a reasonable time.

Provinces negotiating agreements should be accorded equality of treatment with respect to terms and conditions of agreements in relation to any other province that has already concluded an agreement, taking into account the different needs and circumstances of the provinces.

The federal, provincial and territorial governments should commit themselves in a political accord to enter into administrative arrangements to improve efficiency and client service and ensure effective co-ordination of federal Unemployment Insurance and provincial employment functions(*).

As a safeguard, the federal government should be required to negotiate and conclude an agreement within a reasonable time, at the request of any province not requesting the federal government to withdraw, to maintain its labour market development and training programs and activities in that province. A similar safeguard should be available to the Territories.

There should be a constitutional provision for an ongoing federal role in the establishment of national policy objectives for the national aspects of labour market development. National labour market policy objectives would be established through a process which could be set out in the Constitution including the obligation for presentation to

Parliament for debate. Factors to be considered in the establishment of national policy objectives could include items such as national economic conditions, national labour market requirements, international labour market trends and changes in international economic conditions. In establishing national policy objectives, the federal government would take into account the different needs and circumstances of the provinces; and there would be a provision, in the Constitution or in a political accord, committing the federal, provincial and territorial governments to support the development of common occupational standards, in consultation with employer and employee groups(*).

Provinces that negotiated agreements to constrain the federal spending power should be obliged to ensure that their labour market development programs are compatible with the national policy objectives, in the context of different needs and circumstances.

Considerations of service to the public in both official languages should be included in a political accord and be discussed as part of the negotiation of bilateral agreements(*).

The concerns of Aboriginal peoples in this field will be dealt with through the mechanisms set out in item 40 below.

29. Culture

Provinces should have exclusive jurisdiction over cultural matters within the provinces. This should be recognized through an explicit constitutional amendment that also recognizes the continuing responsibility for national cultural institutions, including grants and contributions delivered by these institutions. These changes should not alter the federal fiduciary responsibility for national cultural institutions, including grants and contributions delivered by these institutions. These changes should not alter the federal fiduciary responsibility for Aboriginal people. The non-derogation provisions for Aboriginal peoples set out in item 40 of this document will apply to culture.

30. Forestry

Exclusive provincial jurisdiction over forestry should be recognized and clarifies through an explicit constitutional amendment.

Provincial legislatures should have the authority to constrain federal spending that is directly related to forestry.

This should be accomplished through justiciable intergovernmental agreements, designed to meet the specific circumstances of each province. The mechanism used would be the one set out in item 26 of this document, including a provision for equality of treatment with respect to terms and conditions. Considerations of service to the public in both official languages should be considered a possible part of such agreements(*).

Such an agreement should set the terms for federal withdrawal, including the level and form of financial resources to be transferred. In addition, a political accord could specify the form the compensation would take (i.e. cash transfers, tax points, or others). Alternatively, such an agreement could require the federal government to maintain its spending in that province. There federal government should be obliged to negotiate and conclude such an agreement within a reasonable time(*).

These changes and the ones set out in items 31, 32, 33, 34 and 35 should not alter there federal fiduciary responsibility for Aboriginal people. The provisions set out in item 40 would apply.

31. Mining

Exclusive provincial jurisdiction over mining should be recognized and clarified through an explicit constitutional amendment and the negotiation of federal-provincial agreements. This should be done in the same manner as set out above with respect to forestry(*).

32. Tourism

Exclusive provincial jurisdiction over tourism should be recognized and clarified through an explicit constitutional amendment and the negotiation of federal-provincial agreements. This should be done in the same manner as set out above with respect to forestry(*).

33. Housing

Exclusive provincial jurisdiction over housing should be recognized and clarified through an explicit constitutional amendment and the negotiation of federal-provincial agreements. This should be done in the same manner as set out above with respect to forestry(*).

34. Recreation

Exclusive provincial jurisdiction over recreation should be recognized and clarified through an explicit constitutional amendment and the negotiation of federal-provincial agreements. this should be done in the same manner as set out above with respect to forestry(*).

35. Municipal and Urban Affairs

Exclusive provincial jurisdiction over municipal and urban affairs should be recognized an clarified through an explicit constitutional amendment and the negotiation of federal-provincial agreements. This should be done in the same manner as set out above with respect to forestry(*).

36. Regional Development

In addition to the commitment to regional development to be added to Section 36 of the Constitution Act, 1982 (described in item 5 of this document), a provision should be added to the Constitution that would oblige the federal government to negotiate an agreement at the request of any province with respect to regional development. Such agreements could be protected under the provision set out in item 26 ('Protection of Intergovernmental Agreements'). Regional development should not become a separate head of power in the constitution.

37. Telecommunications

The federal government should be committed to negotiate agreements with the provincial governments to co-ordinate and harmonize the procedures of their respective regulatory agencies in this field. Such agreements could be protected under the provision set out in item 26 ('Protection of Intergovernmental Agreements').

38. Federal power of Disallowance and Reservation

This provision of the Constitution should be repealed. Repeal requires unanimity.

39. Federal Declaratory Power

Section 92 (10) (c) of the Constitution Act, 1867, permits the federal government to declare a 'work' to be for the general advantage of Canada and bring it under the legislative jurisdiction of Parliament. This provision should be amended to ensure that the declaratory power can only be applied to new works or rescinded with respect to past declarations with the explicit consent of the province(s) in which the work is situated. Existing declarations should be left undisturbed unless all of the legislatures affected wish to take action.

40. Aboriginal Peoples' Protection Mechanism

There should be a general non-derogation clause to ensure that division of powers amendments will not affect the rights of the Aboriginal peoples and the jurisdictions and powers of governments of Aboriginal peoples.

IV: FIRST PEOPLES

Note: References to the territories will be added to the legal text with respect to this section, except where clearly inappropriate. Nothing in the amendments would extend the powers of the territorial legislatures.

A. The Inherent Right of Self-government

41. The Inherent Right of Self-Government

The Constitution should be amended to recognize that the Aboriginal peoples of Canada have the inherent right of self-government within Canada. This right should be placed in a new section of the Constitution Act, 1982, Section 35.1(1).

The recognition of the inherent right of self-government should be interpreted in light of the recognition of Aboriginal governments as one of three orders of government in Canada.

A contextual statement should be inserted in the Constitution, as follows;

The exercise of the right of self-government includes the authority of the duly constituted legislative bodies of Aboriginal peoples, each within its own jurisdiction:

(a) to safeguard and develop their languages, cultures, economies, identities, institutions and traditions; and,

(b) to develop, maintain and strengthen their relationship with their lands, waters and environment so as to determine and control their development as peoples according to their own values and priorities and ensure the integrity of their societies.

Before making any final determination of an issue arising from the inherent right of self-government, a court or tribunal should take into account the contextual statement referred to above and should enquire into the efforts that have been made to resolve the issue through negotiations and should be empowered to order the parties to take such steps as are appropriate in the circumstances to effect a negotiated resolution.

42. Delayed Justiciability

The inherent right of self-government should be entrenched in the Constitution. However, its justiciability should be delayed for a five-year period through constitutional language and a political accord(*).

Delaying the justiciability of the right should be coupled with a constitutional provision which would shield Aboriginal rights.

Delaying the justiciability of the right will not make the right contingent and will not affect existing Aboriginal and treaty rights.

The issue of special courts or tribunals should be on the agenda of the First Ministers' Conference on Aboriginal Constitutional Matters referred to in item 53(*).

43. Charter Issues

The Canadian Charter of Rights and Freedoms should apply immediately to governments of Aboriginal peoples.

A technical change should be made to the English text of Sections 3, 4, and 5 of the Canadian Charter of Rights and Freedoms to ensure that it corresponds to the French text.

The legislative bodies of Aboriginal peoples should have access to Section 33 of the Constitution Act, 1982 (the notwithstanding clause) under conditions that re similar to those applying to Parliament and the provincial legislatures but which are appropriate to the circumstances of Aboriginal peoples and their legislative bodies.

44. Land

The specific constitutional provision on the inherent right and the specific constitutional provision on the commitment to negotiate land should not create new Aboriginal rights to land or derogate from existing aboriginal or treaty rights to land, except as provided for in self-government agreements.

B. Method of Exercise of the Right

45. Commitment to Negotiate

There should be a constitutional commitment by the federal and provincial governments and the Indian, Inuit and Métis peoples in the various regions and communities of Canada to negotiate in good faith with the objective of concluding agreements elaborating the relationship between Aboriginal governments and the other orders of government. The negotiations would focus on the implementation of the right of self-government including issues of jurisdiction, lands and resources, and economic and fiscal arrangements.

46. The Process of Negotiation

Political Accord on Negotiation and Implementation
A political accord should be developed to guide the process of self-government negotiations(*).
Equity of Access
All Aboriginal peoples of Canada should have equitable access to the process of negotiation.
Trigger for Negotiations
Self-government negotiations should be initiated by the representatives of Aboriginal peoples when they are prepared to do so.
Provision for Non-Ethnic Governments
Self-government agreements may provide for self-government institutions which are open to the participation of all residents in a region covered by the agreement.
Provision for Different Circumstances
Self-government negotiations should take into consideration the different circumstances of the various Aboriginal peoples.
Provision for Agreements

Self-government agreements should be set out in future treaties, including land claims agreements or amendments to existing treaties, including land claims agreements. In addition, self-government agreements could be set out in other agreements which may contain a declaration that the rights of the Aboriginal peoples are treaty rights, within the meaning of Section 35(1) of the Constitution Act, 1982.

Ratification of Agreements

There should be an approval process for governments and Aboriginal peoples for self-government agreements, involving Parliament, the legislative assemblies of the relevant provinces, territories and the legislative bodies of the Aboriginal peoples. This principle should be expressed in the ratification procedures set out in the specific self-government agreements.

Non-Derogation Clause

There should be an explicit statement in the Constitution that the commitment to negotiate does not make the right of self-government contingent on negotiations or in any way affect the justiciability of the right of self-government.

Dispute Resolution Mechanism

To assist the negotiation process, a dispute resolution mechanism involving mediation and arbitration should be established. Details of this mechanism should be set out in a political accord(*).

47. Legal Transition

A constitutional provision should ensure that federal and provincial laws will continue to apply until they are displaced by laws passed by governments of Aboriginal peoples pursuant to their authority.

A law passed by a government of Aboriginal peoples, or an assertion of its authority based on the inherent right provision may not be inconsistent with those laws which are essential to the preservation of peace, order and good government in Canada.

48. Treaties

With respect to treaties with Aboriginal peoples, the Constitution should be amended as follows:

- Treaty rights should be interpreted in a just, broad and liberal manner taking into account the spirit and intent of the treaties and the context in which the specific treaties were negotiated.
- The Government of Canada should be committed to establishing and participating in good faith in a joint process to clarify or implement treaty rights, or to rectify terms of treaties when agreed to by the parties. The governments of the provinces should also be committed, to the extent that they have jurisdiction, to participation in the above treaty process when invited by the government of Canada and the Aboriginal peoples concerned or where specified in a treaty.

- Participants in this process should have regard, among other things and where appropriate, to the spirit and intent of the treaties as understood by Aboriginal peoples. It should be confirmed that all Aboriginal peoples that possess treaty rights shall have equitable access to this treaty process;
- It should be provided that these treaty amendments shall not extend the authority of any government or legislature, or affect the rights of Aboriginal peoples not party to the treaty concerned.

C. Issues Related to the Exercise of the Right

49. Equity of Access to Section 35 Rights

The Constitution should provide that all of the Aboriginal peoples of Canada have access to those Aboriginal and treaty rights recognized and affirmed in Section 35 of the Constitution Act, 1982, that pertain to them.

50. Financing

Matters relating to the financing of governments of Aboriginal peoples should be dealt with in a political accord. The accord would commit the governments of Aboriginal peoples to:

- Promoting equal opportunities for the well-being of all Aboriginal peoples;
- Furthering economic, social and cultural development and employment opportunities to reduce disparities in opportunities among Aboriginal peoples and between Aboriginal peoples and other Canadians; and
- Providing essential public services at levels reasonably comparable to those available to other Canadians in the vicinity.

It would also commit federal and provincial governments to the principle of providing the governments of Aboriginal peoples with fiscal or other resources, such as land, to assist those governments to govern their own affairs and to meet the commitments listed above, taking into account the levels of services provided to other Canadians in the vicinity and the fiscal capacity of governments of Aboriginal peoples to raise revenues from their own sources.

The issues of financing and its possible inclusion in the Constitution should be ont he agenda of the First Ministers' Conference on Aboriginal Constitutional Matters referred to in item 53(*).

51. Affirmative Action Programs

The Constitution should include a provision which authorizes governments of Aboriginal peoples to undertake affirmative action programs for socially and economically disadvantaged individuals or groups and programs for the advancement of Aboriginal languages and cultures.

52. Gender Equality

Section 35(4) of the Constitution Act, 1982, which guarantees existing Aboriginal and treaty rights equally to male and female persons, should be retained. The issue of gender equality should be on the agenda of the First Ministers' Conference on Aboriginal Constitutional Matters referred to under item 53(*).

53. Future Aboriginal Constitutional Process

The Constitution should be amended to provide for four future First Ministers' Conferences on Aboriginal Constitutional Matters beginning no later than 1996, and following every two years thereafter. These conferences would be in addition to any other First Ministers' Conferences required by the Constitution. The agendas of these conferences would include items identifies in this report and items requested by Aboriginal peoples.

54. Section 91(24)

For greater certainty, a new provision should be added to the Constitution Act, 1867, to ensure that Section 91(24) applies to all Aboriginal peoples.

The new provision would not result in a reduction of existing expenditures on Indians and Inuit or alter the fiduciary and treaty obligations of the federal government for Aboriginal peoples. This would be reflected in a political accord(*).

55. Métis in Alberta/Section 91(24)

The Constitution should be amended to safeguard the legislative authority of the Government of Alberta for Métis and Métis Settlement lands. There was agreement to a proposed amendment to the Alberta Act that would constitutionally protect the status of the land held in fee simple by the Métis Settlements General Council under letters patent from Alberta.

56. Métis Nation Accord(*)

The federal government, the provinces of Ontario, Manitoba, Saskatchewan, Alberta, British Columbia and the Métis National Council have agreed to enter into a legally binding, justiciable and enforceable accord on Métis Nation issues. Technical drafting of the Accord is being completed. The Accord sets out the obligations of the federal and provincial governments and the Métis Nation.

The Accord commits governments to negotiate: self-government agreements; lands and resources; the transfer of the portion of Aboriginal programs and services available to Métis; and cost-sharing arrangements relating to Métis institutions, programs and services.

Provinces and the federal government agree not to reduce existing expenditures on Métis and other Aboriginal people as a result of the Accord or as a result of an amendment to Section 91(24). The Accord defines the Métis for the purposes of the Métis Nation Accord and commits governments to enumerate and register the Métis Nation.

V. THE AMENDING FORMULA

Note: All of the following changes to the amending formula require the unanimous agreement of Parliament and the provincial legislatures.

57. Changes to National Institutions

Amendments to provisions of the Constitution related to the Senate should require unanimous agreement of Parliament and the provincial legislatures, once the current set of amendments related to Senate reform has come into effect. Future amendments affecting the House of Commons which can now be made under s. 42 should also require unanimity.

Sections 41 and 42 of the Constitution Act, 1982, should be amended so that the nomination and appointment process of Supreme Court judges would remain subject to the general (7/50) amending procedure. All other matters related to the Supreme Court, including its entrenchment, its role as the general court of appeal and its composition, would be matters requiring unanimity.

58. Establishment of New Provinces

The current provisions of the amending formula governing the creation of new provinces should be rescinded. They should be replaced by the pre-1982 provisions allowing the creation of new provinces through an Act of Parliament, following consultation with all of the existing provinces at a First Ministers' Conference. New provinces should not have a role in the amending formula without the unanimous consent of all of the provinces and the federal government, with the exception of purely bilateral or unilateral matters described in Sections 38(3), 40, 43, 45 and 46 as it relates to 43, of the Constitution Act, 1982. Any increase in the representation for new provinces in the Senate should also require the unanimous consent of all provinces and the federal government. Territories that become provinces could not lose Senators or members of the House of Commons.

The provision now contained in Section 42(1)(e) of the Constitution Act, 1982, with respect to the extension of provincial boundaries into the Territories should be repealed and replaced by the Constitution Act, 1871, modified in order to require the consent of the Territories.

59. Compensation for Amendments that Transfer Jurisdiction

Where an amendment is made under the general amending formula that transfers legislative powers form provincial legislatures to Parliament, Canada should provide reasonable compensation to any province that opts out of the amendment.

60. Aboriginal Consent

There should be Aboriginal consent to future constitutional amendments that directly refer to the Aboriginal peoples. Discussions are continuing on the mechanism by which this consent would be expressed with a view to agreeing on a mechanism prior to the introduction in Parliament of formal resolutions amending the Constitution.

VI: OTHER ISSUES

Other constitutional issues were discussed during the multilateral meetings.
    The consensus was not to pursue the following issues:

- Personal bankruptcy and insolvency
- Intellectual property
- Interjurisdictional immunity
- Inland fisheries
- Marriage and divorce
- Residual power
- Telecommunications
- Legislative interdesignation
- Changes to the 'notwithstanding clause'
- Section 96 (appointment of judges)
- Section 125 (taxation of federal and provincial governments)
- Section 92(a) (export of natural resources)
- Requiring notice for changes to federal legislation respecting equalization payments
- Property rights
- Implementation of international treaties

Other issues were discussed but were not finally resolved, among which were:

- Requiring notice for changes to federal legislation respecting Established Programs Financing

- Establishing in a political accord a formal federal-provincial consultation process with regard to the negotiation of international treaties and agreements
- Aboriginal participation in intergovernmental agreements respecting the division of powers
- Aboriginal participation in annual First Ministers' Conferences
- Equality of access to the mechanism for protecting intergovernmental agreements
- Establishing a framework for compensation issues with respect to labour market development and training
- Consequential amendments related to Senate reform, including by-elections, floors on House of Commons representation, time limits with respect to the reconciliation process and joint sittings with the House of Commons
- Any other consequential amendments required by changes recommended in this report.

(*) *Asterisks in the text indicate where the consensus is to proceed with a political accord.*

Notes

INTRODUCTION

1 Jonathan Lemco, *Political Stability in Federal Governments* (New York: Praeger 1991).

CHAPTER 1 Quebec's Place in Canada

1 Of course, some anglophones demonstrate a similar degree of anger towards francophones.
2 Perhaps the best books in English exploring the emergence of the Quebec nationalist movement are Kenneth McRoberts, *Quebec: Social Change and Political Crisis*, 3rd ed. (Toronto: McClelland and Stewart 1989); Graham Fraser, *PQ: René Lévesque and the Parti Québécois in Power* (Toronto: Macmillan 1984); and William D. Coleman, *The Independence Movement in Quebec, 1945–1980* (Toronto: University of Toronto Press 1984).
3 For an extended discussion of these points, see Stéphane Dion, 'Explaining Quebec Nationalism,' in R. Kent Weaver, ed., *The Collapse of Canada?* (Washington: Brookings 1992), 77–121.
4 Matthew Fraser, *Quebec Inc.: French-Canadian Entrepreneurs and the New Business Elite* (Toronto: Key Porter 1987), 71.
5 An impassioned defence of the policy of official bilingualism and its successes is offered by Maxwell Yalden, the former commissioner of official languages, in the *Globe and Mail*, 7 September 1990, A17.
6 For a particularly thoughtful journalistic study of the political actors in the Parti Québécois, see Fraser, *P.Q.*
7 This provision of the Charter of Rights and Freedoms (with a five-year time limit beginning in 1982) allows provincial legislatures to override certain sections of the

charter. Ironically, the notwithstanding clause was originally called for by western provinces wary of federal government economic policies.

8 See Joan Fraser, 'The Minorities: Time for Solutions,' *Language and Society*, 17 (March 1986), 16–18.

9 Section 93 of the British North America Act of 1867 established the right to denominational schooling, which tended to follow linguistic lines in Quebec: most Catholic schools were French, and most Protestant schools were English.

10 While 52 per cent of Italian children had attended French schools in 1943, by 1972 this figure had dropped to 9 per cent; Government of Quebec, *Report of the Commission of Inquiry on the Position of the French Language and on Language Rights in Quebec* (Québec: Editeur officiel du Québec 1972).

11 Jews, for example, were defined as Protestants by Quebec law; see Daniel J. Elazar and Harold M. Waller, *Maintaining Consensus: The Canadian Jewish Polity in the Postwar World* (Lanham, Md.: University Press of America 1990), 11, 86–8.

12 Report of the Conseil de la langue française (Quebec 1993).

13 The law has since been amended to allow employers and employees to communicate exclusively in English if both parties agree.

14 This point is more fully developed by Mark O. Rousseau, 'Class and Ethnicity in the Global Economy: Quebec Today' (unpublished manuscript presented at the annual meeting of the Association for Canadian Studies in the United States, New Orleans, 1993).

15 Allan C. Cairns, 'Constitutional Change and the Three Equalities,' in Ronald L. Watts and Douglas M. Brown, eds., *Options for a New Canada* (Toronto: University of Toronto Press 1991), 79.

16 For further discussion, see Alain Dubuc, 'The New Quebec Nationalism,' *The Network*, 2, no. 6–7 (June-July 1992), 14–15, or Pierre Fortin, 'Le choix forié du Quebec: Aspects économique et stratégiques,' in *Les avis des spécialistes invités á répondre aux huit questions posées par la commission*, Document de travail, Numéro 4, Commission sur l'Avenir politique et constitutionel du Québec (Saint-Romuald 1991).

17 For a fuller evaluation of this argument, see Stéphane Dion, 'Why Is Secession Rare? Lessons from Quebec' (mimeograph ed., June 1993), 15–19.

18 For an insightful discussion of this point, see Gordon R. Brown, 'Canadian Federal-Provincial Overlap and Presumed Governmental Inefficiency,' *Publius*, 24 (winter 1994), 21–37.

19 For a further discussion, see Jonathan Lemco, *Political Stability in Federal Governments* (New York: Praeger 1991), chap. 8.

20 See André Blais and Élisabeth Gidengil, 'The Quebec Referendum: Why Did Quebecers Say No?' (unpublished conference paper, annual meetings of the Canadian Political Science Association, Ottawa 1993).

21 Maurice Pinard, 'The Dramatic Reemergence of the Quebec Independence Movement,' *Journal of International Affairs*, 45 no. 2 (winter 1992), 471–97.
22 *Globe and Mail*, 24 February 1993, A1, 2.
23 Daniel Latouche, 'La stratégie québécoise dans le nouvel ordre économique et politique international,' *Les avis des spécialistes invités à répondre aux huit questions posées par la commission*, Document de Travail, Numéro 4, Commission sur l'avenir politique et constitutionnel du Québec (Saint-Romuald 1991), 605.
24 See Cartier Édouard Cloutier, 'Two General Types of Equalitarian Division Behavior: A Game Theoretical Experiment with American, English Canadian, and French Canadian Players' (unpublished PhD dissertation, University of Rochester 1974).
25 For a discussion of this point, see Jonathan Lemco and Peter Regenstreif, 'The Fusion of Powers and the Crisis of Canadian Federalism,' *Publius*, 14, no. 1 (winter 1984), 109–20.
26 For a discussion of the recent history of sovereignty movements in Quebec, see Coleman, *Independence Movement*.
27 *Maclean's*, 12 March 1990, 24.
28 For a discussion of the Environics poll, see Donna Dasko, 'The Ties That Bound: Canadians' Changing Perceptions of the Federal System,' in *The Network*, 2, nos. 6–7 (June–July 1992), 5–11.

CHAPTER 2 From Meech Lake to Charlottetown: The Evolution of Constitutional Proposals

1 The most objective comprehensive volume is Michael Behiels, *The Meech Lake Primer* (Ottawa: University of Ottawa Press 1989). For an excellent and brief overview, see Jeffrey Simpson, 'The Two Canadas,' *Foreign Policy*, no. 81 (winter 1990–1), 71–86.
2 For a discussion, see G.F.G. Stanley, 'Act or Pact: Another Look at Confederation,' *Canadian Historical Association Report*, 1956.
3 For a discussion of this point, see Allan Tupper, 'Meech Lake and Democratic Politics: Some Observations,' *Constitutional Forum*, 2 no. 2 (winter 1991), 26–31.
4 For a discussion, see Stéphane Dion, 'Why Is Secession Rare?'
5 For a discussion of this point, see Richard Sineon and Mary Janigan, eds., 'Introduction,' *Toolkits and Building Blocks: Constructing a New Canada* (Toronto: C.D. Howe Institute 1991), 2–3.
6 Bourassa was interviewed in the *Wall Street Journal*, 17 August 1990, A11.
7 As noted by Jacques Parizeau at the Center for Strategic and International Studies, Washington, 12 November 1991.
8 See, for example, the poll results which reveal that 55 per cent of Quebecers want

to see more functions shifted to the provinces whereas only 8 per cent favour a stronger federal government: *Globe and Mail*, 22 April 1991, A6.

9 The question of whether Quebec can retain these immigrants is another matter. Many Hong Kong Chinese who immigrated first to Quebec have left for Ontario and British Columbia. Altogether, a high percentage of immigrants to Quebec have since left for reasons having to do with the economy and language laws.

10 Daniel Latouche, 'Quebec and Canada: Scenarios for the Future,' *Business in the Contemporary World*, III, no. 1 (autumn 1990), 58–70.

11 For example, see the various studies cited in Stéphane Dion, 'Explaining Quebec Nationalism,' Brookings Institution mimeo, 1 August 1991; or Dion, 'Le nationalism dans la convérgence culturelle,' *'L'engagement intellectuel: mélange en l'honneur de Léon Dion,* ed. Raymond Hudon and Rejéan Pelletier (Quebec: Les Presses de l'université Laval 1991), 291–311.

12 As quoted in 'How a Freer Quebec Could Reshape the Continent,' *Business Week*, 9 July 1990, 40.

13 Bruce Nelan, 'Designing the Future,' *Time*, 9 July 1990, 34.

14 Canadian Press, 'B.C. Wants Sovereignty As Well,' *Globe and Mail*, 29 June 1990, A5.

15 Ibid.

16 For a fuller discussion of western Canadian perceptions of the federal government and its grievances against federal economic and political policies, see Roger Gibbins, ed., *Meech Lake and Canada: Perspectives from the West* (Edmonton: Academic Printing and Publishing 1990).

17 Deborah Jones, 'Vulnerable Provinces in Atlantic Region Fear Isolation if Confederation Crumbles,' *Globe and Mail*, 4 June 1990, B1, B4.

18 For a discussion of these polls, see 'Atlantic Politicians Dislike Idea of Union,' *Globe and Mail*, 25 March 1991, A1-2.

19 *A Quebec Free to Choose,* Report of the Constitutional Committee of the Quebec Liberal Party (28 January 1991).

20 Jeffrey Simpson, *Globe and Mail,* 1 February 1991, A12.

21 For the complete text of the mandate, background, and final recommendations of the Bélanger-Campeau Commission, see Michel Bélanger and Jean Campeau, *The Political and Constitutional Future of Quebec* (Quebec: National Library of Quebec 1991).

22 As reprinted from *Globe and Mail*, 28 June 1991, A6.

23 As discussed in William Claiborne, 'Quebec Sovereignty: What Would Become of Canada?' *Washington Post*, 28 December 1990, A27.

24 Ronald L. Watts, 'Canada's Constitutional Options: An Outline,' in *Options for a New Canada*, ed. Ronald L. Watts and Douglas M. Brown (Toronto: University of Toronto Press 1991), 24–7.

25 *Maclean's*, 7 January 1991, 19.

26 It is a bit odd to refer to 'accords' and 'agreements' and then be forced to note their failures.

27 See Geoffrey York, 'Property Rights Seen as Bargaining Ploy,' *Globe and Mail*, 26 September 1991, A6.

28 For a critical overview of the proposals, see Thomas Walkom, 'Nothing's Going to Happen without a Fight,' *Toronto Star*, 28 September 1991, D5; Jack McArthur, 'Constitution Proposals Are Dangerously Vague,' *Toronto Star*, 29 September 1991, F2; or 'Signposts to Survival,' *Maclean's*, 7 October 1991, 30.

29 '70% of Decided Quebecers Oppose Unity Plan, Poll Says,' *Toronto Star*, 1 October 1991, A1.

30 See the Angus Reid-Southam News survey published in the *Toronto Star*, 4 December 1991, A4.

31 One poll revealed that only 29 per cent of Quebecers, and 18 per cent in the rest of Canada, thought that a 'no' vote would lead to an eventual breakup of the country. See the Maclean's/Decima poll published in *Maclean's*, 2 November 1992.

32 *Maclean's*, 2 November 1992.

33 See the Angus Reid/Southam News Survey published on 7 November 1992.

34 For a discussion of the benefits and costs of the Charlottetown Accord, see Brooke Jeffery Strange Bedfellows, *Trying Times* (Toronto: Key Porter 1993), and Leslie A. Pal and F. Leslie Seidle, 'Constitutional Politics, 1990–2: The Paradox of Participation,' in Susan D. Phillips, ed., *How Ottawa Spends: A More Democratic Canada ...? 1993–1994* (Ottawa: Carleton University Press 1993), chap. 5.

35 For a discussion of this point, see Kenneth McRoberts, 'The Real Failure of the Referendum: the "Quebec Question" Remains Unsolved,' *Canada Watch* (November/December 1992), 75–7.

36 Edward A. Carmichael, 'New Stresses on Confederation Diverging Regional Economics,' *Observation No. 28* (Toronto: C.D. Howe Institute June 1986), 15.

37 See his discussion in Richard Simeon, 'Now the Good News: We Have a Lot in Common,' *Globe and Mail*, 30 April 1991, A15; or Simeon and Mary Janigan, eds., *Toolkits and Building Blocks*.

38 For a discussion of Senate reform, see Jonathan Lemco, 'Senate Reform: A Fruitless Endeavor,' *The Journal of Commonwealth and Comparative Politics*, 24, no. 3 (November 1986).

39 Pierre Fortin speech at the Paul Nitze School of Advanced International Studies of The Johns Hopkins University, Washington, 12 April 1991.

40 For a comparative analysis of asymmetrical federalism, see Ronald Watts's discussion in *Toolkits and Building Blocks*, 133–9. See also Alan Cairns, 'Constitutional Change and the Three Equalities,' *Options for a New Canada*, 90–3.

41 For a broader discussion of this point, see Jonathan Lemco, *Political Stability*.

42 *Globe and Mail*, 14 September 1993, A25.

43 *Financial Post*, 12 March 1990, 15.

44 For a discussion of the implications of 1992, see Michael Calingaert, *The 1992 Challenge from Europe: Development of the European Community's Internal Market* (Washington, D.C.: National Planning Association 1988).

45 For an extended discussion of this point, see Kimon Valaskakis, 'EC Experience Does Not Apply for Sovereigntists,' *Montreal Gazette*, 5 April 1991, B3. See also Thomas Courchene, *In Praise of Renewed Federalism* (Toronto: C.D. Howe Institute 1991), 5–7.

46 For further discussion of the EC's nonapplicability to the Canadian case, see Peter Leslie, *The European Community: A Political Model for Canada* (Ottawa: Federal-Provincial Relations Office 1991).

47 For a discussion of the problems associated with applying the EC model to Quebec, see G. Bruce Doern, *Europe Uniting: The EC Model and Canada's Constitutional Debate* (Toronto: C.D. Howe Institute 1992).

48 'Most Canadians Favor an Assembly on Unity, Poll finds,' *Toronto Star*, 4 June 1991, A1, A22.

49 For a discussion of these scenarios as applied to federations throughout modern history, see Jonathan Lemco, *Political Stability*.

CHAPTER 3 Sovereignty-Association – A Viable Alternative?

1 For an interesting discussion of the stages that sovereignty-association might pass through, see Adalbert Lallier, *Sovereignty-Association: Economic Realism or Utopia?* (Oakville, Ont.: Mosaic 1991). See also Philip Resnick, *Toward a Canada-Quebec Union* (Montreal: McGill-Queen's University Press 1991).

2 Speech by Jacques Parizeau at the Atlantic Council, Washington D.C., 5 March 1993.

3 As quoted in a speech at The Johns Hopkins University–SAIS, Washington D.C., 3 March 1993.

4 Previous works on this subject include: J. Brossard, 'Le droit du peuple québécois à disposer de lui-même au regard de droit international,' *Canadian Year Book in International Law*, 15 (1977); J. Brossard, 'Le droit du peuple québécois à l'autodétermination et à l'indépendance,' *Études internationales*, 8 (1977); J. Brossard, *L'accession à la souveraineté et le cas du Québec* (Montreal 1976); C. Morin, *Quebec vs. Ottawa: The Struggle for Self-Government, 1960–1972* (Montreal: McGill-Queens University Press 1976); D Matas, 'Can Quebec Separate?' *McGill Law Journal*, 21 (1975); D. Cameron, *Nationalism, Self-Determination and the Quebec Question* (Toronto: University of Toronto Press

1974); and R.A. Mayer, 'Legal Aspects of Secession,' *Manitoba Law Journal*, 3 (1968).

5 For a further discussion of these points, see Gregory Marchildon and Edward Maxwell, 'Quebec's Right of Secession under Canadian and International Law,' *Virgina Journal of International Law,* 32 (1992), 141–71.

6 'Secession Scenarios Outlined,' *Globe and Mail*, 29 March 1991, A4.

7 For a listing of these constitutional experiments worldwide, see Lemco, *Political Stability.*

8 See Scott Reid, *Canada Remapped: How the Partition of Quebec Will Reshape the Nation* (Vancouver: Pulp Press 1992), chap. 2.

9 Article 72 of the Constitution (Basic Law) states that: 'The right of free secession from the USSR shall be preserved for each union republic.'

10 The preamble to the Commonwealth of Australia Constitution Act, 1900, states that the colonies 'have agreed to unite into one indissoluble Federal Commonwealth.'

11 For commentary on the U.S. constitution, see J. Powell, 'Joseph Story's Commentaries on the Constitution: A Belated Review,' *Yale Law Journal*, 94 (1985); and A. Amar, 'Of Sovereignty and Federalism,' *Yale Law Journal*, 96 (1987).

12 '[A]lthough the Privy Council has confirmed the provinces in a wide range of powers, it has never said anything to support the right of the Provinces to withdraw from confederation.' J. Corry and J. Hodgetts, *Democratic Government and Politics* (Toronto: University of Toronto Press 1959), 559.

13 See a discussion of this point by Dan Soberman, 'European Integration: Are There Lessons for Canada?' *Options for a New Canada*, ed. Ronald L. Watts and Douglas M. Brown (Toronto: University of Toronto Press 1991), 191–205.

14 As noted in the *Montreal Gazette,* 4 May 1991, B4.

15 'Ottawa, Hull Residents Try to Weigh the Costs,' *Montreal Gazette*, 23 February 1991, B6.

16 The poll was commissioned by the Public Service Alliance of Canada in March 1991; six hundred respondents were sampled. See 'Federal Bureaucrats Uneasy over Future,' *Montreal Gazette*, 10 April 1991, B1.

17 For a comprehensive overview of the legal implications of possible future territorial disputes between Canada and a sovereign Quebec, see David L. Varty, *Who Gets Ungava?* (Vancouver: Varty and Co. 1991).

18 As noted by Angus Reid in an address to the Empire Club of Canada, Toronto, 28 February 1991.

19 Some writers are beginning to consider the possibility of post-sovereignty violence; see Alex Morrison , ed., *Divided We Fall: The National Security Implications of Canadian Constitutional Issues* (Toronto: C.I.S.S. 1991).

20 As discussed in Clyde H. Farnsworth, 'Symposium Tallies Cost of Quebec Separation,' *New York Times*, 6 June 1991, A7. See also Stephen Scott, 'Let's Be Consistent on National Split-Up,' *Montreal Gazette*, 18 June 1991, B3.

21 Submission by international law expert Henri Dorion to the Quebec National Assembly, Quebec, 17 October 1991.

22 For a much fuller discussion of this issue, see Mary Ellen Turpel, 'Does the Road to Quebec Sovereignty Run through Aboriginal Territory?' In Daniel Drache and Roberto Perin, eds., *Negotiating with a Sovereign Quebec* (Toronto: Lorimer 1992), chap. 7.

23 Bill 150: *An Act Respecting the Process for Determining the Political and Constitutional Future of Quebec* (Quebec 1991).

24 As quoted in Terrance Wills, 'Can Canada Dodge Referendum Pitfall?' *Montreal Gazette*, 25 May 1991, B4.

25 Théodore F. Geraets, 'The Problem and its Solution,' *Policy Options*, II, no. 5 (June 1990), 16–17.

26 As noted in Eloise Morin, 'Bourassa Cites Risks in National Referendum,' *Toronto Star*, 20 April 1991, A9.

27 Édouard Cloutier, Jean Guay, and Daniel Latouche, *Le Virage* (Montréal: Québec-Amérique 1992).

28 For a discussion of these poll results, see *Globe and Mail*, 27 December 1989, 1–2.

29 *Montreal Gazette*, 6 August 1990, A7.

30 For a discussion of this point, see 'A Deepening Solitide,' *Maclean's*, 9 April 1990, 21.

31 Robert McKenzie, 'Quebec Poll Boosts Call for Referendum,' *Toronto Star*, 21 November 1990, A11.

32 Edison Stewart, 'Sovereignty-Association's on a Roll,' *Toronto Star*, 26 November 1990, A11.

33 *Montreal Gazette*, 5 January 1991, B3.

34 *Le Devoir*, 18 February 1991.

35 *Toronto Star*, 25 February 1991, A17.

36 See the survey entitled 'Quebec and Canada,' *Globe and Mail*, 22 April 1991, A6. A CBC poll in April also showed diminished support for sovereignty. See 'Poll Suggests Commitment to Canada,' *Globe and Mail*, 29 April 1991, A4.

37 Ibid.

38 Iqop-Le Soleil-CKAC poll, reported in *Le Droit*, 3 June 1991.

39 *Le Journal de Montréal*, 8 June 1991.

40 *Toronto Star*, 26 September 1991, A27.

41 As reported in the *Toronto Star*, 15 October 1991, A2; and *Toronto Star*, 22 December 1991, A17.

42 As discussed in the *Toronto Star*, 18 January 1992, D1.

43 Jacques Parizeau, 'Perspectives on Currency in a Sovereign Quebec,' speech given at a Congress of Forex Canada, Toronto, 19 March 1993.

44 For a further analysis, see André Blais and Élisabeth Gidengil, 'The Quebec Referendum.

CHAPTER 4 Quebec's Economic and Political Development since 1976

1 Matthew Fraser, *Quebec Inc.*, 96.

2 As quoted in McRoberts, *Quebec*, 407.

3 David E.W. Laidler, 'Money after Meech,' *Commentary No. 22* (Toronto: C.D. Howe Institute 1990), 3.

4 Louis Uchitelle, 'Quebec Could Easily Prosper on Its Own, Economists Say,' *New York Times*, 24 June 1990.

5 Ibid.

6 Peter C. Newman, 'Positioning Quebec as the New Switzerland,' *Maclean's*, 17 September 1990.

7 As noted in Peter C. Newman, 'War of the Roses in the New Quebec,' *Maclean's*, 9 July 1990, 37.

8 'Separatism Plays to Mixed Reviews,' *Globe and Mail*, 2 March 1991, B1-2.

9 Jean-Paul Gagné, 'Milieux d'affaires: Meech ou l'indépendence,' *Les Affaires*, 57, no. 19 (1990), 2–3.

10 For example, see the poll published in the 14 June 1992 issue of the *Toronto Star* where only 13 per cent of Quebec business leaders favoured sovereignty, while 80 per cent supported renewed federalism. For a further analysis, see Jean-H. Guay, 'Le patronat: une année de crainte,' in Denis Moniére, ed., *L'année politique au Quebec*. (Montréal: Le Devoir–Québec/Amérique 1992) 181–92, or André Blais and Élisabeth Gidengil, 'The Quebec Referendum.'

11 Jean-François Lisée, *In the Eye of the Eagle* (Toronto: Harper Collins 1990), 283–302.

12 Marc V. Levine, *The Reconquest of Montreal* (Philadelphia: Temple University Press 1990), 221.

13 For an excellent discussion of whether overlapping government activity really leads to inefficiency, see Brown, 'Canadian Federal-Provincial Overlap,' *Publius*, 24 (Winter 1994), 21–37.

14 'Canada's Credit Rating under Pressure,' *Canadian Credit Review*, 6, no. 3 (26 February 1990, Special Edition), 200.

15 David B. Perry and Karin Treff, 'Provincial Budget Roundup, 1990, Part 1,' *Canadian Tax Journal*, 38, no.2 (March/April 1990), 351, 355.

16 *Bank of Canada Review* (Ottawa), October 1990, section H8, p. S110.

17 Patricia Poirier, 'Federalism a Failure, Quebec Chamber Says,' *Globe and Mail*, 8 November 1990.

18 David R. Johnson, 'An Evaluation of the Bank of Canada Zero Inflation Target: Do Michael Wilson and John Crow Agree?' *Canadian Public Policy*, XVI, no. 3 (September 1990), 309–10.

19 Pierre Arbour quoted in the *Montreal Gazette*, 5 September 1993, A1, 2.

20 As reported in *Business Week*, 12 October 1992, 55.

21 For a good discussion of Montreal's sad economic plight, see John McCallum and Chris Green, *Parting as Friends: The Economic Consequences for Quebec* (Toronto: C.D. Howe Institute 1991), chap. 5.

22 'Sex, Politics and Dreams,' *Maclean's*, 7 January 1991, 32.

23 'Recession Bigger Worry than Unity,' *Toronto Star*, 31 January 1991, A12.

24 For example, see the poll entitled 'Quebec and Canada,' *Globe and Mail*, 22 April 1991, A6.

CHAPTER 5 Political Sovereignty for Quebec – The Economic Costs and Benefits

1 'A Strong Vote for Federalism,' *Financial Post*, 20 October 1990, 20.

2 Economic Council of Canada, *A Joint Venture: The Economics of Constitutional Options* (Ottawa 1991).

3 Economic Council of Canada, *Regional Welfare Impacts of Some Alternative Fiscal Arrangements* (Ottawa 1992).

4 See Business Council on National Issues, *Canada's Economic Union* (Ottawa: BCNI 1992).

5 David E.W. Laidler, 'Money after Meech,' *Commentary No. 22* (Toronto: C.D. Howe Institute 1990), 6.

6 'A Strong Vote for Federalism.'

7 Jacques Parizeau, 'The Dynamics of Change in Quebec: A Quarter-Century of Ferment,' in Lansing Lamont and J. Duncan Edmonds, eds., *Friends So Different: Essays on Canada and the United States in the 1980s* (Ottawa: University of Ottawa Press 1989), 200.

8 Speech by Pierre Fortin at the Paul Nitze School of Advanced International Studies, The Johns Hopkins University, Washington, 12 April 1991.

9 See *Montreal Gazette*, 10 July 1992.

10 For further discussion, see Pierre Fortin, 'How Economics Is Shaping the Constitutional Debate in Quebec,' in Robert Young, ed., *Confederation in Crisis* (Toronto: James Lorimer and Co. 1991), 35–44.

11 See a fascinating discussion on this topic by Stéphane Dion, 'Canada Sick of Symbolic Politics,' paper presented at York University, North York, Ontario, February 1992.

12 Ibid, 8.

13 Jay Bryan, 'Meeting Quebec's Demands Could Mean Suicide, Economists Declare,' *Montreal Gazette*, 6 June 1991, A8.

14 For an interesting discussion of the possible consequences of so many anglophones leaving Quebec, see William G. Watson, 'Separation and the English of Quebec,' in John Richards et al., *Survival: Official Language Rights in Canada* (Toronto: C.D. Howe Institute 1992), 104–28.

15 See the Gallup poll in *Toronto Star*, 13 May 1992, A15.

16 Jacques Parizeau, quoted in *Time*, 13 April 1992.

17 These points summarize the pamphlet *La Souveraineté: Pour quoi? Comment?* (Montréal: Parti Québécois 1991).

18 Alan Freeman, 'Breakup Called Costly,' *Globe and Mail*, 7 June 1991, A5.

19 *Globe and Mail*, 22 April 1991, A6.

20 See the Decima Research poll discussed in the *Financial Post*, 29 May 1992, 3.

21 As quoted in Thomas Walkom, 'Two Visions of a Future Canada Day,' *Toronto Star*, 30 June 1990, D1–4.

22 Royal Bank of Canada, *Unity or Disunity: An Economic Analysis of the Benefits and the Costs* (Ottawa 25 September 1992).

23 Shawn McCarthy, 'Quebecers Willing to Pay to Separate, Experts Say,' *Toronto Star*, 6 June 1991, C4.

24 As reported in *Montreal Gazette*, 13 May 1992.

25 Thomas J. Courchene, *In Praise of Renewed Federalism* (Toronto: C.D. Howe Institute 1991).

26 Terence Wills, 'Backlash to Independence Could Leave Quebecers Isolated: Business Leaders,' *Montreal Gazette*, 23 November 1990, B1.

27 'Wise Calls for Prudence,' *Montreal Gazette*, 24 November 1990, A11.

28 'Distinct Quebec Idea a Tough Sell, Survey Indicates,' *Toronto Star*, 21 September 1991, A13.

29 In fact, in one poll 92 per cent of Canadians outside Quebec would not favour giving Quebec special powers unavailable to the other provinces in return for staying in Canada. See the Gallup Canada poll published in the *Toronto Star*, 28 February 1992.

30 David Bercuson and Barry Cooper, *Deconfederation: Canada without Quebec* (Toronto: Key Porter 1991).

31 See, for example, a Decima poll conducted for *Maclean's*, 7 January 1991, a Gallup Canada poll published in the *Toronto Star*, 24 January 1991, A25, or the findings of the Spicer Commission report.

32 See the background report to the Bélanger-Campeau Commission authored by the law professor José Woehrling of the Université de Montréal.

33 See the Gallup Canada poll published in the *Toronto Star*, 13 May 1991, A15; the Southam News Poll published in the *Montreal Gazette*, 5 June 1991, A12; the Gallup Canada poll published in the *Toronto Star*, 11 July 1991, A19; the Angus Reid-Southam News Poll published in the *Toronto Star*, 1 March 1991, A12; or the *Globe and Mail*–CBC News poll published in the *Globe and Mail*, 22 April 1991, A7.

34 See the Léger et Léger poll discussed in the *Globe and Mail*, 3 June 1992.

35 Patrick Grady, *The Economic Consequences of Quebec Sovereignty* (Vancouver: Fraser Institute 1991).

36 Ibid., chap. 5.

37 See 'Quebec and Canada,' *Globe and Mail*, 23 April 1991, A6; and the Southam Unity poll published in *Montreal Gazette*, 7 June 1991, A8.

38 For a discussion, see Jonathan Lemco, 'Senate Reform: A Fruitless Endeavour,' *The Journal of Commonwealth and Comparative Politics*, 24, no. 3 (November 1986), 269–77.

39 For a discussion of the constitutional implications of a sovereign Quebec for Canada, see Roger Gibbins, 'Speculations on a Canada without Quebec,' in Kenneth McRoberts and Patrick J. Monahan, *The Charlottetown Accord, the Referendum, and the Future of Canada* (Toronto: University of Toronto Press 1993), 264–73.

40 As reported in Peggy Curran, 'Sovereignty Carries Hefty Price Tag, Analysts Warn,' *Montreal Gazette*, 11 December 1990, A4.

41 For a discussion of this point, see the Infometrica study entitled 'Atlantic Canada Most Vulnerable to Constitutional Change,' 14 March 1992.

42 See the Infometrica study entitled 'No Clear Winner in Constitutional Wrangling over Fisheries,' 6 May 1992.

43 For discussion of the possible vulnerability of the transfer system after sovereignty, see John McCallum, *Canada's Choice: Crisis of Capital or Renewed Federalism* (Toronto: C.D. Howe Institute, 1992).

44 See the speech by Matthew Barrett, chairman and CEO of the Bank of Montreal, as reported in the *Toronto Star*, 7 May 1991, A9.

45 See the poll reported in the *Financial Post*, 13 May 1991, 4.

46 'Reshaping Country Carries a Price,' *Montreal Gazette*, 8 June 1991, 1, 3.

47 As reported in 'Breakup Called costly,' *Globe and Mail*, 7 June 1991, A5.

48 For discussion of the military implications of Quebec's sovereignty effort, see Joseph T. Jockel, *Security to the North; Canada-U.S. Defense Relations in the 1990s* (East Lansing: Michigan State University Press 1991), chap. 9.

49 As reported in the *Montreal Gazette*, 19 November 1991, A6.

CHAPTER 6 Investment in Quebec after the Failure of the Meech Lake and Charlottetown Accords

1 For further discussion, see a speech by Donald Fullerton, chairman of the Canadian Imperial Bank of Canada, as discussed in the *Globe and Mail*, 22 March 1991, B6.

2 'U.S. Investors Calm on Quebec's Future,' *Montreal Gazette*, 21 February 1991, C3.

3 Ibid.
4 This poll is discussed in 'Quebec Business Sends Mixed Signals, Poll Finds,' *Globe and Mail*, 19 February 1991, A4.
5 'Provigo Chairman Opposes Sovereignty,' *Globe and Mail*, 26 February 1991, B1.
6 'Quebec Business Favors Sovereignty,' *Globe and Mail*, 28 February 1991, B1.
7 Speech by Jacques Parizeau at the Brookings Institution, Washington, D.C., 2 April 1991.
8 See the Southam Business Monitor poll results published in the *Montreal Gazette*, 30 November 1991, D4.
9 In fact, there is evidence to suggest that political uncertainty and the divisive language situation are keeping many Japanese from investing in Quebec. See the report discussed in the *Montreal Gazette*, 24 November 1993, A6.
10 Daniel Latouche, 'La stratégie québécois dans le nouvel ordre économique et politique international,' *Les avis des spécialistes invités à répondre aux huit questions posées par la Commission*, Document de Travail, Numéro 4, Commission sur l'avenir politique et constitutionnel du Québec (Saint-Romuald 1991), 605.
11 For the subsidies issue, see Colleen S. Morton, 'Subsidies Negotiations and the Politics of Trade,' *Canada–U.S. Outlook*, 1, no. 1 (July 1989).
12 This point is discussed in Paul B. Stothart, 'Seven Costs of Quebec Sovereignty,' *Policy Options* (March 1991), 6–7.
13 Ibid.
14 For discussion of the most vulnerable industries, see McCallum and Green, *Parting as Friends*, chap. 6.
15 See the Parti Québécois booklet entitled, *La Souveraineté: Pour qoui? Comment?* (Québec: Parti Québécois 1991).
16 For a brief discussion of this point, see Henry Aubin, 'PQ's Figures for Quebec Sovereignty Do Not Add Up,' *Montreal Gazette*, 3 June 1991, B3.
17 This point is developed in the *Economics of Confederation* series published by the polling and consulting group Infometrica, 11 December 1991.
18 Peter Cook, 'The Battle for the National Stomach,' *Globe and Mail*, 15 May 1991, B2. See also W.H. Furtan and R.S. Gray, 'Agriculture in an Independent Quebec,' in *Broken Links: Trade Relations after a Quebec Secession*, ed. Gordon Ritchie et al. (Toronto: C.D. Howe Institute 1991), 45–57.
19 See 'Quebec Diary Farmers Get Warning,' *Globe and Mail*, 13 December 1991, B4.
20 See *Science Watch* published by the Institute for Scientific Information (July 1992).
21 *Washington Post*, 7 April 1994, A22.
22 For a more complete discussion, see Robert Blohm, 'Quebec's Hydro Hydra: Boondoggling toward Sovereignty,' *Wall Street Journal*, 14 June 1991, A9.
23 I am indebted to Frank Lemco for educating me about the possible implications of sovereignty for small and medium-sized businesses in Quebec.

CHAPTER 7 Quebec Sovereignty and the Debt

1 Canada, Department of Finance, *Federal Budget Report* (Ottawa 20 February 1990), 1.
2 Chambre de commerce du Québec, Comité des affaires constitutionelles, *Rapport sur les aspects économiques sur l'avenir politique et constitutionel du Québec* (27 September 1990), 11–12.
3 Pierre Fortin, 'How Economics Is Shaping the Constitutional Debate in Quebec,' in *Confederation in Crisis*, ed. Robert Young (Toronto: Lorimer 1991), 39.
4 Grant Reuber, 'If Quebec Seceded, Have-Not Provinces Could Really Suffer,' *Globe and Mail*, 9 April, 1990, B2.
5 For a discussion, see Paul Boothe et al., *Closing the Books: Dividing Federal Assets and Debt if Canada Breaks Up* (Toronto: C.D. Howe Institute 1992).
6 For a discussion, see a monograph provided by the Business Council on National Issues entitled *Canada's Economic Union* (Ottawa, April 1992).
7 Ibid., 40.
8 As noted in a speech by Jacques Parizeau, leader of the Parti Québécois, at the Brookings Institution, Washington, D.C., 2 April 1991.
9 See Paul Boothe and Richard Harris, 'The Economics of Constitutional Change: Dividing the Federal Debt,' *Canadian Public Policy*, XVII, no. 4 (1992), 434–44.
10 Côté has made this point in various of his writings. See, for example, Marcel Côté, 'Souveraineté: les coûts de transition,' notes for a Conference Project 90, Module Administration, Université du Québec à Montréal, 24 March 1992.
11 Jeffery Simpson, 'If Quebec Were to Leave, It Would Take a Crushing Debt Load with It,' *Globe and Mail*, 20 December 1990, A16.
12 University of Alberta economist Paul Boothe, quoted in 'Breaking Up Is Hard to Do,' *Globe and Mail*, 26 March 1991, B1–2.
13 This point is made in 'Money Market Has View on Separation,' *Financial Post*, 4 April 1991.
14 Boothe, 'Breaking Up Is Hard to Do.'
15 This discussion is adapted from Boothe, 'Breaking Up Is Hard to Do.'
16 For an extended discussion of this point, see Robert Hajaly, 'Calculating the Cost of Going It Alone,' *Globe and Mail*, 5 June 1991, A19.
17 McCallum and Green, *Parting As Friends*.
18 For a discussion of various studies exploring the issue of assets and debts post-sovereignty, see *The Economics of Quebec Separation: Consequences for Quebec and the Rest of Canada*, published by the Canada West Foundation (Calgary, September 1992).
19 'Quebec Might Fare Better than Canada, Report Says,' *Toronto Star*, 30 March 1991, A16.

CHAPTER 8 Quebec Sovereignty and Currency Concerns

1 'Separate Quebec Would Use Own Dollar Professor Predicts,' *Montreal Gazette*, 5 June 1991, A14.
2 For a detailed discussion of implications of a Quebec currency, see David E.W. Laidler, *Money after Meech*, Commentary No. 22 (Toronto: C.D. Howe Institute 1990). See also Laidler and William Robson, *'Two Nations, One Money?: Canada's Monetary System Following as Quebec Secession* (Toronto: C.D. Howe Institute 1991).
3 Professor Daniel Latouche makes this point in 'Parizeau's Debt Threat Pooh-Poohed,' *Toronto Star*, 22 September 1990, D4.
4 'Keep Strong Ties with Canada, Bourassa Urges,' *Globe and Mail*, 3 September 1990, A1-2.
5 Pierre Fortin's Presentation at Paul Nitze School of Advanced International Studies, The Johns Hopkins University, Washington, D.C., 12 April 1991.
6 'Quebec Would Keep Dollar for Role in Central Bank: Landry,' *Montreal Gazette*, 15 January 1991, A4.
7 This point is discussed in more detail in 'Decentralizing the Central Bank,' *Globe and Mail*, 25 March 1991, B1-2.
8 Frank Dabbs, 'Time to Ponder Post-Meech Bargaining Position,' *Financial Post*, 24 May 1990.
9 Robert Blohm, 'Quebec: North America's Burgeoning Ethnocentric State – Strategic Implications for Americans' (unpublished manuscript, Columbia University 25, February 1993), 3.
10 'Canada-Quebec Economic Union Realistic, Says PQ,' *Suburban* (Montreal), 19 June 1991, A6.
11 Hugh Thorburn, 'Disengagement,' in *Must Canada Fail?* ed. Richard Simeon (Montreal: McGill-Queen's University Press 1977), 214.
12 'Quebec and Canada,' *Globe and Mail*, 22 April 1991, A6.
13 For a discussion of the implications of Quebec's sovereignty for monetary policy, see Patrick Grady, *The Economic Consequences of Quebec Sovereignty* (Vancouver: Fraser Institute 1991); and Laidler and Robson, 'Two Nations, One Money?'

CHAPTER 9 The U.S. View of Post-Sovereignty Quebec–U.S. Relations

1 For a more complete discussion of the bureaucratic actors involved with Canadian affairs, see Joseph T. Jockel, 'If Canada Breaks Up: Implications for U.S. Policy,' *Canadian-American Public Policy*, no. 7 (September 1991), 37–9.
2 A partial listing of declassified U.S. government reports on the evolving Canadian constitutional situation includes:

- NIE (CIA) National Intelligence Estimate #99–61, winter 1961.
- State Department (INR) Research Memorandum, 'Quebec's International Status-Seeking Provokes New Row with Ottawa,' 1 June 1965.
- State Department (INR) Intelligence Note #693, 'DeGaullle to the Aid of Quebec,' 25 August, 1967.
- State Department (INR) Research Memorandum, 'Quebec, Ottawa, and the Confederation – the 1968 Round Begins,' 2 February 1968.
- National Security Council (NSC) – U.S. Government Memorandum, 'Information on Canadian Separatism,' 30 January 1969.
- State Department (INR) Research Memorandum, 'Canada: Implications of Bourassa's Election as Leader of Quebec Liberals,' 21 January 1990.
- State Department (INR) Research Memorandum, 'Canada: Separatism Quiescent but Not Dead,' 23 July 1973.
- State Department (INR) Research Memorandum, 'The Quebec Situation: Outlook and Implications,' August 1977.

3 See the summary report of the Council of American Ambassadors Mission to Canada, 19–22 May 1992.
4 Jean-François Lisée, *In the Eye of the Eagle* (Toronto: Harper Collins 1990). Other useful reviews of Quebec–U.S. relations include Alfred O. Hero, Jr, and Marcel Daneau, eds., *Problems and Opportunities in U.S.–Quebec Relations* (Boulder, Co.: Westview 1984); and Hero and Louis Balthazar, *Contemporary Quebec and the United States, 1960–1985* (Lanham, Md: University Press of America 1988).
5 'Canada: What Next After Meech Lake?' remarks by U.S. Ambassador Edward N. Ney to the Foreign Policy Association, New York, 18 July 1990.
6 Quoted in Carol Goar, 'Four Meech Myths That Need Close Scrutiny,' *Toronto Star*, 28 April 1990, D4.
7 *Globe and Mail*, 15 March 1991, A4.
8 For a discussion, see Jonathan Lemco, 'Quebec's Distinctive Character and the Question of Minority Rights,' in James Crawford, ed., *Language Loyalties: A Sourcebook on the Official Language Controversy* (Chicago: University of Chicago Press 1992); Jonathan Lemco, *Official Language Policy in Canada and the United States: A Route to National Disharmony?* (forthcoming, 1996).
9 At least until they have been recognized internationally.
10 As quoted in Steven J. Woehrel and Arlene E. Wilson, 'Canada's Constitutional Crisis' (Washington: Congressional Research Service 1990).
11 This conclusion was reached after conducting interviews with non-Canadian diplomats, legislative aides, and others in Washington. Interestingly, Quebec government officials are very aggressive in disseminating Quebec-based news clippings to Canada watchers in the United States. They provide regular opportunities to meet with Quebec government officials visiting the United States and

generously support the funding of education courses on Quebec politics, economics, and society.

12 See the discussion by Kimon Valaskakis, 'Neither Canada, Quebec Would Likely Survive Divorce,' *Montreal Gazette*, 20 November 1989, B3.

13 For a complete overview of the poll results, see *Globe and Mail*, 30 October 1990, A7.

14 See the Maclean's/CTV poll published in *Maclean's*, 4 January 1993, 17.

15 See the Gallup Canada poll published in the *Toronto Star*, 7 January 1992, A15.

16 See, for example, Peter Regensreif, *Toronto Star*, 16 July 1980, 1. The Spicer Commission report now calls this into question, however.

17 See Environics polls 1980–91 in citizenship identity. This is discussed in detail in an article by Donna Dasko entitled 'The Ties That Bound: Canadians' Changing Perceptions of the Federal System,' in *The Network* (June–July 1992), 5–11.

18 See the Gallup poll published in the *Toronto Star*, 2 December 1993, A17, and the Maclean's poll in *Maclean's*, 3 January 1994, 11.

19 Al Neuharth, 'O Canada! Cool It; Reject "Rébelmania,"' *USA Today*, 29 June 1990, 11A.

20. 'U.S. Firmly Believes in a Free and United Canada,' Canadian Press Wire Service, 6 June 1990.

21 For example, see the *La Presse* article reviewing the *New York Times* report of Quebec's constitutional position, 'Les frontières d'un Québec indépendant font la manchette aux États-Unis,' *La Presse*, 8 June 1991, F7. See also the furor unleashed in the Quebec press over Mordecai Richler's unflattering portrait of Quebec history in *The New Yorker* of 23 September 1991, or the reaction to a full-page ad in the *New York Times* on 21 October 1991, placed by the U.S.–based James Bay Coalition which compared Hydro-Québec's development project at James Bay to 'The Destruction of the Amazon.' The Quebec government responded to the latter advertisement by placing their own in the *New York Times*, and subsequently calling the original message 'unacceptable, inadmissable and an affront to the pride of all Quebecers.'

22 Results of a comparative survey, 'Canada and the World: An International Perspective on Canada and Canadians,' reported in 'Le Canada est vu froid et inoffensif par les étrangers,' *Le Devoir*, 19 May 1992.

23 Donald K. Alper and Robert L. Monahan, 'Western American Perceptions of Quebec,' *American Review of Canadian Studies*, 22, no. 3 (1992), 387–406.

24 Sheldon Gordon, 'How the U.S. Can Push Canadian Unity,' *New York Times*, 8 September 1990.

25 For a discussion, see 'Canada–U.S. Agricultural Trade: The Current Agenda,' *Canada–U.S. Outlook*, 2, no. 3 (May 1991).

26 'Living with a Freer Quebec,' *Business Week*, 9 July 1990, 88.

27 See the transcript of the speech by Jacques Parizeau, Parti Québécois leader, at the Brookings Institution, Washington, D.C., 2 April 1991.

28 Pierre Fortin, 'Quebec Sovereignty: The Economic Debate and the Role of the Business Community,' notes for a luncheon address at The Johns Hopkins University–SAIS, Washington, D.C., 12 April 1991.

29 See 'Quebec Is Nearing Brink of Disaster, Reisman Says,' *Montreal Gazette,* 1 June 1991, D5.

30 Thomas J. Courchene, *In Praise of Renewed Federalism* (Toronto: C.D. Howe Institute 1991).

31 Jacques Parizeau, 'A Sovereign Quebec: Is It Possible and What Would It Mean?' speech to the Atlantic Council, Washington, D.C., 5 March 1993.

32 For a discussion of the problems associated with accession to NAFTA, see Jonathan Lemco and William B.P. Robson, eds., *Ties beyond Trade: Labor and Environmental Issues under the NAFTA* (Washington and Toronto: Canadian–American Committee 1993); Richard Belous, Jonathan Lemco, and Jay Dunn, *Should NAFTA Be Extended to Include the Rest of Latin America?* (Washington: National Planning Association, forthcoming 1994); and Richard Belous and Jonathan Lemco, eds., *NAFTA as a Model of Development: The Benefits and Costs of Merging High and Low Wage Areas* (Washington, D.C.: National Planning Association, Institute for the Americas, and Friedrich Ebert Foundation 1993).

33 As quoted in the *Globe and Mail*, 19 February 1994, A4.

34 As quoted in the *Montreal Gazette*, 9 April 1991, B1.

35 For a thorough discussion of the prospects for the FTA and NAFTA following Quebec's sovereignty, see Gordon Ritchie et al., *Broken Links; Trade Relations after a Quebec Secession* (Toronto: C.D. Howe Institute 1991).

CHAPTER 10 Where Is the Peaceable Kingdom Headed?

1 One study exploring the conditions associated with political stability and instability in federal countries is by Jonathan Lemco, *Political Stability in Federal Governments* (New York: Praeger 1991).

2 For a fuller discussion, see Jonathan Lemco, *Canada and the Crisis in Central America* (New York: Praeger 1991).

3 André Blais, 'Le clivage linguistique au Canada,' *Recherches sociographiques,* 31 (1991).

4 See the transcript of the speech by Constitutional Affairs Minister Joe Clark to the Canadian Bar Association, Calgary, 18 August 1991.

Index

aboriginal peoples, 39–40, 46, 55; and
  Allaire report, 32, 34, 36; Bélanger-
  Campeau report, 37; Charlottetown
  Agreement, 49, 52; 'distinct society'
  clause, 19; Indian Act, 41; land claims
  of, 70–2, 123, 150–1; Meech Lake
  Accord, 20; self-government by, 48,
  49, 52; in a sovereign Quebec, xiii,
  68–72
Action démocratique, 101
Advisory Committee on Privatization,
  81
aerospace industry, 89, 110–12, 151
affirmative action, 52
agriculture: and agrarian tradition in
  Quebec, 4–5; and Allaire report, 32–3,
  34, 36; in EC, 60; and sovereignty,
  121, 162; dairy farming, 121; federal
  involvement in, 12, 103
Air Canada, 16, 116, 120
airports, 105, 134
Alberta, 27, 29, 33, 55–6, 115, 159; and
  Charlottetown Agreement, 53; Quebec
  sovereignty, 93, 105, 107, 109, 131;
  Reform party, 32; United States, 152.
  See also western provinces
Alcan, 120

Algeria, 68
Allaire, Jean, 101
Allaire report, 32–6, 39; EC as model,
  57–9; and Quebec business class, 117
Alliance Quebec, 10
allophones: and sovereignty, 125; and
  sovereignty-association, 75; children
  of, 9
Alsace, 66
aluminum industry, 82, 89, 151
amending formula, 35, 45, 48, 64
American Law Institute, 150
Angus Reid polls, 70, 76–7, 152
annexation, 151–4
armed services. See defence; military
Assembly of First Nations, 71
Association of Quebec Economists, 104
Atlantic provinces, 15; and boundaries of
  a sovereign Quebec, 70; and migration
  from, 131; post-sovereignty, 93, 107–
  10; unemployment in, 85; union of,
  30–1; U.S. annexation, 152. See also
  entries for provinces; Maritime
  provinces
Australia, 66, 132
Austro-Hungarian Empire, 65
automobile industry, 82, 121, 151

Baltimore Sun, 154
Bangkok Skytrain, 119
Bank of Canada, 46, 130; and federal
    debt, 114; Jacques Parizeau and, 139;
    monetary policy of, 23, 85–6, 139–42;
    post-sovereignty, 25, 105, 140; reform
    of, 35, 59; sovereignty-association, 63.
    See also currency; monetary policy
Bank of Montreal, 120, 166–7
Baseline Research, 31
Basque region of Spain, 14, 65–6
BCNI. *See* Business Council on National
    Issues
Beaudoin-Edwards Committee, 41
beer, GATT rules concerning, 162
Béland, Claude, 117
Bélanger, Michel, 37, 38
Bélanger-Campeau Commission, 23, 33,
    35, 37–40, 72, 129, 138; and EC
    model, 58, 60; and economics of
    sovereignty, 130–2, 134, 135; and
    Meech Lake Accord, 26; briefs by:
    Association of Quebec Economists,
    104, Chamber of Commerce, 86,
    Daniel Latouche, 119, José Woehrling,
    64, PQ, 60
Belgium, 14, 167; Quebec exports to,
    155
Bell Canada, 111, 116, 120
bilingualism, 16; and Bill 101, 6–8;
    Commissioner of Official Languages
    and, 100; federal policy of, 5–6, 56,
    164–5; francophones outside Quebec,
    68; 'notwithstanding' clause, 21; PQ
    policy on, 25; Quebec sovereignty,
    100–1; in a sovereign Quebec, 25–6;
    Spicer Commission report on, 40. *See
    also* language
Bill 75, 80
Bill 101, 6–11, 25, 50

Bill 150, 73
Bill 178, 13, 25
'bipolar federation,' 42
birth rate, Quebec, xiii, 3, 5, 7
Blais, André, 13
Bloc Québécois, 23, 54; and Canada, 32,
    168; and Lucien Bouchard, 12, 58
Blohm, Robert, 141
Bombardier, 84, 89; acquiring Canadair,
    119; pension funds of, 81; in a
    sovereign Quebec, 100
Boothe, Paul, 133
Bouchard, Lucien, 12, 74; and EC model
    for Canada, 58; free trade with United
    States, 160
boundaries, of a sovereign Quebec, xiii,
    69-70, 150
Bourassa, Robert, 47, 55, 73–4; and
    Allaire report, 33; Bank of Canada,
    141; Bélanger-Campeau Commission,
    23, 39; common currency with Canada,
    139, 142; EC model, 57–9; govern-
    ment of, 81; Meech Lake Accord, 23–
    4; 'notwithstanding' clause, 8, 21;
    Société de développement industriel, 4;
    sovereignty, 24, 117
Brazil-U.S. trade, 156, 158–9
Brenner, Reuven, 98
British Columbia, 55, 115; and 1992
    referendum, 53; and Canada Assistance
    Program, 27; and Reform party, 32;
    and United States, 152, 159, 165;
    governed by NDP, 32, 159; migration
    to, 108, 131; post-sovereignty, 93, 107,
    109; premier of, 29, 30; sovereignty-
    association, 30. *See also* western
    provinces
British Judicial Committee of the Privy
    Council, 72
British North American Act of 1867, 66

Brittany, 65, 66
Buchanan, Patrick, 152
Burney, Derek, 115–16
Bush, George, 149, 156, 163
business: and Bill 101, 8–10; federal
    grants and loans to, 128; in a sovereign
    Quebec, 124–7, 144
business class, Quebec, xiii, 14; sover-
    eignty position of, 116–18, 144, 170
Business Council on National Issues, 93–
    6, 104, 130
Business Week, 153, 156

C.D. Howe Institute, 135
Caisse de dépôt et placement du Québec,
    4, 82; and FTA, 161; and trade post-
    sovereignty, 161; contributing to
    Capiteq, 81
caisses populaires. See Desjardins credit
    union group
California: B.C. ties to, 165; market for
    natural gas, 107
Campbell, Kim, 54
Campeau, Jean, 37, 38, 117
Canada Assistance Program, 27
'Canada clause,' 45, 46
Canada Council, 52
Canada Health Act, 110
Canada-U.S. Free Trade Agreement:
    indicating a decentralized Canada, 157,
    165; and Quebec, 82, 84; Congress
    and, 159; ITC report, 161; post-
    sovereignty, 97, 119, 148, 158; U.S.
    government reaction, 156. *See also*
    North American Free Trade Agree-
    ment; trade
Canadair, 112, 119
Canadian Bond Rating Service, 85,
    114–15
Canadian Broadcasting Corporation:

erosion of, 165; poll by, 76;
    Radio-Canada, 52
Canadian Dairy Commission, 121
Canadian Marconi, 112
Canadian National Railways, 120
Canadian Pacific, 116, 120
Canadian Press News Service, 154
Canadian Radio-television and Telecom-
    munications Commission, 47, 52, 57
capital: Canada-Quebec common market,
    138; common currency, 139; flight of
    from Quebec in 1970s, 98; free move-
    ment of, 45, 46, 59; in provincial pen-
    sion fund and *caisses populaires,* 120;
    sovereignty and, 91–92, 106, 109, 117,
    119, 131, 144
Capiteq, 81
Castonguay, Claude, 58
Catalonia, 65
Catholic Church: and abolition of
    religious school boards, 8; Quiet
    Revolution, 4–5
CBC. *See* Canadian Broadcasting
    Corporation
CBRS. *See* Canadian Bond Rating
    Service
CDC. *See* Canadian Dairy Commission
Center for Human Rights (UN), 71
Center on Transnational Corporations
    (UN), 71
Central Intelligence Agency, 84, 146, 148
Centre de recherches sur l'opinion
    publique, 76–9
Charlottetown Agreement, 48–55, 72,
    127, 166, 168, 170; failure of, xi, xiv,
    61, 104; Quebec view of, 167; reaction
    of Wall Street to, 113; and Royal Bank
    report, 102; sovereignty, 78–9;
    sovereignty-association, 63
Charter of Rights and Freedoms, 7, 11,

16, 46, 47, 57, 109; and Allaire report,
32, 34, 35; Charlottetown Agreement,
49; 'distinct society' clause, 20;
immigration, 28; individual vs.
collective rights, 29; Meech Lake
Accord, 19, 26; 1992 referendum, 53;
'notwithstanding' clause, 21; Official
Languages Act, 6; Spicer Commission,
40
Chicago, Toronto link with, 165
Chile: joining NAFTA, 156, 158–60;
U.S. involvement in internal affairs of,
149
Chrétien, Jean, 12–13, 151–2; constitutional program of, 16; government of,
and GST, 128; and sovereignty, 167;
unpopular in Quebec, 23, 32
Churchill Falls, 123
citizenship: 'Canada clause' and, 46; in
EC model, 59; sovereignty and, 25, 68
Civil Code, 19
civil law, xiii, 14, 19, 27; and 'distinct
society' clause, 47. See also justice
civil service: and Bill 101, 8;
anglophones in, 25–6; federal, 68, 100;
in a sovereign Quebec, 144
Clark, Joe, 41, 67, 73
Cleveland, Toronto link with, 165
Clinton, President Bill, 149, 163
clothing industry, 122. See also fashion
industry
Cloutier, Professor Édouard, 74, 75
coast guard, 108, 111
Commission on the political and
constitutional future of Quebec. See
Bélanger-Campeau Commission
Commissioner of Official Languages, 100
common law, 69
Commonwealth of Independent States,
164. See also Soviet Union

communications: and Allaire report, 32,
34, 36; Atlantic provinces, 107–8;
Chamber of Commerce brief on, 37;
FTA, 156; Quebec jurisdiction over,
27, 31; role of EC in, 60. See also
media
Confederation, 59, 70
Conseil du patronat: and skilled labour,
88; and sovereignty, 83, 92, 99–100,
136; business poll, 117; transfer
payments, 97
Conservatives. See Progressive Conservative party
constitution, 43–5, 56–7, 66; Allaire
report and, 32, 34, 35; amendments to,
46, 47, 55, 74, 166; and Charlottetown
Agreement, 50, 54; and minority
education, 9; and a sovereign Quebec,
25, 63–4, 66; Bélanger-Campeau report
and, 38; Canadian public opinion on,
63–4, 109; EC model for, 58; 'notwith-
standing' clause of, 8; Official
Languages Act and, 6; Quebec and, 29,
63; U.S. press coverage of, 154
Constitution Act, 1982, 7, 45, 66, 74; and
Bélanger-Campeau report, 38; Charter
of Rights and Freedoms, 29; Meech
Lake Accord, 19, 26
Cook, Peter, 121
Co-opérants, Les, 86
Core, John, 121
Corporate Research Associates, 31
Corsica, 65-6
Côté, Marcel, 132, 135
Courchene, Thomas, 103–4, 138, 159
Coyne, Deborah, 49, 52–3
Cree, 71–2, 150–1. See also aboriginal
peoples
CROP. See Centre de recherches sur
l'opinion publique

crown corporations, 4, 12

CRTC. *See* Canadian Radio-television and Telecommunications Commission

culture, 43, 46, 92, 102–3; Allaire report and, 32, 34, 36; and 'Canada clause,' 46; and Charlottetown Agreement, 48–9, 50–2, 166; and 'distinct society' clause, 19; and francophones outside Quebec, 165; and labour, 118; and sovereignty, xiii, 24, 100–1; Bélanger-Campeau report and, 39; Canadian, 152; Chamber of Commerce brief on, 37; Corsican case, 66; costs to business, xiii, 118; cultural industries, 14; EC model, 57, 60; protection of, 3–4, 5–7, 13, 81, 165; and language laws, xiii, 7–10; PQ position on, 24–5; trade with United States, 157–8. *See also* language; multiculturalism

Cuomo, Governor Mario, 123, 147–8

currency: and Allaire report, 32–3, 34, 36; and EC model, 57, 59–60, 142; common with Canada, 24–6, 97, 102, 141–3; damaging to Canada, 109; interest rates and, 132; risks of, xiii; sovereignty and, 63, 73, 137–45; veto power of Quebec over, 106; under sovereignty-association, 63, 67; U.S. dollar in Panama, 140. *See also* Bank of Canada; monetary policy

customs, 32–3, 34, 36; Canadian customs union, 121–2; sovereignty and, 25, 58, 99; sovereignty-association and, 62; unions elsewhere, 65. *See also* immigration

Dabbs, Frank, 141

dairy industry: and EC milk prices, 59; Ontario, 121; Quebec, 121, 161

data processing sector, 89

day care, 125

de Gaulle, President Charles, 5

decentralization, Canadian, xii, xiv, 15–17, 27, 32, 42, 165–6; favoured by Quebecers, 43–5, 60; post-sovereignty, 171; and U.S. annexation 151–2

defence: and Allaire report, 32–3, 34, 36; Defense Production Agreement, 130–1; EC model, 57, 59; PAQ program, 55; sovereignty and, xiv, 111–12. *See also* military

Defense Production Agreement, 130–1

deficit, federal, 27, 81, 84–5, 98

Delors, Jacques, 60

Denmark, 132

Department of Indian and Northern Affairs, 41

Deschamps, Yvon, 3

Desjardins credit union group, 82, 117, 120, 161

Detroit, Toronto link with, 165

Deutsche Bank, 133

Devoir, Le, 11, 76

Dion, Stéphane, 4, 98

diplomatic mission, 68; of a sovereign Quebec, 25, 100, 144; under sovereignty-association, 67

'distinct society,' 40, 47–8, 98, 104; and Charlottetown Agreement, 48–9, 50, 52; and Meech Lake Accord, 14, 19, 20; and sovereignty, xiii; and sovereignty-association, 21–2; 'Canada clause' and, 46; constitution and, 44; resembling concessions to Corsica, 65–6; U.S. perception of, 155

District of Columbia, statehood movement of, 153–4

Domtar, 117

Drouin, Richard, 123–4

Dubuc, Alain, 11

Dufour, Ghislain, 136
Durham, Lord, 3

EC. *See* European Community
École polytechnique, pension funds of, 81
Economic Council of Canada, 93, 105, 135
ECU (future European currency), 59–60
education: Allaire report and, 32, 34, 36; anglophone, 26; Bill 101, 6–11; Chamber of Commerce brief on, 37; Charlottetown Agreement and, 166; in EC, 58, 60; higher, 12; federal transfer payments, 27, 97, 128; Quebec, 8, 12, 18, 27, 86, 92, 102–3, 127, 129, 165–6; under sovereignty, 25–6, 100, 125. *See also* manpower training; students
electronics, 110, 151
embassies. *See* diplomatic mission
energy, 150; and Allaire report, 32–3, 34, 36; natural gas, 107, 109; New York state and, 123; oil, 92, 109; Quebec and, 31, 84. *See also* hydroelectricity
Environics Research Group, 17, 77
environment, 60, 89, 118, 150; Allaire report and, 32, 34, 36; and 'Canada clause,' 46; Canada-U.S. agreements and, 156; EC model, 59–60; hydro-electricity and, 71, 123, 159; Quebec small businesses and, 127; sovereignty and, 58, 148
Equality party, 10, 24, 35, 69
equalization payments to provinces, 29, 55, 110, 165; Allaire report on, 32–3, 34, 36; to Quebec, 107, 129, 132
ethnicity, 13; 'Canada clause' and, 46; Charlottetown Agreement, 49; 'distinct society' clause and, 19; Quebec homogeneity, 14, 81; U.S. politics of, 153. *See also* minorities

EU. *See* European Community
Eurofed, 142
European Act, 60
European Community: as model for Canada, 57–61, 65, 169; for Quebec, 103–4, 142
European Union. *See* European Community
Export Development Corporation, 130
Farm Credit Corporation, 130
fashion industry, 89. *See also* clothing industry
Federalism and the French Canadians (Pierre Elliott Trudeau), 6
fertility rate, Quebec, 3
film industry, 3, 161, 165
financial institutions: Allaire report on, 34, 36; Chamber of Commerce brief on, 37; federal policy on, 47, 85; in Quebec, 81–2; post-sovereignty, 124–5
Financial Post, 79
First Boston Corporation, 113–14
First Nations, 41; Assembly of, 71. *See also* aboriginal peoples
fisheries, 150; Allaire report on, 32, 34, 36; and Atlantic provinces, 108
foreign policy: and 1980 referendum, 73; Allaire report on, 32–3, 34, 36; EC model, 57, 59; and PQ position, 24; under sovereignty-association, 67
Foreign Relations Law (United States), 150
forestry, 47, 88–9; and Charlottetown Agreement, 49, 51; pulp and paper, 121; softwood lumber, 163; wood products, 151. *See also* newsprint industry; paper products
Fortin, Pierre, 56, 142; free trade with United States, 158; sovereignty, 97, 135

France: and Algeria, 68; and Quebec, 5, 58, 155; part of trading bloc, 59; regions of and sovereignty-association, 65–6; U.S. trade with, 156
Francophonie, La, 62
Fraser Institute, 29, 105–6
free trade. *See* Canada-U.S. Free Trade Agreement; European Community; North American Free Trade Agreement; trade
Freeman, David, 123
Frontenac (proposed Quebec monetary unit), 137
FTA. *See* Canada-U.S. Free Trade Agreement
Fulbright educational exchange, 147

Galicia, 65
Gallup polls, 76–8, 89, 152
GATT, 162
GDP, Quebec, 81, 101–2, 110, 130, 132
Gendron Commission, 9
Getty, Don, 105
Gidengil, Élisabeth, 13
Globe and Mail, 33–5, 41, 45, 50–2, 83
GNP: Canadian, post-sovereignty, 110; Ontario, 93
Goldman Sachs and Company, 113
Goods and Services Tax, 43, 128, 168
Gordon, Sheldon, 156
Gottlieb, Allan, 151
governor general, as symbol, 16
Grady, Patrick, 105–6, 135
Great Britain: and Ireland, 68; and Quebec, 15, 155; role of in EC, 142
Great Lakes, Toronto and, 165
Great Whale River Power Plant Project, 123, 161. *See also* Hydro-Québec
Greece, 149
Green, Chris, 135

Gregg, Allan, 168
Grey, Julius, 68
Group of Seven, 110
Guam, statehood movement of, 153–4
Guay, Jean, 75
gun control, in Canada, 14

Harris, Richard, 109
health, 27; Allaire report on, 32–3, 34, 36; and anglophone institutions, 25–6; and Bill 101, 8, 10; Canadian system of, 14, 109, 165; in EC, 58–9; federal funding of, 12, 27, 60, 97, 128; in Quebec, 12, 26, 37, 102–3; post-sovereignty, 106, 110, 125, 144; small businesses and, 127
highway rights of way, post-sovereignty, 108. *See also* transport
Holland, 155, 160
House of Commons, reform of, 107, 170; and Charlottetown Agreement, 49, 50
housing, 47; and Allaire report, 34, 36; Charlottetown Agreement, 49, 51
Hull. *See* Ottawa-Hull
Hydro-Québec, 4, 86, 111, 114–15; boundaries issue and, 70; contributing to Capiteq, 81; post-sovereignty, 123, 161; and United States, 113, 151, 161
hydroelectricity, 71, 115, 129; and aboriginal rights, 71–2, 150–1; and sovereignty, 123–4; Canada and, 108, 110; nationalization of, 4–5; significance of for Quebec, 82, 151; United States and NAFTA and, 157, 159, 162

immigration: Allaire report on, 34, 36; and Bill 101, 6–7, 9; and Charlottetown Agreement, 52, 166; francophone, to Quebec, 3, 5, 7; and Meech Lake Accord, 20, 24; to

Quebec, xiii, 8, 18, 22, 27–8, 31, 37, 46, 101, 166, 168; post-sovereignty, 100, 106. *See also* customs
In the Eye of the Eagle (Jean-François Lisée), 148
income security, 34, 36, 58
India, 149
Indian Act, 41. *See also* aboriginal peoples
Infometrica, 97, 102
Institut de recherche sur l'opinion publique, 44
Institut québécois de l'opinion publique, 77
insurance industry, 80, 120
intellectual class, Quebec, 5
intellectual property laws, 103
International Monetary Fund, 110
International Trade Commission, 161
Inuit, 69, 71–2. *See also* aboriginal peoples
Ireland, 68
Israel, 65, 137
Italy: debt of, 128; Quebec exports to, 155; U.S. trade with, 156

James Bay hydroelectric project, 71–2, 150–1; U.S. press coverage of, 159. *See also* Hydro-Québec; hydroelectricity
Japan, 158, 162
job training. *See* manpower training
Johnson, Daniel, 24
Johnson, David R., 86
Johnson, Pierre-Marc, 103
Journal de Québec, 77
justice, 37; Allaire report on, 32, 34, 36; Bill 101 and courts, 8; in EC, 59; language of courts, 25–6; system of in a sovereign Quebec, 69. *See also* civil law

Kennedy, Senator Edward, 147–8

labour: Allaire report on, 32, 34, 36; anglophone, 98-9; and Charlottetown Agreement, 51; federal policy on, 85; free movement of, 45, 109–10, 139; in Quebec, 37, 118, 165–6; post-sovereignty, 98, 131, 138; and trade unions, xiii, 5, 81. *See also* manpower training
Labrador, 72
Laidler, David, 96–7, 138
Lake, Anthony, 149
Lake Ontario, providing Toronto-U.S. link, 165
L'Allier, Jean-Paul, 13
Landry, Bernard, 140
language, 46, 92, 109, 167; Allaire recommendations on, 33, 36; and Official Languages Act, 6; and sovereignty issue, xiii, 7, 13, 100–1, 165; Bélanger-Campeau recommendations on, 39; Charlottetown Agreement and, 48–9, 50; constitutional powers and, 29; Corsican issue of, 66; 'distinct society' clause and, 19; Meech Lake Accord and, 26; minority language rights, 101; 'notwithstanding' clause and, 21; provinces and, 56; in Quebec, 3–4, 7, 18, 81, 102, 124; –, and anglophones, 34, 98-9; –, and Cree, 150; –, and immigrants, 28; –, and labour, 118; –, and laws, xiii, 3, 6–9, 126; PQ policy on, 25; during Quiet Revolution, 5; Spicer Commission and, 41; trade with United States, 157–8. *See also* bilingualism; culture; multiculturalism
Latin America, Canadian trade with, 165
Latouche, Daniel, 11, 75, 119

Laurin, Camille, 7, 8
Lavalin, 82, 86, 100, 119
Lesage, Jean, 4
Lévesque, René, 101, 113, 149
Levine, Marc, 84
Liberal party, 54, 59; and Jean Chrétien, 32; Meech Lake Accord, 21, 23; referendum, 73–4
– in Quebec: Allaire report, 32, 33, 34–5; and Bélanger-Campeau Commission, 35; Constitutional Committee of, 33, 34; Lesage and Bourassa governments, 4; nationalism, 5; sovereignty, 54–5, 77–8; sovereignty-association, 24, 76
liquor industry, 161
Lisée, Jean-François, 148–9
Locher, Uli, 87

McCallum, John, 135, 135
McKenna, Frank, 30
Maclean's, 89
magnesium products, 162
Manitoba: and 1992 referendum, 53; decentralization, 107; Meech Lake Accord, 19, 20, 44; post-sovereignty, 93, 131. *See also* western provinces
manpower training: and Charlottetown Agreement, 49, 51; federal investment in, 12; provincial responsibility for, 46, 47; in Quebec, 24, 26–8; post-sovereignty, 125. *See also* labour
Maritime provinces: and Ontario, 16; Quebec, 72, 105; common market among, 30–1; federal government and, 40, 56, 139. *See also* Atlantic provinces; entries for provinces
media, 47, 89; and Allaire report, 33; and Meech Lake Accord, 20, 44; and referendum campaign, 168;

anglophone, 25–6; CBC, 165; Cree lobby of, 150–1; CRTC and, 47, 52, 57; Quebec, 3, 7; post-sovereignty, 25–6, 100; Radio-Canada, 52; United States: coverage of Canada-Quebec, 152–4, 156
medicare, 27, 32–3, 165. *See also* health
Meech Lake Accord, 20–3, 27–9, 40, 48–9, 50–2, 64, 133, 168; Allaire report and, 33; and 'distinct society,' 14, 19; Bélanger-Campeau Commission and, 37; economic effects of, 83, 113, 115–16; failure of, 7, 16, 24, 26–7, 30–2, 41, 44, 98; Quebec reaction to, xiii, 4, 25, 75, 79, 167; and sovereignty-association, 63; seen from United States, 149
Merck, 122
Mercredi, Ovide, 71
Merkin, William, 161
Merrill Lynch, 83, 113–14, 166
Mexico: Canadian trade with, 165; as NAFTA member, 82, 148, 156, 160; trade with post-sovereignty, 159
military: implications of sovereignty for, 25–6, 68, 111–12, 144; PQ position on, 24; under sovereignty-association, 42, 67. *See also* defence
mining, 47; and Charlottetown Agreement, 49, 51; sovereignty, 121; Cree rights to minerals, 150–1
minorities, 18; and Bélanger-Campeau report, 35; and 'distinct society' clause, 19, 20; Bill 101, 8, 10; boundaries issue, 69; education of, 9; language policy and, 7, 13, 101, 109; PQ policy on, 25; in a sovereign Quebec, 125; visible, 52. *See also* ethnicity
Mitchell, Senator George, 147–8

Mohawks, 71, 151. *See also* aboriginal peoples

monetary policy, Canadian, 98; EC, 142; internationally, 65; sovereignty and, xiii, 91, 105–6, 132, 137, 139–40, 142, 143; under sovereignty-association, 62. *See also* Bank of Canada; currency

Montreal: aerospace industry, 111; and Montreal Expos, 120–1; and Toronto, 31; Bank of Montreal and, 166–7; economic decline of, 81, 86–7, 89; federal civil servants in, 68; head offices in, 116; language and, 6, 10; pharmaceuticals, 122; regional government of, 115; and sovereignty, 69; unemployment, 85, 87–8

Montreal Catholic School Commission, 9

Montreal Expos, sale of, 120–1

Montreal Gazette, 10

Montreal Urban Community, 115

Moody's Investor Service, 83, 115

Mouvement Desjardins. *See* Desjardins credit union group

Moynihan, Senator Daniel Patrick, 148

Mulroney, Brian, 26, 153; and 1984 election, 48; decentralization, 16; federal-provincial powers, 59; George Bush, 163; Meech Lake Accord, 19–21, 28, 32; referendum, 53, 73; sovereignty, 100, 119, 137

Multi-Fiber Agreement, 122

Multi-Reso, 77

multiculturalism, 11, 18; and Official Languages Act, 6; Spicer Commission, 40. *See also* culture; language

multinational companies, 16, 83; and Hydro-Québec, 161

municipal affairs, 27, 34, 36, 49, 51

Nadeau, Bertin, 117

National Action Committee on the Status of Women, 49–52

national anthem, as symbol, 16

National Assembly (Quebec): and Bélanger-Campeau recommendations, 38, 39; Constitution Act of 1982, 26; post-sovereignty, 25–6

National Energy Policy, 55–6

National Film Board, 165

National Security Council. *See* U.S. National Security Council

nationalism, Quebec, 5, 6, 13, 170

nationalization of industry, during Quiet Revolution, 4

NATO. *See* North Atlantic Treaty Organization

natural gas, 107, 109

natural resources, 55–6; and Allaire recommendations, 34, 36; and U.S. annexation of Canada, 152

Neuharth, Al, 154

New Brunswick, 20; bilingualism in, 6; and common market for Maritimes, 30–1; Jean Chrétien representing constituency of, 23. *See also* Atlantic provinces; Maritime provinces

New Democratic Party: Action Group of, 41; and 1993 election, 54; U.S. annexation of Canada, 153; governing B.C., 32, 159; governing Ontario, 139, 159; Meech Lake Accord and, 21, 32; post-sovereignty, 107

New England, and Atlantic Canada, 108

New France, and boundaries issue, 70

New York Power Authority, 71, 123

New York state, 123–4, 151, 155

New York Times, 148, 153, 156

Newfoundland: and Meech Lake Accord, 19–20, 44; Quebec sovereignty, 108; Churchill Falls, 123; collective orientation of, 14; Labrador and, 72; standard of living in, 88, 102. *See also* Atlantic provinces

newsprint industry, 110. *See also* forestry; paper products; pulp and paper

Ney, Edward, 149, 154

NORAD. *See* North American Air Defence Agreement

North American Air Defence Agreement, 25, 62, 111; implications for FTA, 156

North American Free Trade Agreement, 168; membership in, 159–60; Quebec support for, 63, 65, 82; and sovereignty, 110, 131, 144, 156, 162, 168; United States and, xii, 158; ITC report, 161. *See also* Canada-U.S. Free Trade Agreement; trade

North Atlantic Treaty Organization, 25, 62, 111

'notwithstanding' clause, 8, 20, 31, 35

Nova Scotia, 20, 30-1. *See also* Atlantic provinces; Maritime provinces

NSC. *See* United States National Security Council

Oberstar, Congressman James, 148

OECD. See Organization for Economic Co-operation and Development

Oerlikon Aerospace, 112

Office de la langue française, 9

Official Languages Act, 6

oil industry, 92, 109

Ontario, 15–16, 20, 31, 55, 152-3, 158; dominating Canada, 64, 106; economy of, 27, 88–9, 92-3, 94–6, 120, 139, 166; GATT, 162; migration to, 108, 131; monetary policy, 140–1; NDP and, 32, 107, 159; post-sovereignty, 29, 99, 101, 104, 107, 109–10, 131;

Quebec and, 63, 80, 84, 105, 115–16; unemployment in, 87, 88, 116, 118; U.S. branch plants in, 158

Ontario Milk Marketing Board, 121

Option Canada, 70

Order of Engineers of Quebec, 81

Oregon, B.C. ties to, 165

Organization for Economic Co-operation and Development, 115

Organization of American States, 62

Ottawa-Hull, 6, 68–9, 100

Panama, and U.S. dollar, 140

paper products, 82, 151, 157

PAQ. *See* Parti Action Québec

Parizeau, Jacques, xi, 24, 74, 128-9; and English language, 101; debts, 131, 133; monetary policy, 137, 139–42; PQ policy, 12; referendum, 167; Régime d'épargne-actions, 80; sovereignty, 78, 99, 117; sovereignty-association, 63; Toronto-Montreal co-dependency, 31; trade, 99, 159, 161-2; transfer payments, 97; United States, 157

Parti Action Québec, 55

Parti Québécois, 12, 14, 119, 121, 140–1, 152, 164; and Bélanger-Campeau Commission, 35; Bill 101, 6-7, 9; Cree land claims, 71; EC model, 60; election of, 4, 54–5, 80, 167; Meech Lake Accord, 23; minorities, 25, 101; sovereign Quebec, 77–8, 105

– Canada and, 68, 129, 141–2; language of, 25–6, 100–1; legal system of, 69; military of, 111; monetary policy of, 140; and sovereignty-association, 24–5, 63

Parting as Friends: The Economic Consequences for Quebec (John McCallum and Chris Green), 135

passport, Quebec, 25, 68. *See also* citizenship
Péladeau, Pierre, 117–18
pensions, 12, 118, 166; federal civil service, 130–1; old age, 101, 165; pension funds, 4, 27, 81, 120; and sovereignty, 102, 106, 125
Peterson, David, 106–7
Petro-Canada, sale of, 128
pharmaceutical industry: affected by sovereignty, 121, 122; and GATT, 162; Montreal and, 89
Picard, André, 52
Pittsburgh, Toronto link with, 165
police: in EC, 58; Quebec, 12
Political and Constitutional Future of Quebec, The, 38
polls: and decentralized nature of Canada, 16–17; and mood of Canadians, 167; during referendum campaign, 168; of business, 83, 105, 117; of economists, 109; of United States and Canada, 152–3, 155; on Atlantic union, 31; on the economy, 89; on Mulroney Conservatives, 32; on sovereignty, xii, 74–79, 101–2, 106, 108–9, 143
population, Quebec, 3, 7, 99, 165
ports, sovereignty and, 105
post office, 25, 134; Allaire recommendations on, 34, 36; EC model, 59
press. *See* media
Presse, La, 11, 77
prime minister, as symbol, 16
Prince Edward Island, 30–1, 50. *See also* Atlantic provinces; Maritime provinces
Progressive Conservative party: and 1993 election, 54; Meech Lake Accord, 23, 32; public opinion on, 32
property: federal, division of upon sovereignty, 105, 131, 134; rights, and

Charter amendments, 46; intellectual 103; values, and a sovereign Quebec, 106. *See also* post office
Protestant School Board of Greater Montreal, 8
Proulx, Pierre-Paul, 101, 110
Provigo, 117
public security, 34, 36
public works, 31. *See also* post office; property
Puerto Rico, statehood movement of, 153–4
pulp and paper industry, 121; newsprint, 110. *See also* paper products
Purvis, Douglas, 109

'Quebec, Inc.,' 81
Quebec Chamber of Commerce, 37, 86, 137
Quebec Charter of Human Rights and Freedoms (proposed), 34
Quebec Federation of Labour, 81
Quebecor, 117–18
queen, as symbol, 16
Quiet Revolution, 4–5, 81, 86

race. *See* ethnicity; minorities
Radio-Canada, 52. *See also* Canadian Broadcasting Corporation; media
Rae, Premier Bob, 31, 61
rail: and decentralization, 27; sovereignty, 108, 131; Via Rail, 16, 165
Raynauld, André, 107
recession, 89, 116, 118, 127, 168; and federal debt, 128; and sovereignty, 102, 106, 168–9; foreign investment 116; in Montreal, 81; in Ontario, 93; in United States, 89, 167; nationalism and, 170
recreation and sports, 34, 36, 49, 51

referendum: (1980), 44, 67, 73, 79, 168; (1992), 53–4, 72–4, 102; (1995, predicted), 167–8; and Allaire recommendations, 32, 34; Bélanger-Campeau recommendations, 35, 37, 38, 39; on sovereignty, 40, 63, 77–8, 116; PQ position on, 23–4, 54–5

Reform party, 168; and 1993 election, 54; opposed to Charlottetown Agreement, 49, 52–3; sign of alienation, 30, 32, 167

Régime d'épargne-actions, 80

regional development, 60; Allaire recommendations on, 32, 34, 36; and Charlottetown Agreement, 52; EC and, 58

Reid, Angus, 70, 168. See also Angus Reid polls

Reisman, Simon, 158–9

religion: and abolition of religious school boards, 8; 'Canada clause,' 46; Catholic Church, 4–5

Rémillard, Gil, 37, 73

republic, Quebec as, 25

research and development: Allaire recommendations on, 34, 36; and federal government, 12, 85; sovereignty, 122–3, 125; Chamber of Commerce brief on, 37. See also science and technology

Reuber, Grant, 129

roads, EC and, 58. See also transport

Royal Bank of Canada, 102, 120

Royal Commission on Bilingualism and Biculturalism, 5

Saloman Brothers, 113

Saskatchewan: decentralization and, 107; NDP government of, 32;

post-sovereignty, 93, 131. See also western provinces

Schering-Plough, 122

schools. See education; students

Schuman, Robert, 59

science and technology, 32, 60, 122–3. See also research and development

Scotland, 65

Scott, Ian, 15–16

Scott, Stephen, 70

Scowen, Reed, 151

Seagram's, 120

Securities and Exchange Commission (U.S.), 115

semi-conductors, export of, 151

Senate: abolition of, 32, 35; post-sovereignty, 106–7; Quebec representation in, 57; reform of, 29, 37, 41, 44–5, 46, 47–9, 50, 56, 170

sexual equality, 49–52. See also women

Shaping Canada's Future Together, 45–8

shipbuilding industry, 121

sign laws, 13, 98–9; Bill 101, 6, 8; Bill 178, 25; post-sovereignty, 126; PQ policy on, 25–6; U.S. press coverage of, 154

Simeon, Richard, 56

Simpson, Jeffrey, 33–5, 133

SNC-Lavalin, 100. See also Lavalin

social affairs, Quebec, 32, 34, 36, 37

Socialist party, of France, 66

Société de développement industriel, 4

Société générale de financement du Québec, 4

Société québécoise d'initiatives petrolières, 4

'soft' industries, 122

softwood lumber issue, 163. See also forestry

Soleil, Le, 75

SOM polls, 54, 78
Sonnen, Carl, 102
sovereignty, 43, 54–5, 64–5, 68–9, 170;
  aboriginal groups and, 68; Allaire
  recommendations on, 33, 34; and free
  trade, 131, 155–63; and referenda:
  1980, 73; 1992, 53–4; anglophones
  and, 68; Bélanger-Campeau recommendations on, 35–9, 38; boundaries
  and, 69–72; BQ and, 54; business
  community, 80, 82–3, 116–17, 124–7;
  costs of, 67–8, 103, 105; currency,
  137–45; deficit, 132–5, 135; economic
  effects of, 82, 91–112, 116, 119–21,
  128–36, 144–45, 166; federal civil
  servants, 100; health care, 110; Jacques
  Parizeau and, xi, 63; language, 100–1;
  legal system under, 69; nationalists
  and, 83; outside Quebec, 117; PQ and,
  63; public opinion on, xii, 74–79;
  referendum on, 37, 39–40, 167;
  transition to, 101–12, 125; United
  States and, 116, 146–63, 152, 155. See
  also sovereignty-association
sovereignty-association, xi, 13, 24, 62–
  79, 103–4, 169; and 1980 referendum,
  42, 73; Canada and, 106; costs of, 67–
  8, 105; 'distinct society,' 21–2; for
  B.C., 30; EC model for, 57; economics
  of, 99–100, 116–17, 124–7; internationally, 65–7, 164; PQ and, 23; public
  opinion on, 44–5, 74–9, 167–8; U.S.
  State Department evaluation of, 148.
  See also sovereignty
Soviet Union, xiii, 66, 147, 164
Spain: and Group of Seven, 110; regions
  of and sovereignty-association, 65
Spar Aerospace, 89
'special status': affirmative action and,
  52; for Quebec, 53, 56; for Quebec and
  aboriginal peoples, 49

Spicer, Keith, 39
Spicer Commission, 39–41, 45, 67, 107,
  153
sports. See recreation and sports
St Lawrence Seaway, 130–1
Standard and Poor's Corporation, 115
stock exchange, Quebec, 14
stock market: and national referendum,
  53; Quebec and Canada post-sovereignty, 106; Quebec investment in, 80
student loans, 130
students, Quebec: Bill 101 and, 10; high
  school, 165–6; anglophone, 87; in
  Montreal, 86; and nationalism, 5. See
  also education
Sununu, John, 147–8
Supreme Court: appointment of judges to,
  44, 47; and Charlottetown Agreement,
  49, 50; Quebec representation on, 57
Switzerland, 165
'symbolic atonement,' 98

Task Force on Job Opportunities for
  English-speaking Youth, 98–9
taxation: in Canada, 12, 14, 23–4, 26–7,
  89; Charlottetown Agreement and, 48;
  EC and, 57, 60; Meech Lake Accord
  and, 27; post-sovereignty, 109;
– in Quebec, 89, 118, 120; and 1980
  referendum, 73; Allaire recommendations on, 32, 34, 36; incentives to
  business, 80–1; post-sovereignty, 25,
  58, 78, 97, 99, 101, 106–7, 126, 132–
  3, 135, 139, 145; shrinking base for,
  165; sovereignty-association and, 24,
  62
telecommunications, 34, 36; and
  Charlottetown Agreement, 52; CRTC
  and, 47, 52, 57; Quebec control of, 26
television. See media
textile industry, 121–2

Time, 153
Toronto: and U.S. Great Lakes cities,
165; and Montreal, 31, 116, 166–7
Toronto Dominion Bank, 83
tourism, 47; Allaire recommendations on,
34, 36; and Charlottetown Agreement,
49, 51; Office de la langue française
and, 9; Quebec autonomy over, 102–3;
Quebec-Canada post-sovereignty, 96
trade: Canadian, xi, 109–10, 118, 150;
with Quebec, 58, 96–7, 106, 138–9;
with United States, 147–8; Quebec,
with United States, 150, 155–63;
sovereignty and, xi–xii, 43, 92, 106;
sovereignty-association and, 42, 62, 67.
See also Canada-U.S. Free Trade
Agreement; European Community;
North American Free Trade Agreement
trade union movement, Quebec, xiii, 5;
Quebec Federation of Labour, 81
transfer payments: to Atlantic provinces,
108; and federal deficit, 27, 128–9;
indexation of, 86; to Quebec, 84, 93,
97; immigration and, 28; sovereignty
and, 101, 106, 108, 132, 144
transport: between Canada and Quebec,
32, 34, 36, 96; between Canada and
United States, 156; between Quebec
and Atlantic provinces, 107–8; in EC,
58–9; ferry services, 47; industry,
Montreal, 89; sovereignty and, 110;
rail, 27, 108, 131, 165
Treasury Department (U.S.), 84
Trudeau, Pierre Elliott: and bilingualism
and biculturalism, 5–6; Charlottetown
Agreement, 49, 52–3; on divisibility of
Quebec, 70; National Energy Policy of,
55–6

unemployment, 118; among youth, 88;
and foreign investment, 83–4; in
Canada, 89, 96, 167; Ontario, 87;
Quebec, 85, 116, 118, 120, 166;
Montreal, 87, 87–8; monetary policy
and, 140–1; sovereignty and, xiii, 97,
100, 102, 109, 126, 145
unemployment insurance, 14, 27, 96, 103,
165; Allaire recommendations on, 34,
36; Bélanger-Campeau testimony, 26;
Chamber of Commerce, 37;
Charlottetown Agreement and, 49;
Montreal, 88; Quebec, 97, 120
United Empire Loyalists, 152
United Nations: Canadian influence in
post-sovereignty, 110; Center for
Human Rights, 71; Center on
Transnational Corporations, 71; and
Quebec: aboriginal peoples of, 71,
150–1; post-sovereignty, 25, 111;
under sovereignty-association, 62
United States, 16–17; aboriginal lobby in
Washington, 150–1; and Atlantic
Canada, 108; and B.C., 165; and
Canada, 60–1, 83, 107, 111, 115–16,
134, 144, 156, 171; and Ontario, 92,
107, 165; and Quebec, 65, 82–4, 91,
113, 117; Bill 101 and, 10; constitution
of, 66–7; currency of, 137, 138, 140,
143–4; debt of, 132; hydroelectricity
exports to, 123–4; industrial takeover
by, 125; migration to, 87, 108; and
military, 111; Panama and, 140;
post-sovereignty, xi–xii, 23, 97, 124,
146–63, 169; preventing sovereignty,
149; recession in, 89, 167; secession
from, 69; and sovereignty-association,
62, 67; statehood movements in, 153–
4; study by, 84; trade with, 99, 119,
155–63, 165; and western provinces,
56, 165. *See also* Canada-U.S. Free
Trade Agreement; North American
Free Trade Agreement

U.S. Commerce Department: during
  Bush-Mulroney era, 163; interest in
  Canada, 147; trade law and GATT, 162
U.S. English (interest group), 149
U.S. Foreign Relations Law, 150
U.S. National Security Council, 83, 146,
  163
U.S. Securities and Exchange Commis-
  sion, 115
U.S. State Department: during
  Bush-Mulroney era, 163; and U.S.–
  Canada issues, 147; investigating
  Canada, 146, 148; Quebec, 84
U.S. Treasury Department, 84
U.S.A. Today, 154

Vaillancourt, François, 102
Vander Zalm, Bill, 30
Via Rail, 16, 165
Virginia, secession of West Virginia
  from, 69

Walker, Michael, 29
Wall Street, ties with Quebec, 113
Wall Street Journal, 153
Washington Post, 153
Washington state, B.C. ties to, 165

Watts, Professor Ronald, 42
welfare: federal funding for, 27, 128; in
  Quebec, 88, 97
West Germany: Deutsche Bank of, 133;
  part of trading bloc, 59
West Virginia, secession of from
  Virginia, 69
western provinces, 15, 54; and Canada
  joining United States, 152; and
  monetary policy, 139; and NDP, 107;
  and Ontario, 92, 106; and Quebec, 39,
  92, 117, 120; federal government and,
  29–30, 40, 56, 103; post-sovereignty,
  104, 107. *See also* entries for provinces
Wilson, Michael, 128
wine industry, 161
Woehrling, José, 64
women: affirmative action and, 52; and
  'Canada clause,' 46; Charlottetown
  Agreement, 49–52; Meech Lake
  Accord, 20; Quebec birth rate, 5
wood products, 151. *See also* forestry
World Bank, 110
World Trade Agreement (WTA), 110, 131

youth, Quebec, 98–9, 165
Yugoslavia, former, xiii, 164